THE

BURN RAT

DIET

THE

BURN RATE

DIET

Burn Fat and

Boost Vitality

Stephen R. Van Schoyck, Ph.D.

Thorsons

To Diane, Keele, Kimberley, Dain, Kerry, and Keith.
Thank you for who you are and what you give.

Thorsons
An Imprint of HarperCollins*Publishers*
77–85 Fulham Palace Road
Hammersmith, London W6 8JB

The Thorsons website address is:
www.thorsons.com

and *Thorsons*

are trademarks
of HarperCollins*Publishers* Ltd

First published by HarperResource Inc. 2001
This edition published by Thorsons 2002

10 9 8 7 6 5 4 3 2 1

© Stephen R. Van Schoyck Ph.D. 2001

Stephen R. Van Schoyck Ph.D. asserts the moral
right to be identified as the author of this work

A catalogue record of this book is
available from the British Library

ISBN 0 00 712296 9

Printed and bound in Great Britain by
Omnia Books Limited, Glasgow

Contents

Preface

It never made sense to me. Patients with weight problems would tell me they were overweight because they ate too much, ate the wrong things, ate under stress, and didn't exercise enough. Yet when I questioned them further, every pattern they described was similar to the way my whole family had lived. We ate all the wrong things at the wrong times. My family used to eat hors d'oeuvres before dinner—cheese, pepperoni, chips and dip, crackers, and so on. Then we would eat a big dinner, usually steak and potatoes with plenty of butter and sour cream. We ate lots of snacks in front of the TV at night and hit the local ice cream stand for a hot fudge sundae at least once a week. And that didn't include the level of food intake at a picnic or party. I couldn't even begin to count the calories. It was normal to us. Yet I never had any problems with weight control.

Something was wrong with what my patients were saying. Either they had a warped perspective, or I had worse eating problems than they had and I never knew it. I always had a big appetite, especially as a kid. I remember the beef stew that a Polish cook, Annie, made for my family. She would make two pots each time—one for the family and one for me. I was always known as the kid with the huge appetite. But because I was never over-weight, nobody saw any problem with what I was eating.

In 1982, when I became the director of several weight control clinics, I brought this life experience to the treatment of weight control. Of course, I also had received rigorous scientific training in the biology, psychology, and exercise physiology of weight control. I had read all the leading research in the field, talked with many of the leading researchers, and knew the treatment being offered from a clinical standpoint. Later I came to realize that the difference between me and the other medical practitioners in my field was that I had no personal experience or vested interest in any one approach to dieting and weight control. While you might think this would make me the wrong person to treat weight prob-lems, quite the opposite was true. First, I did not start with the assumption that all overweight people are lazy and lack self-control. I had no preconceived ideas to warp my thinking or perspective. Personally, I was a blank slate, free to be objective as a scientist. I had only my observations and a desire to help my patients with their weight control efforts.

Second, lacking personal experience with weight control, I knew I had to listen extra carefully to what my patients said. What surprised me was that the patients weren't listening to themselves. Some knew that they ate less than many of their thin friends, but they still would blame themselves for lacking self-control. Some exercised regularly but still didn't lose weight, so they blamed themselves for not trying hard enough. Most of my patients were used to blaming themselves and had become quite expert at doing so. Their self-respect had been distorted by the traditional notion that fat people overeat and don't exercise. Because my patients bought into this stereotype, there was a large gap between what they reported and how they explained what they reported. They were so tyrannized by the fat stereotype that they were not only embarrassed about their weight, but also ashamed. Everything was their fault. Some could lose weight but still feel like they didn't lose enough. They might retain water for a variety of reasons but be convinced their weight gain was due to the piece or two of choco-late cake they had eaten the night before. While dieting, they would go through several weeks of no weight loss and feel they

were doing something wrong, despite following the diet to the letter. I decided to find an explanation that made better sense of
these experiences than simply blaming the patient.

As I tracked the food intakes of my patients at the clinic, I discovered that the vast majority of them actually ate normally. The
classic stereotype of the patient who eats more than the average
person was rare. Certainly fewer than 20 percent of my patients
actually overate. Yet if you listened to what they said about themselves, they all believed that something was wrong with their eating. They were overweight, so they assumed that they were eating
too much. After tracking the amount they were eating and measuring their energy requirements, they saw that the data proved
otherwise. Most people had confused eating *more than average*
with eating *more than their body could tolerate*. Eating the same
as the average person caused most patients to gain weight.

I was appalled at the distorted relationship to food that my
patients had developed because of their weight problems. I mar-
veled at the fact that the hors d'oeuvres we ate in my family were
called "binges" by my patients. Second helpings like the ones that
I ate were perceived as self-indulgent—living to eat rather than
eating to live—by my patients. It seemed as if everyone, friends
and professionals alike, was part of a conspiracy to perpetuate this
erroneous perception. It puzzled me that my medical colleagues
seemed to accept their patients' self-reports as gospel truths. They
believed without question that their patients were overeating. I,
instead, used to wonder how my patients' perspectives had gotten
so warped. After all, they were eating the way that had been called
normal in my family. How could they think they were doing something wrong?

The overwhelming need for a revised perception of patients'
behavior, one free of the stereotypes and biases, has led me to
write this book. I have helped hundreds of patients in my fifteen
years of clinical practice in weight control, and I can't believe that
nobody is listening to the patients' experience. When patients tell
me jokingly that they gain weight when they smell food, I know
that they are telling me that eating and exercise have less to do
with their weight control than others may think. I have come to
understand that *metabolism* is the most critical feature in weight

control and is the single greatest contributor to changes in body weight. It is not the "excuse" that overweight people use to justify their poor weight control. It is the truth that I can prove with a "metabolic cart," a piece of medical equipment that measures metabolic rate by analyzing the content of a person's breath, a reliable and independent measure of energy requirements. I have hundreds of patient files that contain the data from the metabolic cart on which I base my diet recommendations for each individual patient. Using my knowledge of physiology and nutrition, plus the essential information about each patient's metabolism, I am able to help people of all shapes and sizes in all walks of life lose weight and start enjoying themselves again. They use the power of the Burn Rate Diet to get the extra weight off and to keep it off—to triumph over the fat stereotype forever.

Recently, I had to make a decision about what to do with all the information I have gathered about weight loss and metabolism. I could have written a scientific paper, submitted it for publication in a medical journal, and then waited for the information to trickle down through the media. The more I thought about it, however, the more I felt that the information would be lost among all the biases that the world and the scientific community seem to hold about weight control. In the end, I decided that it was more important to tell the story of my success with my overweight patients than to publish my scientific data. I wanted you—the people who struggle with weight day in and day out—to have access to the truth about weight loss and weight control. So here are my observations and conclusions.

It is said that the truth will set you free. Listen to what I have to say, open your mind to eliminate your own biases about weight control, and decide for yourself where the truth really lies.

THE INTERNET CONNECTION

In conjunction with this book, I am very pleased to offer readers access to my Web site at **www.burnratediet.com**.While this book can stand alone, the Web site is an extremely valuable resource. With the use of Internet technology, *The Burn Rate Diet* is able to achieve a level of personalization for the general reader that has not been possible previously. Using the Web site, you will be able to calculate your personal Body Burn Rate, determine an appropriate weight goal, and plan the exact meals that fulfill your individual hour-to-hour energy requirements and suit your personal tastes. Through the Web site you will be able to create meal plans that are as individual as those I create for the patients in my office. I believe that this Internet connection is revolutionary, and that it makes all other diet books obsolete.

1

Toward a New Understanding of Ourselves and Our Bodies

Many of the people who call me don't know or care what kind of doctor I am. They call because they want to lose weight and have heard about my approach to weight control through a friend, their doctor, or the media. Whether they need to lose 15 pounds or 150, they immediately want to know how I am going to make them thinner. When they ask me, "So how is your program any different?" I believe they are really asking me not only how I can make them thin, but also how I can make them feel better about themselves. Then they ask me other questions about my approach to weight control to make sure that I am reputable, that I am not going to hurt them, and that I won't make them do too much work, or repeat the same kind of diet that didn't work for them in the past. They focus only on my dieting methods and assume that weight loss will automatically cause them to feel better about themselves.

THEME AND VARIATIONS: YOUR STORY

I share my patients' desire for them to lose weight and feel better. It gives me satisfaction to do my job and to see my patients' lives be improved. I know how much they want to be healthier. They would not have spent their hard-earned money and time following one diet plan after another if they didn't want to be healthy. With the Burn Rate Diet, weight loss makes my patients feel mentally stronger and healthier, improves their self-esteem, and improves medical conditions such as hypertension and diabetes.

Most of my patients' previous attempts to make themselves healthier have ended up making them worse. Time after time, a patient's weight control history shows that each period of dieting was followed by a period of weight regain. Usually people ended up weighing more after a diet than they did before they started. The saddest part of the story is that they blame themselves. They have become desperate from the embarrassment and all the failed attempts. In addition to physically feeling the strain of carrying extra weight, they are tired of having their weight make them feel bad. It hurts to stand out in a crowd and not be able to fit into the clothes they like to wear. They really want to be relieved of this psychological burden as much as, or even more than, the burden of their larger size. They want to feel better about themselves and who they are.

My approach to weight control solves all of these problems. You can lose weight and keep it off. You can be thinner and feel better about yourself. You won't have to hide or feel apologetic anymore. The first step is to realize that you can't lose weight the way that you have tried before. It can't be done with the next magical diet or by using a one-size-fits-all approach. There is magic in my approach, but it is the magic of treating you as an individual with energy requirements that are different than anyone else's, and with a psychological makeup based on who you are and what you alone have experienced.

You are unique and deserve to be treated that way. It's a simple fact that all people are different. Cookie cutter diets that treat all people the same way can't possibly work for everyone. A diet that causes one person to lose weight may cause another to gain the same amount of weight. Have you ever had the experience of being given a "great new diet" by a friend who lost 15 pounds in two weeks, only to gain 3 pounds on the same diet in the first week?

The methods used to control weight have to be as individualized as the people who use them. Some of you have been overweight your whole lives. As a fat child, you may have lived with the taunts and jeers of other children. You may have started dieting with diet pills when you were a teenager. You may have followed each new diet guru and gone from low fat to high protein by way of crazy diets that included nothing but soup or fruit or sugar cubes or eggs. I've heard it all! Or you may have exercised your heart out but stayed the same shape. You may have multiple diet books collecting dust on your shelves, proof of your failure. Even worse, you probably blame yourself, and feel more desperate and ashamed with each failure.

Some of you may have become overweight as adults. The struggle with weight control may have begun for you with getting older, stopping smoking, pregnancy, menopause, a medical problem, medication, or some other cause. In most cases, the problem started out small, like gaining 15 to 20 pounds after getting married. The weight may have disappeared with the first diet that you tried, and may have even stayed off for awhile. When it returned, however, a new problem emerged. Each diet attempt, whether successful or not, was followed by weight gain, making you heavier than when you started. You probably blamed yourself and were willing to try anything that gave you some hope. You most likely started each diet with the same enthusiasm as the one before, each time convinced that this was the last time you were going to lose weight. Above all, you believed that if you got back to what you used to weigh, you would finally have enough motivation to keep it off for good.

WHAT'S THE PROBLEM?

My approach to weight control is based on what I have learned from the thousands of patients I have treated. While each person is unique and must be treated that way, there are some common mistakes that nearly all of my patients have made. Whether they want to lose 10 pounds or 200 pounds, almost all believe that *they* are the problem. They believe that they simply eat too much and don't exercise enough. All of them believe that weight loss is good for them, despite having regained more weight each time they tried to reduce their body size. All are convinced that they have a problem with willpower or self-control, and blame themselves for each diet failure. Nobody blames the weight loss programs. No one stopped to ask whether the weight loss they wanted could be provided by the lifestyle that would be required to maintain it.

I don't want you to repeat those same mistakes. I want your Burn Rate Diet experience to benefit you and do you no harm. Some diet books are published simply because they offer magical solutions that sound good, not because they contain any truth. I believe people are only truly helped when they receive what they need. Sometimes what you need isn't the same as what you want. If you try and try to lose weight but regain it plus more each time, you get desperate. You lose confidence in yourself. You become vulnerable to believing that some magic diet or pill will be the answer. False hope starts to feel better than no hope, so you want a crash diet that will fix your weight problem fast.

There is another path to success. This way is based on real hope rather than false hope. Real hope involves an honest examination of the facts and realistic compromise if necessary. I believe it is far healthier to lose 30 pounds and keep it off than lose 50 pounds and regain 60. You may think that you will feel better about yourself if you lose all 50, but your satisfaction will be short-lived. The happiness of losing weight will quickly give way to the depression and increased self-blame of the next failure as the weight is regained.

Some people are blessed with a metabolic rate that does not require them to make such a compromise. A fast metabolism makes it easier for them to live as thin as they want to be. These lucky individuals usually do not have a weight problem. If they get a little heavy, it's easier for them to lose the extra weight. Other people are not so fortunate. Some have to yield to the demands of their energy requirements. Faced with this, some think, "If that's the case, then I don't want to even find out what it is reasonable for me to weigh." Don't shy away from the facts, thinking it is better not to know. Knowledge is power. It frees you to solve the problem once and for all. This book will show you how to plan your meals for weight loss, and it will even help you make some emotional adjustments if they are required. Real hope is stronger than false hope. Only if you face the facts head-on can you succeed and permanently feel better about yourself.

Real answers begin with the ability to trust yourself. Most of my patients do not trust their food choices. Some feel they are addicted to food or at least doubt the strength of their own willpower. Many wonder why they make the same poor choices over and over and why they may be hurting themselves with food. I don't believe that my patients are out to hurt themselves. While I recognize the value in original Freudian thought, I agree with many of my colleagues who think Freud was wrong to believe people have a death wish. For example, I do not believe that people who eat under stress are unconsciously motivated to destroy themselves by becoming obese. There is another explanation, and just because it's simpler doesn't mean it's wrong. For many people, food provides stress relief. When they get stressed, they eat to calm down. The result, getting fat, is not their intention and certainly not desirable to them.

If you believe that you are already doing the best you can, a whole new approach to weight loss and weight control opens up. You can trust your motivation to be thin and will not need more encouragement. In fact, what you need is to have your motivation protected from the external and internal influences that stop you from trusting yourself. You don't need a diet guru who wants to be your cheerleader and you don't need a policeman. You may think that you need both, but my patients have shown me the danger of putting someone else in charge of your diet. If you don't trust yourself, you won't be successful long term. Cheerleading only helps if it is clear why you need a cheerleader. If it is to help you do what you believe you lack the ability to do, then a cheerleader will hurt rather than help. You will rely on the cheerleader and will never come to believe in yourself. Needing a policeman is the same thing. If you cannot control yourself, and need other people to stop you from following your urges, what happens when they go away?

Trusting yourself means that you trust your natural eating habits. I find that my patients actually have exercised far more self-control than the average person has in an attempt to control their weight. Most diets are rigid and inflexible, which is one reason they don't work in the long term. Any truly effective food plan needs to be based on your natural tendencies, likes, and dislikes. Diets based on restriction and food elimination make no sense psychologically. You can live with restriction for short periods of time. Ultimately, though, weight control is more like running a marathon. You don't want to sprint the whole way; you need to pace yourself. In terms of food intake, you need to plan to eat what you can't live without, and build a diet around that. In this way, the psychology of restriction gives way to the psychology of permission.

I will encourage you to adopt many other beliefs to live thinner for life. For example, you don't need somebody telling you that you need to be a certain weight on a chart that is not relevant to you. Your body size cannot be reduced to a simple height-to-weight ratio. You are an individual, with your own bone density, shape, and size that are as unique as your fingerprint.

You also don't need somebody telling you to eat rice cakes for the rest of your life. You don't need to be made to feel guilty for liking desserts, chocolate, fast food, cookies, gravy, or anything else that tastes good. You don't eat only to stay alive. You eat for taste and pleasure, and to socialize. "Breaking bread" together is a powerful experience to share with others. Why else do you have friends over to your house to share your food, your style of cooking, your wine, and your home? Each is an important expression of yourself. Dining out with friends is a shared experience that deepens the friendship. To reduce eating to nutrition alone is no different than reducing sex to procreation. Eating food only to stay alive is as absurd as having sex only to make children.

THE SOLUTION: THE BURN RATE DIET

The Burn Rate Diet is my answer to what you need to permanently live thinner and healthier. Taking a whole different approach to weight control eliminates weight cycling. The essence of my approach is that you are treated with dignity. With the use of computer technology, I can now offer you an approach to weight control that is truly personalized. It is time to treat yourself as the individual that you are. While my Burn Rate Principles remain the same for everyone, each Burn Rate Diet is created individually, using the information in this book and certain calculations performed at my Web site.

The psychology of weight control in *The Burn Rate Diet* is based on real hope instead of false hope, on making compromises in your goals if needed, on trusting your choices with food, and on eliminating fear, guilt, and shame. Dignity replaces desperation, allowing you to restore your natural relationship to food. This in turn gives you a wider range of options to solve the challenges posed by your energy requirements. Because it is possible to flex the Burn Rate Diet from day to day, you will be better able to handle the inevitable highs and lows that are part of the weight control struggle.

THE BIOPSYCHOLOGY OF BURN RATE

An important part of this book concerns what I call the *biopsychology* of dieting. Weight control is a mind/body issue. Self-control is less important in weight control than the biology of metabolism. *The Burn Rate Diet* introduces a new biopsychology of dieting to help ensure success for every reader. The Burn Rate Diet frees you from the burden of guilt and the shame of past failures and allows you to recreate a natural relationship to food.

Weight control is effective only when you can stick to the plan. The key is getting your emotions and your behavior in tune. *The Burn Rate Diet* helps you restructure your approach to weight management by introducing a new psychology of managing the body's burn rate. Other diets are based on willpower and self-control. These approaches never work long term and basically act as a "double whammy." You stay overweight and feel worse than ever. In *The Burn Rate Diet*, a scientific understanding of metabolism and a psychological understanding of issues related to weight and eating replace the assumptions that have hurt you in the past. False hope is replaced by real hope.

I have identified eight Burn Rate Principles of weight control. They are discussed fully in the next chapter. These principles correspond to certain physical changes that cause changes in Body

Burn Rate, such as aging, pregnancy, increase in muscle mass, and weight cycling. The new biopsychology of weight control offered by *The Burn Rate Diet* explains and helps you manage such psychological issues as overeating, stress eating, relapsing, failing to exercise, and so on.

Consider the plight of the average patient who walks into my office. When I ask, "Why do you think you are overweight?" he or she inevitably offers explanations like, "I eat too much," " I eat the wrong things," "I don't exercise enough," or "I'm addicted to food." As I listen to these patients, I often wonder how they *know* that they overeat, or that their eating is abnormal. Most of my patients tell me that they think they should be eating like a thin person. When I ask them to describe the average thin person's diet, they describe a diet that is devoid of any eating for pleasure or joy. But this "skinny diet" is a myth. Research by doctors and psychologists has shown that there is no difference in the eating habits of thin and fat people. There are just as many overweight people who eat too much as there are thin people who stuff candy in their desk drawer to nibble all day long. Heavy people assume that thin people live on grapefruit and Melba toast. By extension, they themselves must be heavy because they like to eat muffins and bagels. It follows that the fat person is weak, lazy, and has no self-control. People with a history of poor weight control feel wretched about being heavy and believe it's all their fault.

The Burn Rate Diet shows that weight control is based on metabolism. "Fault" is removed from the equation. Knowledge replaces the guilt and shame. Consistent with the mind/body approach, it is your responsibility to manage your biology. With the Burn Rate Diet, you are free to eat for both pleasure and nutrition. Eating foods in moderation means sometimes eating a lot and sometimes eating a little. This approach brings with it the freedom to eat guilt-free. The biopsychology of Burn Rate banishes burnout forever.

THE NUTRITION OF THE BURN RATE DIET

The nutrition in your Burn Rate Diet creates weight control, creates optimum appetite control, boosts your energy and vitality, and

restores your natural relationship to food. Prior diets have emphasized one food component over another, such as high protein, low
fat, or high carbohydrate. By contrast, in *The Burn Rate Diet*, carbohydrate, protein, and fat are all viewed as different fuels for the
human engine. I have found that the key to weight loss and
appetite control is to combine these different elements of food
into a healthy diet that is uniquely suited to each dieter's metabolism. Using this book and my Web site, you will be able to create a
diet that takes into account your metabolic rate, food preferences,
optimum diet composition, and the perfect timing of your meals
and snacks. No two Burn Rate Diets are the same. Weight control
is tied to individual body metabolism in a way that truly personal-
izes the diet for each and every reader. Matching the right fuel mix
to your metabolic engine enables you to avoid hunger, live thinner,
and maintain a high performance level in work, love, and play.

"Fat is back" is a core concept of the Burn Rate Diet. By this I
don't mean *being* fat, but rather making sure enough fat is present
in your diet to ensure ideal appetite control. Giving the body a
steady supply of energy from the burning of fats—both body fat
and fat from the food we eat—can control hunger. The Burn Rate
Meal Plans are designed to ensure that energy is supplied over the
entire interval between meals. Fat from the body is also used as an
energy supply, especially in the morning. The body uses stored
body fat to meet its energy needs during sleep. As I will discuss
later, the Burn Rate Breakfast is created to integrate both energy
sources, the burning of body fat at night and the burning of breakfast food during the morning. This same concept is applied to the
Burn Rate Sport Snacks that are designed to provide the ideal
energy supply for sports performance. Fat plays an essential role
in living comfortably without hunger on fewer calories as well as in
providing a steady supply of energy to maximize athletic performance. Because the ideal fuel mix for our metabolic engine
includes a healthy amount of fat, the Burn Rate Diet reverses the
trend toward fat-free foods and makes weight control easier and
more palatable. Imagine a proven, scientifically sound diet that
actually includes bacon and veal parmigiana!

The Burn Rate Meal Plans include a healthy amount of fat at
breakfast and lunch. As long as they are part of an overall meal

plan, I even advocate a return to the old breakfast of eggs and bacon or other breakfast meats. Likewise, lunches on the Burn Rate Diet are larger than seasoned dieters expect, with foods like pizza, French fries, and even the occasional hot dog all being given their proper place. While remaining consistent with the nutritional guidelines of the medical community, the Burn Rate Diet not only frees you from the excessively low fat intakes currently advocated by many popular diet books, but also ensures successful dieting by giving the body the fat it needs.

The Burn Rate Diet presents a new nutritional framework for weight control based on the energy requirements of the body and the energy contained in food. Each of us has a different rate at which we burn fuel. I call this the Body Burn Rate. It is another name for metabolic rate and it defines the total energy needs of the body. You will determine your personal burn rate by following a reference diet, called the Burn Rate Test Diet (see chapter 4), for a period of two weeks, and then entering your resulting weight changes at my Web site, **www.burnratediet.com**. The site's computer programs then determine your burn rate. After your Body Burn Rate has been established, you can plan your energy intake to match your burn rate by using either the tables in this book or the Web site.

The Burn Rate Diet includes Burn Rate Meal Plans that are individualized to match each person's Body Burn Rate to the right fuel mix. Here it is important to recognize that carbohydrate, protein, and fat are burned over different time intervals. You will design meal plans that control appetite by taking advantage of the burn rate differences in food. In addition, you will be able to choose foods you like to eat, and to set mealtimes that suit your lifestyle.

FINDING YOUR GOAL WEIGHT

I advocate a new approach to selecting goal weight. This method is based on the fact that we are all individuals, uniquely designed to be a certain body size. We all have a natural weight that we would weigh if we all ate the average amount of calories per day for our sex and age. The problem is that some of us need to live on fewer calories than average to weigh less than our natural weight in order to be healthier or thinner. This is the hardest, coldest fact about weight control, and the one that many people refuse to face. The less you weigh, the less you get to eat. Each body size is associated with a different Body Burn Rate. You must choose a goal weight with a corresponding burn rate that enables you to eat a reasonable amount of food. This is essential to maintain your new weight and prevent weight cycling.

I believe that your Body Burn Rate, not some crazy ideal that may or may not be right for you, should dictate your correct goal weight. Ideal weight is not simply a number on a chart; it is a realistic goal based on each person's metabolism and current weight. Being realistic may be hard for you. You may have to choose a goal weight that is higher than you wanted. I am continuously amazed at the emotional intensity of my patients' reactions to setting their goal weight. If I recommend a weight that is consistent with their hopes and dreams, their relief is enormous. If I recommend less weight loss than they wanted, their sense of loss is equally large. Many people, especially in the United States, have a very unrealistic view of their ideal body. It is based on magazines and models that link power to sex and thinness. We have forgotten along the way that people are made in different shapes and sizes, and that our bodies are not our source of power. We aren't meant to all be the same. Who you are and the ability to represent this are your source of power. Your body is your vessel and only needs to be made as healthy as it can be to represent you.

When you really consider it, the choice is obvious. If you must make an adjustment, isn't it better to compromise and achieve success, than to reach for the unreasonable and hurt yourself in the end? The path of false hope leads straight into the proverbial "brick wall." Take the real path dictated by your burn rate and you will have real success.

You can use the Burn Rate Diet Web site to determine your ideal weight. This process is more complex than picking a number that sounds good. Your Body Burn Rate actually falls as you lose weight. Therefore, your goal weight is calculated by predicting the drop in Body Burn Rate that will occur with weight loss. Your predicted Body Burn Rate will determine your recommended daily calorie intake. For weight loss, your level of intake will be less than your current Body Burn Rate. If you keep restricting your intake, your Body Burn Rate will keep dropping with weight loss until your daily intake of calories matches your lower Body Burn Rate. At this point, you will be at your goal weight.

There is a limit, however, to how much food restriction is psychologically reasonable. In general, the lower the intake, the higher the stress. Daily calorie restriction can be mild, moderate, or severe. I do not believe that it is healthy or conducive to long-term success to attempt to live on a severely restricted diet. It is remarkable that many of my patients have been able to live at these highly restrictive levels for several months at a time. But in the end, the stress overwhelms them and their weight climbs to levels associated with more reasonable food intake.

I want you to avoid this mistake. I discourage my patients from choosing an unrealistic goal weight that would be difficult to meet and to keep. On the Web site, a graph will be created for you that shows how your Body Burn Rate will drop with your reduction in body weight and the recommended range for your goal weight. The computer will predict the rate of weight loss that will occur. Eventually, you reach a point at which you are no longer losing weight on your calorie-restricted diet. This is the optimal goal weight for you. In this way, you will live at a level of daily calorie intake that is comfortable for you. There is no roller coaster of intensive dieting followed by going off the diet. How you get to your goal weight will be how you stay there. By selecting the right weight, you can balance the desire to be thinner with a stress level that you can tolerate.

PAMELA'S STORY: POUNDS FROM PREGNANCY

Pam was a forty-five-year-old woman who had battled a weight problem her whole adult life. She had never been fat as a child and didn't start to gain weight until she got married in her early twenties. She blamed herself for the weight gain, feeling that she "let herself go" after being married. She started having children, and ended up holding onto 10 pounds with each of her three pregnancies. Now, as she was entering menopause, the accumulated effect was nearly 50 pounds. Her husband found her less attractive the heavier she got, and their relationship had deteriorated. Her doctor was on her case because at her last physical her blood sugar and blood pressure both had been borderline high.

It was not as if Pam hadn't been aware of her own weight gain. She had gone on too many diets to count. Each time she would lose the weight and feel terrific. Unfortunately, this good feeling would eventually give way to a renewed depression as she regained the weight. All along, she blamed herself for "letting herself go" and for lacking the willpower to be thin like her friends.

When she came into my office, Pam immediately burst into tears. She said, "I'm a very competent woman. I run an office and a home. I've raised three children. This is the one thing that I've not been able to do, and I'm so embarrassed about being fat."

Pam's weight had held steady for the past several years, but she wasn't happy with her size. I measured her Body Burn Rate by using the metabolic cart. Afterward, I met with Pam to review the results. Pam's energy requirements fell in the normal range. Since her weight had been stable for the past few years, I knew that her eating matched her energy requirements. Also, since Pam's burn rate was in the normal range, I knew her eating was also in the normal range. This match meant that her weight gain was not due to eating more than the average person her age. I described to Pam how the aging process and multiple pregnancies most likely had caused a drop in her burn rate over the years. By eating like the average person, she had taken in more calories than her declining burn rate had required. Pam's weight gain over the past thirty years had more to do with changes in her Body Burn Rate than with a problem with her eating habits during that time. As Pam aged, her average level of food intake stayed the same, but it became increasingly higher in proportion to her lowered Body Burn Rate. This difference between food intake and energy need was deposited as fat. After each diet, Pam's body size would increase until her food intake, which was still just average, matched a new higher weight. Unfortunately, with each diet, her body reset her "set point" at a higher weight.

Pam needed to settle on an appropriate goal weight. I explained how energy requirements fall with loss of body weight, and predicted that a 50-pound weight loss would require her to severely undereat, a fact that most likely contributed to her past diet failures. I recommended that she lose not 50 but only 25 pounds. This would enable her to live on a more reasonable amount of calories and give her a higher chance of maintaining her weight loss.

The relief on Pam's face was remarkable. She again burst into tears, but this time for a different reason. She said, "Now I finally understand. All these years I have been blaming myself for no reason. Now maybe I can once and for all take the monkey off my back and focus on my health."

Understanding Body Burn Rate cuts far deeper psychologically than just the relief that Pam experienced. The Burn Rate Diet frees you from such vicious cycles as eating a treat and then feeling guilty, or overcontrolling behavior—such as rigid, inflexible dieting; excessive exercise; use of the latest fad diet foods; weight loss goals set too high—followed by impulsive behavior. Unlike treatments that assume that being overweight is due to overeating, *The Burn Rate Diet* offers a different explanation. *Overcontrol* is the problem, not the lack of control that is commonly assumed.

NANCY'S STORY: PUTTING THE I IN ICE CREAM

Nancy was a patient who was caught in the cycle of deprivation followed by "cheating." She described herself as a compulsive overeater, and she believed she had gained 30 pounds because of her eating habits. Whenever she got upset, Nancy would eat ice cream until the container was empty. However, she never ate it all in one sitting. She would eat it one spoonful at a time throughout the day. I asked her if there was ever a time that she ate ice cream and enjoyed it, or didn't feel guilty. She said no. I then recommended that she eat nothing but ice cream for one of her meals. She looked horrified and said, "But I won't be able to stop! Once I get started, I will eat the whole thing." In fact, the first time she *did* eat ice cream for dinner, she did eat the whole container. The anxiety of eating the ice cream caused her to eat until there was nothing left. But that didn't continue. The next time, she ate the amount she had served herself, and actually enjoyed it. Thereafter, she ate ice cream regularly as part of her Burn Rate Diet. Understanding her Body Burn Rate enabled her to judge the amount she could eat, and she did not gain any weight despite eating the ice cream. She satisfied her craving, and now she knew that she could have ice cream whenever she wanted. After several weeks, she didn't care to eat it because she found that she would rather spend her calories on something else.

Nancy's story is an example of how anxiety about eating can cause overeating. It is also an example of how the psychology of permission can overcome the desire to overeat. Nancy ultimately learned to trust her desire to weigh less while taking into account her Body Burn Rate. Instead of seeing herself as addicted to food and unable to control herself, she learned to trust her motivation and self-control organized around her Body Burn Rate. Nancy successfully reduced her burden of shame and restored her natural relationship to food.

THE SEARCH FOR THE WHOLE TRUTH: DIETING IN AMERICA

Now that you have been introduced to some of the concepts in this book, I hope that you can see that the Burn Rate Diet is novel and may work for you where other diets have not. As I said before, I do not want this book to be just another diet book that contradicts all the other approaches. I wanted it to help you understand the pieces of truth that are contained in each dieting method that has preceded mine. Once you integrate these truths with each other and with Burn Rate concepts, you will come to believe as completely as I do in the Burn Rate approach.

This book does not dangle a magical solution before people distressed by dieting. Instead, it puts everything together. When I first meet them, my patients are confused by the array of opinions and ideas about dieting that seem so contradictory. Weight loss is explained not by magic, but by science. When the science is explained and understood, it all makes sense. I will show you how the ideas in this book integrate the ideas of the past and extend them into a new understanding of our bodies and ourselves.

HISTORY OF DIETING IN AMERICA

Dieting in America in the past twenty-five years can be described as reactive and volatile. The public is offered one nutritional craze after another, with several years of confusion between each diet. Each new craze is usually a direct reaction to the particular concerns expressed by the medical community and by the government through the office of the Surgeon General.

The cholesterol controversy is a good example. Cholesterol got a bad name when it was linked to heart attacks. A campaign to educate people about cholesterol scared people into eating differently. Despite the evidence that the majority of high cholesterol cases may not respond to changes in dietary cholesterol intake, many people continue to check the nutrition labels to avoid foods with high levels of cholesterol. Even eggs, the traditional American breakfast staple, have gotten a bad reputation. Regardless of the fact that many people's cholesterol levels would not be affected by eating eggs several times per week, most consumers fear that eggs will contribute to a heart attack.

Fat, too, has gotten a bad rap. People know that blocked arteries can lead to heart attack. Many people view fat as sludge that will clog their pipes, hurt their heart, and possibly kill them. Without understanding the big picture, they make an assumption that all fat is bad. This just isn't true.

The net effect of the cholesterol educational effort has been that people associate fat intake with fear. This fear is further increased by the medical community's efforts to stem the rising incidence of obesity in America, now estimated to affect well over 30 percent of the population. By familiarizing people with the health risks of obesity, health professionals have given people the impression that all dietary fat is bad and should be avoided at all costs. It is an easy association to make. Fat makes fat. Eat less fat, and you will be less fat. Unfortunately, there is more to the story. Low-fat foods, say a box of fat-free cookies, can actually have more calories because of its sugar content than regular cookies.

THE HIGH PROTEIN CRAZE

Once people are influenced nutritionally in a given direction, a wave of diet books arrives to exploit that issue and diet gurus stake their claim to the next magical solution. In the 1980s, an awareness of the health risks of obesity, coupled with an obsession with

fitness as the next American frontier, fueled interest in high protein diets. Diets such as Optifast, the liquid protein shake that
Oprah Winfrey used to lose weight in the late 1980s, and *Dr.
Atkins' Diet Revolution* by Dr. Robert Atkins featured protein as
"good" diet food. Carbohydrate was the "bad" food that made you
fat. Steak was good for you, but bread and potatoes made you fat.
An appealing feature of the high protein diets was the idea that
you could eat as much as you wanted of certain foods because they
had no calories. The high-protein approach spawned the idea of
"free foods," foods that could be eaten in unlimited quantities
without causing weight gain. With protein diets, you could eat as
many vegetables as you wanted. Vegetables were treated as if they
had no calories.

Oprah Winfrey's highly publicized failure to maintain her size
6 figure caused a dramatic shift in the marketplace. Many dieters
became skeptical and confused, and the liquid protein diet programs became associated with failure. Dr. Atkins's approach, high
protein and all the vegetables you wanted, was tainted by association. In addition, it became known that water loss, coupled with
the loss of essential electrolytes, created the potential for heart
attacks in individuals while on these diets. Eventually the public
lumped all high protein diets together and saw them all as health
risks. Protein fell into disrepute for the next ten years.

In the past five years, America has rekindled its love affair with
high protein. Protein is once again considered a good food, despite
the failure of the high protein diets. Protein is associated with
muscle mass development. Eat muscle, gain muscle is an agree-
able idea, and "free" foods are attractive. *Protein Power* by Drs.
Michael and Mary Eades is a remake of the high protein dieting of
the 1980s, with a severe limitation on carbohydrate intake. Even
Dr. Atkins's old diet has been recycled as *Dr. Atkins' New Diet
Revolution*.

Value in the High Protein Approach

Protein has its place in dieting and weight control. As demonstrated by the research on very low calorie diets, a high protein
intake can prevent the loss of muscle mass during dieting. These

types of diets, often using a liquid protein form, were called "protein sparing fasts" by the medical community because they spared the body from the loss of protein that usually occurs in muscle during periods of severe calorie restriction.

I do not debate the importance of protein as a protective mechanism during dieting, but I do question the value of modified fasting, especially from a psychological standpoint. These low calorie, highly structured diets create an abnormal pattern of eating. Modified fasting achieves the short-term goal of promoting fat loss without protein loss, but most medical professionals do not want their patients on a high protein fast for more than sixteen weeks. It is not a diet they can follow for life. Eventually, patients have to live on a balanced diet and learn how to be flexible. When they get to this point, nearly all patients on this type of diet regain their weight.

I know of many physicians who do not want their patients on a modified fasting diet at all because of the unnatural demands that it imposes on the body. High protein diets create a strong diuretic effect, causing high levels of fluid loss very quickly. As the body breaks down body fat for energy, ketone molecules are formed. During fasting, the body uses these ketones as fuel. The byproducts of ketone metabolism are excreted in the urine and eliminated through your breath, which is why people who fast tend to have bad breath. With frequent urination, you run the risk of dehydration and the loss of essential water-soluble minerals like potassium and sodium that are needed for heart and muscle functioning. If fasting causes potassium levels to fall too low, you are vulnerable to heart failure.

My experience with high protein diets has taught me several important things. First, if you believe in modified fasting, which I do not recommend, a high protein intake is necessary. Second, high protein diets cause a temporary loss of body fluid. You must differentiate between weight loss due to the breakdown of body fat and weight loss due to increased urination. It is easy to confuse the two because they both cause the scale to change. One is a false weight loss and the other is real. Third, there is no such thing as "free" foods. All foods have calories and contribute to energy intake. Finally, high protein diets have helped to clarify the role of ketones as an energy source in the body. Fasting diets have given us the opportunity to observe how people live on severely restricted intakes by burning ketones. Different levels of carbohydrate in the fasting diets have provided information about appetite control as well as about the relationship between glucose and ketones. These diets have shown us how the body can switch from one fuel source to another. The use of ketones as a fuel source has been incorporated in the Burn Rate Diet and is explained in more detail in the next chapter.

THE HIGH CARBOHYDRATE - LOW FAT APPROACH

With the evidence mounting that high protein diets had poor long-term success rates, plus the Surgeon General's warnings regarding the impact of high fat intake on cardiovascular disease, diets that emphasized low fat and high carbohydrate came into vogue in the 1980s. This approach seemed to promote good health and long life, and it made intuitive sense. Eating carbohydrate was encouraged and actually written into nutritional law by the experts when the Basic Four Food Groups were replaced by the Food Pyramid, with over 55 percent of the diet based on carbohydrate. Fat intake was readily connected to body fat. Dieters became convinced that if a lot of fat is bad, then cutting out all fat is good. Diets were based on counting grams of fat, and fat-free versions of innumerable food products were introduced. Some products that always were fat free began to advertise themselves as such.

As time went on, carbohydrates began to get a bad name. Carbohydrate intake was tied to lethargy, with some people even positing the possibility of carbohydrate addiction. Several diet books, including *The Carbohydrate Addict's Diet* by Drs. Richard and Rachel Heller and *Sugar Busters!* by H. L. Steward et. al. led this assault on the good name of carbohydrate. These authors saw carbohydrates such as white bread and sugar as contributing to cravings, overeating, and yo-yo weight cycling.

Value of the High Carbohydrate / Low Fat Approach

Carbohydrate is in fact the core of the human diet. The Mediterranean diet has its pasta, the Asians and Latins have their rice, and the Europeans have their bread. The scientific community recommends that carbohydrate should be at least 55 percent of our daily caloric intake. In the Burn Rate Diet, you can choose a carbohydrate intake of 50, 55, or 60 percent depending on your dietary needs.

Recent research has indicated that 42 percent of the calories in the average American's diet comes from fat. While there was certainly a need to emphasize fat reduction to reach a healthier goal of 30 percent fat intake, the emphasis on low fat became overdone. Some researchers claimed that fat intakes below 15 percent were capable of reversing heart disease, a very attractive notion to those who have had a heart attack, or those who have heart disease in their family. This would give them some control over their heart trouble. Here, too, though, the research has not borne out the expectation. Extremely low fat intake does not guarantee freedom from heart disease.

We know that carbohydrate consumption is linked to the regulation of blood sugar and its impact on appetite control. Understanding how the body uses carbohydrates contributes to our knowledge about effective appetite control. We now understand that a rise in blood sugar promotes the insulin reaction to store sugar, and that the release of insulin stimulates appetite. This mechanism is factored into the Burn Rate Diet by linking carbohydrate intake to each individual's Body Burn Rate.

The diet mentality in America has always emphasized one food component to the exclusion of others. It is time to rethink our approach to weight control and to find the proper place for all the elements in food. This is core to the Burn Rate Diet, where all foods are given their proper role in weight and appetite control.

IT'S WHEN YOU EAT THAT MATTERS

Carbohydrates have a definite impact on blood sugar. Carbohydrate moves into the system very fast. If you keep eating carbohydrate at very short intervals, there is an overabundance of energy available. The body deals with this very efficiently by turning the extra calories into fat. Maintaining the proper time intervals prevents overload and is important to keeping a steady supply of energy that is the key to appetite control. If you can control your appetite, restricting your calorie intake is made much easier. In this way, *when* you eat affects weight regulation as much as *what* you eat. But, like any other valid scientific concept, diet gurus can warp this simple truth.

Despite having almost no scientific credibility, *Fit for Life* by Harvey and Marilyn Diamond embodied the concept that weight control was based on both when and what you ate. This book was widely accepted and sold millions of copies. The public liked the idea that the combination and timing of foods was more significant than the amount you ate. The *Fit for Life* diet consisted of consuming fruits and meats in patterns that mimicked the diet of our ape ancestors. For example, protein is to be avoided until a certain time of the day, and only fruit is to be eaten in the morning. Many readers found this diet plausible and appealing. Eventually, dieters found that the *Fit for Life* diet's emphasis on food combinations and the timing of food intake was difficult to follow. Worse, this approach did not meet with long-term success.

The Value of Timing Your Eating

The concept that *when* you eat is as important as *what* you eat is a significant contribution to diet literature, but not for the reasons that the authors of *Fit for Life* suggested. In his widely popular diet book, *The Zone,* Barry Sears argued that carbohydrate intake causes variations in blood sugar that interfere with human performance. He advocated the careful managing of carbohydrate along with a level of protein intake consistent with each dieter's muscle mass. The purpose was to stabilize blood sugar levels and to maximize performance by ensuring a steady supply of energy.

The Burn Rate Diet also provides a steady supply of energy. In addition, I have extended the idea of timing food intake. Not only do you time the intervals between your meals (and snacks), but also the timing is linked to the burn rates of the different foods and to your Body Burn Rate. The Burn Rate Diet accommodates the individual variations that exist for each dieter. Fat, protein, *and* carbohydrates are all important, as is your own metabolism. This level of individuation has never been available in a commercial diet book until now.

The Burn Rate Diet is completely individualized to your particular habits, tastes, and energy requirements. It is the first diet that is based solely on who you are, and how your body responds. It is the one and only diet that is based on your own Body Burn Rate. It is as unique as you are.

In the next section, I will explain in more detail how changes in your Burn Rate may have affected your weight control efforts to date. I will then help you plan your own Burn Rate Diet. Taking control of your weight is only several chapters away.

2

Biological Principles in Weight Control

The Burn Rate Diet involves a total mind/body shift in your approach to dieting and weight management, centered on the idea that changes in body weight are more often than not the result of changes in Body Burn Rate, and not the result of changes in food intake. This means that both the corporate lawyer who suddenly realizes he has a "spare tire" and the mother of three kids who wishes she were at her prepregnancy weight are not necessarily eating more than they always have. This is a novel concept, and as I've said, it flies in the face of the belief that many of my patients have about themselves—fat people are weak, lazy, and have no self-control.

My patients blame themselves because they are used to doing so. American society harbors a bias against fat people. Any overweight person who has applied to college or a job knows the effects of the social bias against fat people. The bias carries over into the medical community. Doctors don't believe what their patients report about their eating. I remember one case of 350-pound diabetic woman who had to be hospitalized because her blood sugar levels were so high. She was placed on the standard 1,200-calorie diet while in the hospital and *gained weight*. Her physician actually had the audacity to accuse her of hiding candy bars in her nightstand!

AMANDA'S STORY: DOUBTING HER DIET

Overweight children suffer the same fate. Pediatricians automatically question overweight children's reports about their eating habits. Take the case of a child I'll call Amanda, an eleven-year-old girl who was 5 feet 5 inches and 175 pounds. At the beginning of puberty, she was often the target of taunts and teasing about her weight by her schoolmates. After breaking down in front of the school nurse during one particularly bad episode, she was referred to me. Both mother and daughter were convinced that Amanda's weight problem was due to her overeating and lack of exercise. They were both skeptical at first of my initial impression from her diet history. I was concerned that Amanda's Body Burn Rate was low. Sure enough, I measured it and found it to be one of the lowest I had ever measured in a child. I referred her to her pediatrician for a checkup to make sure that her low Body Burn Rate was not caused by some medical or glandular problem. This is rarely the case, but needs to be considered. Even after reviewing my report and evaluating Amanda's metabolism, the pediatrician questioned her mother about Amanda's eating habits. When her mother confirmed that Amanda seemed to eat less than her friends did, the doctor asked what she ate for lunch at school. Amanda responded that she usually had a sandwich, a piece of fruit, and bottled water. The doctor turned to the mother and said, "You never know what else they eat at school. My kids trade school lunches all the time!" With that comment the doctor invalidated Amanda's experience and reinforced her false notion that her weight problem was her fault.

This reaction by doctors isn't limited to patients who are children. Nearly all of my adult patients hate to go to the doctor. They hate getting on the scale for a very valid reason. No matter what ails them, once they get on the scale, their body weight is the cause of their medical problem. They don't feel that the doctor will listen to them or give them credibility. Body size blocks out reason and masks the true meaning of their symptoms. It is more evidence of the strength of the bias that exists in our society against the overweight.

Why couldn't the doctor believe Amanda? Why do all my patients feel mistreated by their physicians? The stereotype says that fat people overeat, are lazy, and use metabolism as an excuse for their problem. In America, we have very little tolerance for such weakness. Our country is the strongest and most powerful nation in the world because Americans are strong people. We are not a nation of lazy, fat people. We are a nation of adventurous risk takers, a place where competition brings out the best in people. We look up to athletes whose strength and courage are seen as prized possessions, attributes to emulate.

Doctors and researchers in America are not immune from cultural stereotyping in which strength is valued and weakness is loathed. The message is everywhere. Even children's books contain derogatory comments about fat people. I remember reading one to my daughter one night that had characters called Mr. Thin and Mr. Fat. Mr. Fat was seen with his work desk full of candy, chips, and other snacks. Mr. Thin was depicted as rugged and athletic. The bias and the blame are all around us.

Is it any wonder, then, that this bias invades the thinking of medical researchers and health care practitioners alike? The clinical bias of Amanda's doctor mirrors the thinking of much of the medical community. This bias influences the way in which medical people deal with the issue of ideal body weight. The bias can be seen in the new standard that has been adopted to define obesity. In the past several years, the medical community has adopted the Body Mass Index (BMI) as the standard measurement for ideal body weight. BMI is a calculated figure that relates weight to height. If you weigh 220 and are six feet tall, your BMI is 30. This is bad news for you, because the acceptable ratio for a healthy weight is a BMI between 19 and 25. For a person who is six feet tall, this BMI range corresponds to a body weight of 140 to 184 pounds. You are considered overweight beyond 184 pounds. There is no allowance for differences in bone mass, age, or metabolism. The previous standard, the Metropolitan Height and Weight Tables, had categories for small, medium, and large frame. These were eliminated by the use of BMI.

The fact that individual differences were eliminated reveals the bias. There is no adjustment for individual variables in weight. We have become fat phobics. Overweight people are treated as if they are all the same, although we know for a fact that age causes a decline in Body Burn Rate. Using the BMI, the fifty-five-year-old postmenopausal woman is measured by the same standard as the eleven-year-old girl.

I am 5 feet 8 inches tall and weigh 185 pounds. As a two-sport athlete in college, in the best physical shape of my life at nineteen years old, I weighed 175 pounds. Twenty-eight years later, I have gained 10 pounds. Many would consider that weight change to be usual and normal for a man my age. But by the new standard, my BMI is 28, and in order to meet the standard, I would have to lose 10 pounds and weigh the same at forty-seven years of age as I did at nineteen. That makes no sense to me. In addition, the amount of food that I would have to live on to be that weight would be too frustrating and stressful. And what would I gain? Increased health? Probably not, since the incidence of disease associated with excess weight does not become significant until you are 120 percent of the ideal, and some would argue it is not significant until you exceed 130 percent of the ideal. For me, there is nothing to be gained by trying to lose the weight but a lot of stress in my life for no reason.

Not only does the attitude toward body weight affect clinical recommendations, but it also affects the research on obesity. The press will report the results of any study that supports the link between obesity and inactivity in children. For example, a study may find that overweight kids watch more TV than their thin peers. Here is the evidence everyone has been waiting for. Fat kids really are couch potatoes. If you repeat the study and measure energy regulation, you will find that fat children expend far more energy in the course of their day than their friends do. The energy required to move their larger bodies all day long far exceeds the calories that the thin children might burn by playing baseball instead of watching TV. Or the thin child may be swinging on a swing or reading, instead of watching TV. There are not a whole lot of calories burned by swinging or reading, so the thin child should look like his friend, the couch potato. Only a few studies have been done that monitor energy patterns and attempt to respond to the stereotypes we hold about overweight children and adults. In fact, when these studies are done, they find that the fat children do expend more energy at the end of the day than normal-weight children!

The fact that researchers jump to the conclusions that support the bias against fat is easy to understand. Typically, nobody will challenge their research. Heads will nod in agreement because we have all been trained in our culture to believe exactly what the research has now supposedly confirmed. Overweight kids are lazy and inactive, and are to blame for their condition.

Here is another example of how research is interpreted to support a common belief. A researcher wants to examine the effects of high fat intake on weight loss. He or she already believes that eating more fat will result in less weight loss than a low fat, high carbohydrate diet. As we think we all know, eating fat makes you fat, so let's prove that to the world. The researcher takes two groups of subjects, Group A and Group B, and puts them on two different diets for a month. Group A gets 1,200 calories with a 40 percent fat intake diet, while Group B gets 1,200 calories with 30 percent fat. When the results are evaluated after the end of the month, lo and behold, Group B has lost more weight. The researchers conclude that higher fat intakes are associated with slower weight loss. The media reports the conclusions of the study, and the public becomes a little more fat phobic than before.

So what's wrong with the conclusion? Seems reasonable enough, right? Look again. There are numerous other conclusions that may be drawn from the study. For one, Body Burn Rate differences between the two groups could explain the results. The metabolism of the research subjects was not even measured, nor were the subjects matched in each group to control this factor. To validate this study, you would have to switch diets between the two groups, and have both Group A and Group B try each diet for a month. You would also have to remeasure Body Burn Rates after one month on the diet to make sure that the drop in body weight didn't change the average burn rate of either group. Not only that, you would have to make sure that each group contained more than thirty people, to ensure statistical significance.

Can you imagine the press reporting all these concerns to the public on a quick TV report on the news? I can't. It is far easier to report that high fat diets make you fat. This appears far more newsworthy and gets your attention because it confirms what you already believe. It is an easy sell, but far from the truth.

There is quality medical research being done that does ask the right questions and tries to avoid simple conclusions that confuse the issues. These studies are not typically picked up by the evening news because they are too complex and more difficult to report. Can you imagine a newscaster saying, "There was a study done with overweight children regarding the amount of TV they watch. It was found that overweight kids burned more energy than the average kid does in a day, but researchers still need more evidence to support the conclusions. The researchers did say that the pre-liminary evidence suggests that overweight children need much help from their families and doctors to battle the problem." Sounds too depressing and honest for the evening news, doesn't it?

Or how about this news bite from the TV reporter: "A new study reported that there was no difference found between the rate of weight loss on high fat and low fat diets. Investigators were planning future studies to examine the impact of metabolism on weight loss." I think that sound bite would end up on the cutting room floor.

In the following section, I will discuss the medical research that is not typically picked up by the media. Research is limited by the narrowness of the questions that each study is designed to answer. It provides possible answers only to the specific question that the study is designed to answer. That is why numerous studies are required to definitively answer one question alone, and why the overall trends from many studies need to be examined. The circumstances in people's lives aren't nearly that controlled. Clini-cal experience becomes important in answering questions that have no applicable research. Clinical knowledge is based on watching the patterns in thousands of people's lives and attempt-ing to provide answers for the common patterns and, even harder, answers for those that are unique.

To me, it makes sense to blend the current conclusions of the research with clinical experience. To do my job well, I must know the overall direction of research and blend it with my observations of thousands of patients to come up with an answer.

Both the research and my clinical observations of real people support the idea that many biological factors, especially Body Burn Rate changes, can cause changes in body weight. From my clinical experience and reading of the research, I have derived the eight Burn Rate Principles of Weight Management. I will discuss each principle below, including the research base where it exists, and the clinical experiences that have led me to these conclusions.

 Burn Rate Principle #1:
Energy requirements are different for different people.

Some people have a high Body Burn Rate, some people have a low Body Burn Rate, and the vast majority of people have a moderate Body Burn Rate.

While this fact may seem intuitively obvious, it is rarely applied to the stereotype of the overeating overweight person. You don't look at a fat person and wonder whether he or she has a low burn rate. You look at a fat person and wonder what he or she has been eating.

Recognition of this simple fact that people are different in energy regulation has been confirmed in relatively obscure research. One study done in the late 1960s was called the "Vermont Overfeeding Study" (Sims, E., and Horton, E. *American Journal of Clinical Nutrition*, 1968, 21, 1455). Prisoners were paid money to gain weight. The more weight they gained, the more money they made. Many discovered to their dismay that they were unable to gain weight despite eating the same higher-calorie diet. Even when encouraged to eat as much as they wanted, many could not gain weight, despite eating more than 12,000 calories per day! Others gained weight quickly with a relatively modest increase in their intake.

Another study a decade later was done by the Wooleys, a husband-and-wife team at the University of Cincinnati in Ohio (Wooley, S., Wooley, O., and Dyrenforth, S. *Journal of Applied*

Behavioral Analysis, 1979, *12,* 3). They noticed that the majority of research over the prior twenty years had attempted to answer the question "Why do fat people eat more than thin people?" Based on their own life experience, the Wooleys' research was designed to question the assumption that there are eating differences between fat and thin people. They found no difference between fat and thin people on numerous eating variables. For each group, there was a match. Some overweight people ate a lot. Some thin people ate as much or more. Some overweight people ate less than normal. Some thin people ate less than average, too.

Medical researchers have been very slow to accept the simple premise that what you weigh may have very little to do with activity or eating, and may have a lot to do with individual differences in Body Burn Rates. One of the most comprehensive articles on metabolism and weight control ever published appeared in 1991 in the *Journal of the Society of Behavioral Medicine.* In this article, Drs. Shah and Jeffrey of the University of Minnesota did a review of 132 studies. The title of their article alone gives us some indication of the resistance to accept metabolic factors in weight control: "Is Obesity Due to Overeating and Inactivity, or to a Defective Metabolic Rate? A Review." In that article, they address the role of eating and exercise and conclude that there is little relationship between how much you eat or how active you are and what you weigh.

That conclusion leaves us with a problem. Most health professionals believe that the increase in obesity in America is due to increased food intake. They point to fast foods with high fat content, sugar-filled beverages, and huge portion sizes to explain why Americans are getting fatter every day. Their solution is to get people to eat less, or consume fewer calories. Fat-free, sugar-free, or fat-blocking foods are some examples of the efforts to reduce the calories in food. But if how much we eat is only slightly related to what we weigh, then these solutions will only have a slight effect. I believe we need to address the burn rate issue. We need to identify those who are at risk for weight gain, and educate them about how to cope with a low Body Burn Rate before they get into trouble with weight control.

In order to identify individuals with low burn rates, the first step is not to round up everyone who is overweight. Body size should not be confused with burn rate. Most overweight people have a normal burn rate at their current larger size. It is after weight loss that the lower burn rate becomes exposed (see Burn Rate Principle #2, on page 32).

In order to appreciate the full impact of burn rate on obesity in the population, we need to make another assumption. I am not aware of any research about the distribution of burn rates, but I firmly believe my clinical observation will be borne out by future research. Many variables—for example, intelligence, hair color, left-handedness—exist in the human population. Some are called "normally distributed variables" because the distribution pattern forms a bell-shaped curve on a graph. This means that the greatest number of people share some trait in common. I believe Body Burn Rate is a normally distributed variable. On the graph, at the center of the bell, are the vast majority of people who have burn rates close to the average. The farther you go from average, meaning the edges of the bell shape, the lower is the incidence of that trait in the population. Since a bell shape is equal on both ends, the number of people who have a low burn rate equals the number of people who have a high burn rate. This means that if people were all to eat the same amount of food per day, some would gain weight, some would lose weight, and most would stay the same. The body weights would be equally distributed in the population, with an equal percentage of overweight and underweight.

I believe we can understand the increase in obesity in this country by looking at the effect of the food supply, specifically on those who have low burn rates. Because of increased food abundance, it is safe to assume that the average calorie intake was higher in 1990 than it was in 1890. In addition, because of modern conveniences and the automobile, there is less walking, bicycling, and physical activity in general. The net effect is to reduce the need for calories even while daily intake has increased.

When the average calorie intake was lower, there were fewer overweight people. However, though there is no research to support this, I would predict that there were many thin and unhealthy people in the 1890s who were malnourished and underfed. With prosperity, we created an energy-rich environment that exposed people with a low burn rate to a higher average daily intake of food. These are the people today who are overweight.

African American women have nearly twice the incidence of obesity than the equivalent white population. Researchers originally thought this was due to higher fat consumption because of poorer quality meats and a higher intake of high-fat convenience foods in the average African American diet. While these may be legitimate factors, burn rate differences were not even considered. It was only recently that Dr. Thomas Wadden and his research group at the University of Pennsylvania examined the role of metabolism. They found that the average Body Burn Rate of black women was significantly lower than that of white women, strongly suggesting that biological factors were at least as important as nutritional factors. (Foster, G., Wadden, T., and Vogt, R. *Obesity Research*, 1997, 5, 1).

Once burn rate differences are given the credibility they deserve, a different approach to reducing the incidence of obesity in America can be suggested. Since people with low burn rates at any point in their development are susceptible to obesity, the early detection of low burn rate could be achieved by including metabolic testing in the annual physicals of adults and children. Those with a low burn rate could be offered education and treatments like the plan offered by the Burn Rate Diet to effectively manage their superefficient metabolism. Metabolic screening might prevent the psychological cycles that lead overweight people to falsely blame themselves, or pursue unrealistic weight loss strategies with short-term outcomes.

Burn Rate Principle #2:
Changes in body weight cause changes in Body Burn Rate in the same direction.

As body weight drops, the Body Burn Rate falls. Conversely, as body weight increases, the Body Burn Rate increases. In other words, the less you weigh, the less you get to eat. The more you weigh, the more you get to eat.

Research in the 1950s on the post-obese condition (after weight loss) found that the drop in metabolic rate amounted to nearly 40 percent (Keys, A., et al., *Biology of Human Starvation,* Minneapolis: University of Minnesota Press, 1950). One of the most recent studies to examine this issue was a 1995 study by Drs. Leibel, Rosenbaum, and Hirsch at Rockefeller University in New York (*New England Journal of Medicine,* 1995, 332, 621). They examined the drop in burn rate that was associated with a 10 percent loss of body weight. Loss of weight caused burn rate to drop by 12 to 16 calories for each drop of 10 pounds. They also confirmed the mechanisms that appeared to be operating in the Vermont Overfeeding Study almost 30 years ago.

The fact that weight gain and weight loss affect metabolism has been known for fifty years, yet it has made little impact on the consciousness of the average physician or, most importantly, on the average person on the street. The concept did achieve greater acceptance with the development of the set-point theory of weight control in the 1980s. University of Wisconsin researcher Dr. Richard Keesey, Dr. Albert Stunkard of the University of Pennsylvania, and many others were supporters of the idea that energy regulation mechanisms in the body, not calorie control, were the ultimate determinants of body size.

The set-point theory stated that each person has a natural weight based on his or her genetics and energy regulation. "Natural weight" can be considered what your body will weigh if you eat the same calorie intake as the average man or woman. The body defends against changes in that weight by adjusting its calorie requirements downward as you try to weigh less than your natural weight, and upward as you try to increase your weight. The previously mentioned 1995 Rockefeller University study added support to the theory and demonstrated that burn rate changes are caused by weight loss below a person's set point.

Changes in muscle mass can also change the relationship of body weight to burn rate. Muscle is an active tissue that requires energy. The more muscle you have, the higher your daily total energy requirement, and therefore the higher your burn rate. As I stated earlier, there is no doubt that increasing muscle mass will increase your Body Burn Rate, but it is a difficult task for many because of the time commitment required, and also because of the hormone differences between men and women. There is also the unknown issue of whether the reduction in burn rate caused by weight loss will offset the increase created by adding more muscle. Further research is needed on these effects to determine their usefulness in controlling your burn rate.

 Burn Rate Principle #3:
Weight cycling causes a reduction in
Body Burn Rate.

Studies that examined the effectiveness of dieting have shown that nearly all people eventually regain the weight they lose, and very often they will gain even more. The weight loss and gain cycle, also called "yo-yo dieting," can be unhealthy for several reasons. A study done by Dr. Kelly Brownell of Yale University (*New England Journal of Medicine,* 1991, *324,* 1839) found that people with many weight changes or large weight changes have significantly greater risk for heart disease and premature death than those whose weights are stable. In 1994, the National Institutes of Health created a National Task Force on the Prevention and Treatment of Obesity whose conclusions were published in the *Journal of the American Medical Association* in October 1994. They noted in this review that yo-yo dieting can make subsequent dieting more difficult, and may be associated with increased health risks.

Not only can weight cycling make you unhealthy, it can make you fatter. There are *permanent* changes in Body Burn Rate that occur when lost weight is regained. With every weight loss, both fat and muscle are lost. Some diets are more effective than others in promoting fat loss alone, but inevitably some muscle mass is lost with all diets. More muscle tissue is lost with rapid weight losses than with slower weight losses. Unfortunately, when lost weight (including muscle) is regained, it is gained as a result of eating and therefore is gained as fat alone. When the body loses muscle mass, its daily total energy requirements are reduced. When the person returns to his or her original weight, he or she now has to eat less than before just to maintain the original weight. If the person returns to old eating habits and the same daily calorie level, he or she will quickly become both fatter (higher fat percentage) and bigger (higher body weight)!

Burn Rate Principle #4:
Obesity in childhood is created by a low Body Burn
Rate at normal weight.

Studies involving the Pima Indian tribe in Arizona have shed some
light on the role of burn rate in childhood obesity. The Pima Indi-
ans have lower burn rates than the white population. There has
been an alarming increase in obesity in this tribe as their way of
life has been influenced by the modern American culture. The rise
in weight has been attributed to increased calorie intake and its
more pronounced effect on individuals with low burn rates. Studies on Pima children have noted that a low burn rate at birth predicted which children would be overweight at one year of age
(Ravussin, E., and Swinburn, B. *Lancet,* 1992, *340,* 404). This
study begins to provide support for the idea that changes in burn
rate, even more than food intake, determine when a child
becomes overweight.

I am not aware of any research that has tracked changes in
Body Burn Rate for children, so I will share with you my observations of children whom I have treated. Some were brought to me
as overweight preadolescents; others were referred to me because
of severe eating disorders. My treatment involved continuous testing of their burn rates through gas exchange analysis with a metabolic cart. These cases reinforced my belief that each person's
Body Burn Rate changes throughout periods of growth and development. For example, a decrease in Body Burn Rate may be
caused by an internal regulatory mechanism, such as hormones,
that promotes fat storage. The trigger would most likely have been
genetically predetermined to kick in at that particular stage in the
child's growth. For example, the body may be preparing to store
energy to fuel a future growth spurt. In this case, it knows what it
is doing. If the child reduces his or her calorie intake to match the
lower burn rate, he or she may have insufficient energy stores to
fuel future growth.

I expect future research to confirm several observations I have
made with overweight children. Like adults, overweight children
often have a normal Body Burn Rate when their weight is in the
obese weight range. When they reduce their weight to the normal

range, their Body Burn Rate drops to below normal, which means they burn fewer calories than the average child does. If a child were truly overeating, the results would be different. The Body Burn Rate would be above average at the obese weight, and normal at the average weight. By determining Body Burn Rate, it is possible to differentiate the child with low metabolism from the child who truly eats too much.

All overweight children can use the Burn Rate Diet. I encourage girls prior to the onset of menses to eat within the normal range of calorie intake while increasing their activity level for general health and fitness. After the onset of menses, and especially when full growth has been achieved, adolescent girls need to learn how to live with their Body Burn Rate. I use similar guidelines for boys, allowing for their different growth patterns. The Burn Rate Diet is a plan that can help adolescents cope with their natural metabolism, and achieve a new level of understanding of themselves and their bodies.

Burn Rate Principle #5:
Adults gain weight as they grow older because of the decrease in Body Burn Rate with age.

It is natural for adults to gain weight as they age. Most believe it occurs because they eat more and exercise less. In most cases, the opposite is true. Most people eat less in their thirties or forties than they did in their teens or twenties. Moreover, declining activity levels do not affect the daily calorie expenditure sufficiently to explain this change in body weight. For example, if you were exercising three times per week and stopped, the net calorie impact would be about 150 calories per day, or 450 calories per week. The increase in body weight with aging is due to both the natural decline in energy requirements and an associated drop in Body Burn Rate. Average recommended calorie intakes are reduced for both men and women across different age groups (*Recommended Dietary Allowances,* National Academy of Sciences, 1989). While many elderly fight the gain in weight, recent research results indicate that being slightly overweight helps people to live longer (Berg, F., *Healthy Weight Journal,* 1996, *10,* 7). The increased weight may protect against medical conditions that affect the elderly. For example, the extra padding provided at higher weights might reduce the impact of a fall, helping to prevent hip fractures. The greatest life expectancy was found to occur in adults over seventy years old with a BMI in the range of 25 to 32, corresponding to 30 to 40 pounds overweight. (This begs the question of why we call an optimal body size "overweight.") This is in contrast to younger adults, whose optimal BMI is 19 to 25, as I mentioned earlier.

Burn Rate Principle #6:
Hormones affect Body Burn Rate.

Hormone changes in women, especially during pregnancy and menopause, are known to affect body weight. Dr. Rena Wing and her colleagues at the University of Pittsburgh in 1991 found that 20 percent of women between the ages of forty-two and fifty-three (that is, premenopausal and menopausal women) gained 10 pounds or more, with 5 pounds being the average weight gain (*Archives of Internal Medicine*, 1991, *151*, 97). The authors suggest that the weight gain may be caused by a decrease in burn rate. This finding is consistent with other research that found that a decrease in estrogen in postmenopausal women is associated with a decrease in Body Burn Rate. These findings support the conclusion that there may be a link between menopause, with its decrease in estrogen, and a decline in burn rate.

Weight gain patterns during pregnancy and their long-term impact on the mother's weight suggest a relationship between fat cells, hormones, and weight gain. First, there may be a relationship between fat cells and burn rate. The greater the number of fat cells you have, the higher will be your set point. This means that your natural weight will tend to be higher if you have higher numbers of fat cells. As you lose weight, fat is removed from fat cells, causing them to shrink. It is conceivable that the cells release hormones that cause a reduction in burn rate as a mechanism to defend the body's set point.

During pregnancy, the energy demands to feed both fetus and mother may exert a biological pressure on the body to store more energy. This could be accomplished by increasing the number of fat cells during pregnancy. The effect of this increase in the number of fat cells would show up after the birth of the child. The mother would now be different in her energy regulation systems. Her body's set point would be set at a higher weight, and her body would regulate her weight at a higher level than before the pregnancy.

This may explain why the amount of weight retained by mothers after pregnancy depends on when they gained the weight. Women who gained weight early in their pregnancy are more likely to retain that weight. Fetal daily calorie requirements are low prior to the twentieth week of pregnancy. As a result, weight gained during that time is added to the fat reserves of the mother (Berg, F. *Healthy Weight Journal*, 1997, *11*, 45). As fetal growth increases after the twentieth week, more of the mother's intake ends up contributing to the development of the fetus. Any increase in fat cells created prior to the twentieth week could cause the resetting of the mother's set point. Even if she returned to her prepregnancy level of eating and activity after delivery, she would regulate her weight at a higher level than before pregnancy because of the changes in her energy regulation systems.

I believe research will indicate that women entering menopause gain weight dependent on their estrogen levels. Women with lower estrogen levels will need to eat less food after menopause to maintain their premenopausal weight. Changes in Body Burn Rate can be managed by following the Burn Rate Diet. By tracking their weight and Body Burn Rate, women will be able to make the necessary adjustments in eating and activity to compensate.

 Burn Rate Principle #7:
Stopping smoking, and other biochemical changes, may cause a change in Body Burn Rate.

Weight gains associated with stopping smoking provide a perfect example of how changes in body weight can be misunderstood. Nearly all my patients who smoke have mentioned that one of the fears they have about quitting is that they will gain weight. Many have tried to quit numerous times and experienced a weight gain each time. Without fail, when I ask them why they gain weight, they tell me that they eat more to compensate for the absence of their cigarettes. One patient said to me, "Doctor, we smokers need to have something in our mouth. If you take away our cigarettes, then we have to put something else in our mouth all the time."

There is, however, another mechanism at work that is the true culprit in the weight gain associated with quitting smoking. Nicotine, the active component in cigarettes, causes an elevation in Body Burn Rate (*International Journal of Obesity*, 1991, *15*, 813). When you stop smoking, your Body Burn Rate is no longer artificially stimulated, and your weight can increase by 10 to 15 percent without any increase in your eating. For example, if you weighed 160 pounds when you decided to quit, I predict, based on Burn Rate Principles, that you would gain 24 pounds if you continued the same eating habits. If you gained more weight than that, then it would be due to increased eating in response to stress. When I review a patient's weight control history, and find that they have quit smoking at some point, I do the calculations and predict the weight gain in the next year after stopping smoking. It is rare to find that the weight gain is due to overeating at all. Nearly all my patients have gained the exact amount of weight that my 15 percent rule predicts!

It is interesting to note that I have never had a patient who explained his or her weight gain to me in this fashion. Every single one of them attributed the cause of their weight gain after quitting smoking to increased eating. They all believed that if they could just get their eating under control, then they would be able to return to their former weight. Not one realized that they were asking themselves to eat *less* than they did before to weigh *the same* as when they smoked.

Because of the changes in burn rate created by nicotine, ex-smokers need to change their approach to weight control. They need to redefine what is a reasonable weight and to experiment with living at different levels of calorie restriction and activity. Ultimately, they will find the right balance in calorie intake and activity to regulate their weight in the most reasonable way.

Nicotine is not the only drug or biochemical event that can change your Body Burn Rate. Thyroid stimulating hormone, or TSH, is a hormone released by the thyroid that activates hormone-producing glands. If your body fails to produce sufficient TSH, all the hormone systems will be sluggish. Low TSH affects energy regulation. Less energy is needed in this condition, and the Body Burn Rate drops.

Low TSH is the medical condition referred to as an underactive thyroid or hypothyroidism. It is unusual among the patients referred to me, but it needs to be ruled out, or corrected if it exists. It can be assessed by a blood test, and medication can be prescribed to increase the TSH in the system. In many cases, this treatment will cause the Body Burn Rate to increase, and to regulate body weight at a lower level than prior to treatment. An overactive thyroid can cause an increase in Body Burn Rate, and require a high intake of food to avoid becoming too thin.

Burn Rate Principle # 8:
A decrease in Body Burn Rate is associated with a corresponding increase in stress.

This principle is important to understand because it sets a limit on weight control based on psychology as well as biology. There is no research I can quote you to illustrate this point. It is based solely on my observations of thousands of patients who have tried unsuccessfully to manage their weight at levels of food intake that are unreasonable. People with a low Body Burn Rate who select a low goal weight must eat in an excessively restrictive fashion. Not only is this impossible to keep up long term, but also at some point it becomes psychologically unhealthy to live in that manner.

Severe calorie restriction can cause serious psychological damage. In the Keys et al. study published in 1950 on the effects of starvation cited earlier, the psychological effects of cutting the men's rations in half (to 1,570 calories) were observed. They became preoccupied with thinking about food to the point of distraction and were unable to concentrate on their work. They would hoard food, or find pleasure in watching others eat, or would read cookbooks or books on nutrition when they had shown no interest before, and would display many other obsessional features about eating. Consumption of coffee and tea rose so dramatically that the men had to be limited to nine cups per day! Gum chewing became excessive. High levels of hunger were associated with episodes of binge eating for some, followed by periods of severe guilt and self-blame. Some of the men experienced significant emotional and personality changes, including depression, anxiety, irritability, and apathy. One man became so depressed that he jacked up his car and let it fall on his hand to deliberately crush three of his fingers (Garner, D. *Healthy Weight Journal*, 1998, *12*, 68)!

While I have not had a patient go to those lengths, I have observed the food preoccupations, the high levels of self-blame, and the emotional changes that accompany severe levels of food restriction. At some point, it is psychologically unhealthy to live below a certain level of food intake. I recommend no fewer than 1,800 calories per day for men and 1,500 calories per day for women. While you may be able to live for brief periods of time at lower levels, the psychological strain becomes excessive over time. Even worse, in the end, you will blame yourself for failing to do the impossible, and make yourself more miserable in the process. Body weights that require a restricted food intake will most likely not be maintained over an extended period of time.

SUSAN'S STORY: LOSING WEIGHT, GAINING CONTROL

The case of Susan, a binge eater, illustrates what can happen when you try to live at a level of calorie restriction that is too severe. At her first visit, I measured Susan's burn rate by indirect calorimetry with the metabolic cart. At her current weight of 200 pounds, her Body Burn Rate was in the low normal range, requiring an intake of 1,900 calories per day. In the past, Susan had attempted to maintain her weight at 150 pounds, only to find that once she reached this goal she would periodically binge eat. At 150 pounds, her Body Burn Rate dropped well below normal and required an intake of 1,500 calories per day. She binged because she couldn't manage the calorie restriction dictated by her low Body Burn Rate. It exceeded her frustration tolerance. Her behavior resembled that of the men in the starvation study. She became preoccupied with food, and became overwhelmed by all the excessive attention to her eating.

Susan's problems weren't just related to her low food intake. Her life problems also got in the way. She was frustrated by her boyfriend's emotional distance, parents who were a constant source of criticism and demand for attention, and a job for which she was given too much responsibility without the authority to carry it out. These collective problems only served to add more stress to a situation that evoked high levels of frustration due to excessive food restriction. It was just too much to handle and Susan would start to binge.

As we continued to work together, Susan tried hard to find some different solutions. The first was to take the pressure off about her body weight. She agreed to adjust her goal weight to 175 pounds, and let her metabolism dictate her final weight. She challenged her mother's behavior, and made some demands on her boyfriend to emotionally participate in the relationship. She also quit her job. Susan was still occasionally vulnerable to food binges, but they occurred far less frequently and for shorter periods of time. Her eating became more controlled, and her weight started to drop toward her revised goal.

SUMMARY

I have found that these Eight Burn Rate Principles of Weight Management explain changes in body weight for 95 percent of my patients. The person who truly overeats without any associated changes in Body Burn Rate is very rare. I have treated only a handful of those patients. I believe that you, too, are like most of my patients and are affected by these Burn Rate Principles. In the subsequent chapters, I will show you how to apply these guidelines to your weight control. You will identify your Body Burn Rate and create your individualized Burn Rate Diet. I will then discuss how Burn Rate Principles can reshape your approach to weight control, much as they have helped change my patients' lives and their bodies. I hope you will see yourself in many of their experiences and come to learn something about the role of burn rate in your weight control.

3

The Human Engine

Many of my patients raise an eyebrow when I compare their weight management to the fuel system of a car. My female patients especially don't appreciate the comparison, and are not enthused about relating their bodies to a gasoline engine. It is, however, an analogy that makes sense, and one my patients come to appreciate when they realize its importance in weight control.

A human body burns fuel much like a gasoline engine. The body drives muscles and neurons for work and thought. It needs fuel to operate, and the proper fuel can make a large difference in the way the body operates. Use the wrong fuel and neither the body nor the car works well. Use the correct fuel and both operate at maximum efficiency. Without enough fuel, both run out of gas. Take on too much fuel, and both need a spare tank.

The human engine is wonderful in its design. Unlike a car engine, where combustion occurs in the chambers, the burning of fuel takes place throughout the cells in the body. Cell parts called *mitochondria* are the individual furnaces of the body. These furnaces burn two basic fuels. The primary fuel, *glucose* (sugar), comes from the food that we eat. The secondary fuel, *ketones,* are created from stored body fat. The body uses these two energy sources to create all the biochemical reactions required to grow, move, and think.

The sum total of the energy required for all these chemical interactions is called the *basal metabolic rate* (BMR). Basal metabolism is similar to the idle speed of a car. The human engine is constantly running, though it expends more energy when greater work is required of it. Our muscles act as the accelerator. They are active tissues that require extra energy to move a mass through a distance. The bigger the mass, or the greater the distance, the greater will be the work requirement of the body. While work calls for an increase in total energy required, BMR is only one part of the total energy requirement and does not change with the level of work. It may be increased temporarily under certain conditions, like heating the body in cold weather, fever, and possibly for a short period after intensive exercise. Outside of these specific conditions, the BMR is constant and unchanged.

Work in the body is expressed as energy units called kilocalories (1,000 calories). A calorie is the energy required to heat one milliliter of water one degree centigrade. It is a scientific reference point that is used the world over to measure energy in chemical systems. The energy requirement of basal metabolic rate is expressed in calories per day. The work done by muscle movement during exercise or activities of daily living can also be measured in calories. For example, walking one mile burns 100 calories of energy for the average person.

There are a variety of direct and indirect methods to measure the idle speed of the body's engine, or basal metabolic rate. Some measurements are made directly by determining the total heat of the body. Indirect methods rely on measuring respiratory gases, that is, our oxygen intake and carbon dioxide output. There are also mathematical equations that yield approximations of BMR based on height, weight, and age.

Muscular activity and BMR are just two of the human engine's energy requirements. Energy is also required to break down and restructure the molecules of food we eat. Food contains three energy sources: carbohydrate, protein, and fat. These are broken down respectively into glucose, amino acids, and fatty acids for absorption by the body. You will use the Burn Rate Test Diet in chapter 4 to determine your total daily energy requirement, which is the sum of the energy amounts you use for basal metabolism, muscular activity during daily living, and digestion.

BODY BURN RATE

The total daily energy requirement of your body determines the amount of food needed by your body's engine. Like people, car engines are different. Some get many miles to the gallon. Some are gas-guzzlers. For a car we call this the fuel economy rating. Much like the automobile, each body has a fuel economy rating. In the body, the fuel economy rating is based on the person's metabolic rate.

I recall one patient who could not understand why she kept gaining weight. She reported that she ate the same as or less than her friends did. She never snacked on appetizers, had only one glass of wine when everyone else had two or three, always ordered the lowest calorie entrée, and never ate dessert. She concluded that she gained weight even when she smelled food. She had a very efficient fuel economy rating. For her, a little fuel went a long way.

Each individual at any given age and weight burns a certain number of calories per hour. I call this energy requirement the Body Burn Rate. It includes the energy for BMR, digestion, and the muscular activities of daily living. It does not include the energy required for exercise or for intensive, sustained labor. Your burn rate is different during the day and at night. Metabolism, food breakdown, and activity all add to the energy requirements of the body during the day. At night, with virtually no activity other than sleep, and little food digestion occurring, your Body Burn Rate is the same as your basal metabolism.

If metabolism is like an engine, then food is the fuel that runs the human engine. Food, like gasoline, is a fuel that can be rated. Gasoline is given octane ratings to indicate its power. Food also can be categorized according to its burn rate.

The burn rate of food is determined by how quickly it can be converted into energy. All food that is consumed is broken down into other units for absorption. Foods vary in this rate of breakdown based on their complexity. *Carbohydrate* provides glucose, the basic fuel of the body, in the shortest amount of time and in the least complicated manner. Carbohydrate is composed of units of glucose that can be split easily into glucose molecules for ready absorption into the bloodstream. Because this process doesn't take long, carbohydrate has what I call a fast burn rate.

Protein consists of amino acids linked together in a variety of combinations. The amino acids that the body needs are absorbed into the bloodstream and used, while any excess is converted to glucose. Many of my patients are surprised to learn that extra protein is converted by the body into sugar. Protein has a medium burn rate. Its breakdown requires more time than the simple splitting of the glucose units in carbohydrate.

Fat takes the longest to convert from ingested food to energy. The breakdown process of fat takes three times longer than that of glucose, making fat the slowest burning fuel. This is a result of the complex chemical process required to convert ingested fat into either stored fat or ketones for fuel.

BODY BURN RATE AND WEIGHT CONTROL

A variety of factors determine the burn rate of the body. Your personal Body Burn Rate will vary throughout your life. For example, the daily energy requirements of the body diminish with age. Hormones are also known to have an impact on burn rate. Childbearing and menopause can affect a woman's burn rate.

I had one patient, Alice, who came to me after being on four different weight control programs in the past ten years. With each one she ended up gaining more than she lost. She'd never had a weight problem until she turned forty, and it had gotten worse as time went on. Alice came to me believing that her weight problem reflected a change in her eating and exercise habits. She didn't realize that her weight gain was biological in origin until I measured her burn rate and found it to be lower than normal. Her burn rate had changed in response to the declining hormone production that precedes menopause, so the eating habits that had been appropriate when she was younger now were causing her to gain weight. I was able to help her adjust to this fact and live comfortably at her most reasonable "new" weight.

Burn rate also can vary with changes in body size. Each person has a *natural weight*. I define natural weight as the amount you will weigh if you eat like the average person of your age and sex. You may, like many of my patients, eat normally but weigh more than your friends. Your body has mechanisms in place to defend that weight, including a certain amount of body fat. When you try to live thinner than your natural weight, your body responds by dropping its burn rate. This allows the body to preserve body fat, the fuel in its spare tank. Similarly, as body weight rises, burn rate increases. In this way, the body protects itself from weight gain above the natural weight for that body. This mechanism has been referred to as the body's set point. When necessary, the body will change its burn rate to restore the natural weight.

I recall one patient, Mike, who had battled with his weight his whole life. When he came to see me, he was 150 pounds overweight according to the charts, and had lost over 100 pounds four times in his life. Each time, he would regain more than he lost. When I measured his burn rate, and tracked it during the course of one of his weight losses, I found that it dropped significantly each time Mike started dieting. After a 60-pound loss, his burn rate had fallen to the point where he required only the bare minimum I recommend for men, 1,800 calories/day. This was an important fact for Mike to realize. In the past, he would always go beyond this point to lose the full 100 pounds. By doing that, his burn rate most likely dropped, requiring 1,400 calories/day or less. This level of food intake is unrealistic and requires an excessive restriction long term. Mike clearly realized that losing those final 40 pounds was not in his best interest. He lost the 60 pounds, was able to feel good at that new weight, and avoided future rollercoaster rides by maintaining his weight at 1,800 kcals/day. While the extra weight he carried was not ideal, Mike reduced his health risk with intensive and regular exercise.

GLUCOSE, THE PRIMARY FUEL

Now that we've covered the importance of total energy requirements to weight control, I want to discuss in more detail how the human body uses fuel. Once we understand how food is taken in, how it is stored, and how and when it is used, we can learn to adjust the fuel mix of the food we eat to control appetite and regulate body weight.

Glucose is the preferred fuel of the body. Glucose is a sugar molecule that stores energy. It is found in food either in its basic form, simple sugar, or as a series of glucose chains called complex carbohydrates. These chains of sugar units form foods such as cereal, rice, pasta, bread, and potatoes. To a much smaller extent, complex carbohydrates are also present in vegetables and fruit. Fruits and vegetables also contain many other basic sugars, such as fructose. Fruits, vegetables, and complex carbohydrates provide the basic fuel of the body, and are the staples of diets throughout the world.

When we eat any type of food, it is broken down in the stomach and intestines into its component parts. The useful parts, such as glucose units, amino acids, vitamin and mineral complexes, and fatty acids are absorbed into the bloodstream. Glucose and other nutrients are transported in the blood to the cells for use. If the cells do not need the glucose at that time, the sugar is stored in the muscle tissue, in the liver, and in fat cells. In the muscles and liver, the glucose is stored as a series of glucose units called *glycogen*. In the fat cells, the excess sugar is converted into *triglyceride* molecules. Note that excess sugar is converted into fat. This explains why a no-fat food isn't necessarily fat-free in the long run!

As a fuel, glucose has its strengths and weaknesses. Its strengths are its ready availability and ease of storage. Glucose can be ingested directly as simple sugar. When we eat sugar in any form, from table sugar to candy, the glucose can be readily absorbed into the bloodstream as individual glucose molecules. Complex carbohydrates, with their chains of glucose units, need to be broken down into the individual molecules prior to absorption. This is why complex carbohydrates take longer to absorb into the bloodstream than simple sugars. Sugar is absorbed into the blood in less than twenty minutes, while complex carbohydrates require two hours to be completely broken down and absorbed. This simple fact explains why many of my patients are hungry two hours after eating a meal that consists exclusively of complex carbohydrates. The body has processed all the sugar and is looking around for more.

I remember one patient named Bob who could never turn down donuts or bagels at the office. Unknown to Bob, one reason was that his typical breakfast consisted of a bowl of cereal with skim milk and a piece of fruit. Bob thought he was eating healthfully, but this carbohydrate-heavy meal was absorbed and stored in two hours. If Bob ate that breakfast at 7:00 A.M., then the glucose from the meal was absorbed, used, or stored by 9:00 A.M. It was no wonder that he was hungry by 10:00 A.M. when the donuts and the bagels arrived.

Unfortunately, the same thing would happen to Bob in the afternoon. Two hours after his low-fat sandwich, he would be hungry again. He would then eat a piece of candy, which would give him a short energy burst for twenty minutes, followed by more hunger. An hour later, he would eat another piece of candy. This cycle would go on and on, convincing Bob that he was addicted to carbohydrate foods. He would refer to himself as a "sugar addict" without realizing his true problem.

Both simple and complex carbohydrates provide energy as glucose. The body converts any extra glucose into fat. The same is true of protein and fat. Eat more calories as protein or fat, and the excess will eventually end up as stored fat. However, with protein and fat, the process takes longer than it does with complex carbohydrates. The food must first be broken down into absorbable units of protein, glycerol, and fatty acids. These are transported to the liver, where they are converted into either glucose for immediate use or fat for storage.

I find that many of my patients are confused about the body's energy requirements. Because of the amount of misinformation about nutrition, it is easy for someone to believe that *what* we eat is more important than *how much* we eat. It is easy to think that eating muscle creates muscle, or that eating fat makes you fat. The truth is that eating too much of anything—carbohydrate, protein, or fat—over and beyond what your energy needs require will result in an increase in fat storage in the body.

As I mentioned earlier, excess sugar is stored by the body in muscle tissue, in the liver, and in the fat cells. Changes in blood sugar levels can trigger each of the storage systems; glucose is stored as blood sugar levels rise or released if blood sugar falls.

Each of the storage systems has a different rate of delivery of glucose. That is, each level of storage enables energy to be supplied over different time intervals. This is how we avoid the problem of having to eat all the time.

Glycogen storage in the muscles can be considered the basic fuel tank in the car. Under high exertion, it is rapidly depleted. When the muscle tank is empty, a spare tank needs to be activated. This is where Mother Nature demonstrates her engineering genius. She designed *two* spare tanks—one that can readily supply glucose, and a second that supplies an alternative fuel from body fat. The spare tank for glucose is the storage of glycogen in the liver. When the body activates the glycogen in the liver, it is using up its final source of glucose in the body. This spare tank can deliver glucose for three to six hours, depending on the amount of energy that is being expended. The second spare tank is body fat, which provides the alternative fuel called ketones. This spare tank provides energy for hours to days and weeks at a time when no food is eaten.

Under normal circumstances, the coordinated use of these three energy storage systems is critical to providing an even flow of energy to the body. A constant and uninterrupted energy supply is the key to appetite control, body weight regulation, and peak human performance. These storage systems provide energy in between meals.

Candy can activate the storage systems for glucose. The ease of absorption of sugar can result in rapid rises in blood sugar. It is one of those times when the simple law is true: Eat sugar and you get sugar in the blood. This rise in blood sugar must be controlled because glucose can become toxic to the system at high levels. This is why people with uncontrolled diabetes risk tissue and nerve damage from high sugar levels.

The body produces insulin to control the rise in glucose in the blood. As blood sugar rises, insulin is released from the pancreas to store the excess glucose. Over time, as more glucose is stored, the levels of both sugar and insulin in the blood start to drop. We experience this drop as fatigue and hunger that act as signals to the body that no more fuel is available. In this sense, insulin acts as the fuel gauge in the system. It signals when the tank is empty and activates the hunger mechanisms to ensure that we refuel.

KETONES, THE ALTERNATIVE FUEL

Glucose is not the only fuel used by the body. Human engines can also burn ketones, molecules that are produced from the breakdown of body fat. Body fat has different properties than glucose. Understanding how the body uses these fuels, both alone and mixed together, provides us with many options for regulating our body weight, appetite, and energy level.

When excess glucose is stored as body fat, it is not released again as glucose. Once it is converted into a fat molecule, it is released into the system as a ketone molecule. The release is slow to develop, allowing the body to nearly deplete its preferred fuel, glucose, before it shifts to ketones.

I became acutely aware of the effects of ketones on the human body when I was the director of several hospital weight control programs in the 1980s. The patients in these programs were put on fasting diets that required medical supervision. Dieters would follow a semistarvation diet of 600 to 800 calories a day of high protein with a severe carbohydrate restriction. The purpose of the protein was to protect the patient from the loss of muscle mass. The limitation on carbohydrates caused the body to burn body fat almost exclusively. Ketones would build to high levels in the blood in a short period of time, resulting in appetite suppression.

Over an eight-year span, I personally participated in the treatment of over two thousand patients on this type of diet. I was surprised by their different reactions. For one, I couldn't believe how good many of these patients felt while on the diet. Many reported that they experienced no hunger. I found their overall good health while nearly starving to be remarkable. How could somebody feel so good and eat so little?

I attributed their positive response to the availability of their back-up fuel supply. They were literally "living off the fat of the land." Body fat was being turned into ketones as the energy source for the body's needs. The exclusive reliance on ketones as a fuel supply avoided the rise and fall of blood sugar levels that occur when food is eaten. The energy supply was constant and uniform. My patients experienced no hunger and reported that they didn't even think about eating. Some even had to be urged to eat the protein they needed because they didn't want to eat at all. Their bodies had adapted to using ketones as fuel, and they had an abundant supply.

The buildup of ketones had different effects on each dieter's body. These included frequent urination, bad breath, and headaches. A few patients complained of fatigue. These effects occurred to varying degrees in different patients. Some tolerated ketones better than others. Some took a long time to feel the absence of appetite. Others felt it right away. Headaches ranged from mild to severe, with some patients having an onset within a few hours of ketone production while others never developed a headache.

These varying reactions occur because people differ genetically in how they use the two-fuel system. Some people burn glucose effectively, but don't use ketones well. They may experience nausea in the absence of glucose. For example, I have some patients who don't feel good when they wake up in the morning. These patients are probably more sensitive to the presence of ketones and experience adverse reactions as ketones build up overnight. Some patients are the exact opposite. They skip breakfast and don't report any hunger until the afternoon. These people use ketones effectively and don't report any ill effects from skipping meals.

One patient who had a difficult time with ketone adaptation was Jane. While following a normal diet, Jane reported to me that she felt nauseated every morning. No matter what she tried, nothing seemed to solve the problem. My best guess was that she had an intolerance to ketones, and needed to prevent the overnight buildup if she wanted to feel better in the morning. I recommended that she eat a bowl of cottage cheese before going to bed because digesting the protein and fat would delay the onset of ketone production. It worked. She reported that she felt much better in the morning and no longer felt any stomach distress.

Contrast Jane with another patient. Tony feels better when he doesn't eat breakfast. He typically has no breakfast, a small lunch, and a large dinner. Tony noticed that when he did eat breakfast, he would eat an even larger lunch because he would feel really hungry. Then, he would still have a large dinner. Tony adapted readily to the ketones produced during sleep after food was no longer available. His system worked better when he relied on ketones throughout the morning, and introduced the glucose system gradually by eating a small lunch.

I needed to consider both fuel sources, glucose and ketones, in planning meals for Tony and Jane. I based decisions about whether or not breakfast should be skipped, the type of breakfast that should be eaten, when to exercise, and what to eat before exercise on their individual reactions to the two-fuel system. Tony's effective use of ketones, in contrast to the commonly accepted rules of healthy eating, enables him to save the calories from breakfast and to live thinner and healthier for it.

When an engine uses two fuels, the transition between fuels often reduces performance. There may be a gap in time when one fuel runs low and the other is needed, or the engine may require time to make adjustments so it will burn as efficiently with one fuel as the other. Mechanics refer to this problem as the engine "running rough."

The same is true of the human engine. There is often a period of time when the body's performance is impaired as it makes the transition to a new fuel source. Another important factor is how much of each fuel is available at any given time. Some people's engines run well on low levels of ketones, but they experience trouble, such as headaches and/or fatigue, during the transition to higher levels of ketones. However, some people are able to adapt and operate very effectively on ketones at any level. The challenge is to find a way to use both fuels comfortably. This is the key to effective appetite and weight control.

MIXING TWO FUELS: GLUCOSE AND KETONES

Throughout the day, the average person shifts from one fuel source to another. Consider what occurs at the end of the day. Ketone production is activated at different times depending on the composition of your dinner, your Body Burn Rate, and the timing of your last meal or snack. If you ate a big meal late in the evening, then ketone production is low in the morning. The food is metabolized over a six-hour period before ketone production is significantly activated. If you sleep for eight hours, the last two hours would be fueled by ketones. If you ate the same meal earlier, with a small night snack of carbohydrate such as pretzels or a piece of fruit, then ketone production is higher in the morning. The fuel from the snack would be burned in two hours, leaving six hours of night metabolic functioning to be fueled by ketones.

My patients on the fasting diets had large individual differences in their responses to ketones. In an effective diet and particularly in long-term weight control, these individual differences need to be accommodated. The most significant factor is the Body Burn Rate. In subsequent chapters, you will learn how to determine your own Body Burn Rate, and how to individualize your diet to best meet your energy requirements. You will also learn how to experiment with different evening snacks to change your ketone level in the morning.

For the average person, breakfast is the first time during the day that the body needs to make the transition in fuel sources. Throughout the night, the body has exhausted any glucose it took in prior to sleep. When you introduce glucose back into the system during breakfast, your body ceases ketone production and switches to its preferred fuel, glucose. This is especially true if you consume a fast-burning fuel like cereal or orange juice that introduces glucose into the bloodstream quickly. As the preferred fuel becomes quickly available, there is no longer any need for the body to use ketones.

If the influx of glucose into the system is slower, ketone production will continue and both fuels will be used simultaneously. The basic principle of the Burn Rate Diet is to slowly decrease the rate of ketone production by the gradual introduction of glucose. This can be accomplished by eating foods that contain protein and fat rather than carbohydrate for breakfast. Since protein and fat take longer to be utilized, glucose is fed slowly into the system. Ketone production continues, providing two fuels for the body during the morning hours.

I learned about the effects of glucose on ketone production from observing my patients on the fasting diet. Their carbohydrate intake was highly restricted to prevent the shutdown of ketone production. Each dieter was given an allowance of 30 grams of carbohydrate per day. This would allow ketone production to stay elevated, thus suppressing appetite as the fat melted away.

Patients varied widely in their tolerance for carbohydrates. Some could eat double the gram limit and still report no appetite, indicating that their ketone level remained high despite the increase in carbohydrate. Others were highly sensitive to the slightest increase above 30 grams per day. A few needed to be restricted to 20 grams, and a handful had to have no carbohydrate at all to achieve the desired effect of ketone production.

The use of ketones as fuel is a double-edged sword. On a fasting diet, ketone production stabilizes the dieter's energy supply and controls appetite. In a normal, balanced diet, burning body fat for energy has a cumulative effect on appetite. Body fat is the last reserve for the body. When it is reduced, a strong signal, experienced as a strong surge of appetite, tells the body to refill the spare tank. Once carbohydrate has been introduced and ketone production falls, the body signals the need to refill the storage tank by an increase in hunger. The availability of glucose signals to the body that food is now present, and ketones are no longer needed.

THE URGE TO EAT

I have had much personal experience with the strength of the urge to eat. My wife, who has lived with me for twenty-five years, has told me, "You're like a bear when you don't eat." One of my children is the same way. Her mood slowly turns ugly the longer she goes without food. She becomes her usual sunny self once she has eaten.

This type of mood swing is just one illustration of the impact of hunger on the human body and mind. Food cravings are another. Many of my patients report that they crave a particular kind of food, like a donut or potato chips, whenever they get hungry. When they try to ignore the craving, it only seems to get worse. The more they try to not think about it, the more they think about it. The obsession with the food makes them feel crazy. They feel they think about food too much, or even describe themselves as addicted to food, as if they have been taken over by some powerful force of unknown origin.

Appetite control is difficult under normal circumstances. It is even harder as we lose weight and try to live at a weight below our natural set point. The farther below our natural weight we try to live, the less food we get to eat, and the more we have to battle hunger. The longer we fight hunger, the more tired we become of the fight. As the hunger grows, our resistance to food decreases. It is a tiresome and exhausting process.

Appetite is the body's signal that your energy supply is running low. As your blood sugar drops, a signal is sent to your brain to trigger appetite. You experience this reaction as an increase in the urge to eat. Corresponding chemical messengers are sent to the secondary fuel system, which is stored fat. The body activates the process of converting stored fat into ketones for energy. This process is associated with an even greater urge to eat. People feel "famished" and they often overeat in this state.

Fortunately, there is a way to win this fight with appetite. By matching your body's burn rate to the burn rate of the foods you eat, you can reduce the strength of the hunger signals. Also, you can use the two fuels of the body, glucose and ketones, in combinations that keep your energy supply at a high level and keep hunger from your door. In this chapter, I will show you how to mix and match these foods and fuels to reduce appetite and enable you to eat less and live thinner.

THE OLD FARMER

The old farmer was a man who needed plenty of energy. He typically got up before sunrise, fed the animals, milked the cows, and then came in for breakfast. He hadn't eaten since his late night snack about nine o'clock the night before. Since he rose at 5:00 A.M., he had gone eight hours since eating any food. Any hint of glucose from his food had disappeared from his bloodstream over two hours before he woke up. Because the body needs energy even while sleeping, he had to create the new fuel, ketones, by burning body fat to fuel his burn rate while he slept. He was using that fuel as he arose.

The old farmer may not have been that hungry when he first got up. However, the work of his early morning chores reduced the ketone levels in his blood, and he got hungrier the more he worked. He knew that a big day of activity lay ahead of him. He may have had to bale hay, mend fences, plant or pick crops, and many other physically demanding jobs. He needed a hearty meal to keep him going.

At 7:00 A.M., the old farmer's wife called him inside. She served him eggs, bacon, sausage or scrapple, toast, muffins, and maybe some side dish of oatmeal or grits. He ate three eggs, five sausages, and seven strips of bacon. He put real homemade butter on his toast or muffin until it dripped.

The old farmer has just eaten what is considered poison in today's world. His intake of fat alone in that one meal may exceed 50 grams. Today his doctor would be advising him to eat only two eggs per week and to watch his cholesterol. His friends at the health club would be telling him that he is going to die if he doesn't switch to cereal or maybe a granola bar for breakfast.

The farmer knew from years of experience what he was doing. He knew that if he didn't eat all that high-fat food, he would be hungry by ten o'clock. He didn't have time to return to his house to eat a midmorning snack. He also couldn't afford to be hungry or tired, with all the physical chores he had to do. He knew he needed food that "sticks to your ribs" to keep him going.

The farmer's wisdom has gotten lost along the way, buried by the research on cardiovascular disease and the guidelines regarding proper nutrition. From studies regarding the impact of lifestyle on disease, we know that heart disease can be controlled with exercise, a low fat diet, and proper cholesterol management.

But what about the old farmer? Did he die of heart disease from his diet? Probably not, unless it was genetic and his father, mother, aunt, or uncle died of heart disease. He may or may not have had high cholesterol levels. His high cholesterol intake may have given him abnormal levels in his blood, but only if he was genetically predisposed. He certainly got his fair share of exercise in his normal activities of daily living, so the higher fat intake may not have mattered. He may have struggled with his weight, but I doubt it. Even if he had a low Body Burn Rate, the calories burned in his activities of daily living most likely compensated for it. In fact, many farmers may have had the opposite problem.

Those with high metabolic rates were probably too lean and had trouble eating enough calories to keep the meat on their bones.

So, with our wealth of modern medical knowledge, do we think the old farmer should change his meals? Should he be eating a granola bar or a high-fiber cereal with a banana for breakfast? Today the wisdom of the farmer's diet needs to be blended with the medical research on genetics and heart disease. Both the farmer and the nonfarmer need to base their diet on their genetic background. People first need to consult with a doctor to assess their cardiac risk profile. If their cholesterol levels are within normal range, and there is no known disease risk in the family, they are free to incorporate the ideas learned by the old farmer. In fact, *The Burn Rate Diet* combines the ideas of the old farmer with the concepts of modern medical technology. It's possible to eat a scaled-down version of the farmer's breakfast and still be within the guidelines that are recommended by all the leading nutrition authorities.

Food That Sticks to the Ribs

The old farmer ate food that "stuck to his ribs" for a good reason. The old farmer knew the foods that would prevent him from tiring and that would keep his hunger at bay. While he did not know it, the farmer's choices were based on the burn rate of foods. He knew how to properly distribute the fat in his diet to maximize his appetite control. The fat we eat takes six hours to be completely transformed into glucose in the blood. The supply is slow but steady throughout the six-hour period.

So why not eat all fat? The explanation is that the glucose levels would not rise fast enough to meet your body's energy needs. If you ate nothing but fatty foods, you might not feel hungry at the end of the six hours, but you would feel lethargic at the start. If the old farmer ate only bacon for breakfast, he wouldn't feel like getting up from his chair to attend to the chores. He would need a quick start with an energy supply to last him. He required a mixture of foods to supply a constant supply of glucose for his muscles to do their work.

APPETITE CONTROL

Like the old farmer, you need a steady stream of energy to prevent becoming tired and hungry. A fuel mixture that provides a steady supply of energy is the key to appetite and weight control. We can live on fewer total calories when we eat a mixture of foods that keeps our appetite in check. To help you understand how to accomplish this level of appetite control, I explain below the mechanisms that affect appetite and the optimal fuel mixtures that provide us with a steady stream of energy.

Appetite Control and What We Eat

Burn rate determines the speed at which glucose is consumed. However, the type of foods we eat determines the rate that glucose becomes available to the body. Foods that have a fast burn rate, like simple sugars or complex carbohydrates, are consumed or stored very quickly. This is why eating a candy bar gives us a quick rise in energy, followed by a quick drop into feeling tired and lethargic.

Protein and fat have, respectively, medium and slow burn rates. As a result, these fuels provide a steady stream of glucose slowly fed into the bloodstream on a constant basis. Avoiding an overload of glucose prevents the blood sugar roller-coaster ride of insulin release and glucose storage. Ideally, the blending of these three food types, each with a different burn rate, provides a steady stream of the right amount of glucose to match the Body Burn Rate. When the body's needs are being met, you don't feel hungry. This maintains full appetite control throughout the time interval required.

Appetite Control and Ketones

As mentioned earlier, when blood sugar drops, the body begins to burn body fat and produces ketone molecules that can be burned to supply energy. There are two problems with this energy source. The first is that it is slow to get started. Glucose must be low for a period of time before fat oxidation is initiated. Typically, low glucose levels occur during sleep. The last food you eat before going to bed is either burned or stored within two to six hours. The maximum figure is based on the six-hour burn rate of fat, the longest burning fuel. The longer the interval without a glucose supply, the greater will be the level of ketones in the blood. The body appears to anticipate the need for fuel and increases the ketone supply in response to the absence of glucose.

The second problem with ketones, one I mentioned earlier, is that there is a wide range of individual tolerances for the use of ketones. High levels can be associated with fatigue, headache, or even lightheadedness. People who are highly sensitive to ketones are not able to effectively use them for energy. Ketone tolerance is an individual matter that can best be determined by trial and error.

The first step in determining your ketone tolerance would be to determine your Body Burn Rate. You will learn how to calculate your Body Burn Rate in chapter 4. The second step is to match the fuel mixture of the foods you eat with your Body Burn Rate. This match will provide you with a steady stream of glucose while avoiding the overload that activates the insulin reaction. In chapter 5 you'll learn how to categorize foods by their dominant type of fuel, a novel organizing principle that you will use in meal planning. Chapters 6 and 7 will offer you an opportunity to experiment with different meals and snacks. Trial-and-error adjustments of your late night snacks will enable you to determine your tolerance for ketones.

The Burn Rate Diet accounts for individual differences in use of glucose and ketones, enabling you to maximize your appetite control and live at the lowest weight possible for you. The Burn Rate Diet that you will ultimately follow will depend on your individual Body Burn Rate. In the next chapter, I will show you how to determine your own Body Burn Rate with the Burn Rate Test Diet.

4

The Burn Rate Test Diet

The Burn Rate Test Diet is a structured meal plan you will follow for two weeks in order to determine your individual Body Burn Rate. In this chapter, I will show you how to use the Test Diet and how to interpret the results. After that, you will create your own individualized Burn Rate Diet by using the Web site.

WHAT'S A TEST DIET?

Unlike the usual diet that is designed for weight loss, the Burn Rate Test Diet has a different purpose. It is designed to provide you with the means to measure your Body Burn Rate. You will carefully follow a series of menu plans for fourteen days, and record the weight changes that you experience during that time. Your final weight change indicates whether your Body Burn Rate is higher or lower than the calorie level of the Test Diet, and by how much.

Once you know your Body Burn Rate, you can determine your ideal or goal weight and construct your individualized Burn Rate Diet to achieve that weight. Your personal Burn Rate Diet is based not only on your Body Burn Rate but also on your food preferences, the burn rate of those foods, the diet composition (percentage of carbohydrate, protein, and fat) you desire, and the time intervals of your eating.

While this may all sound overwhelming and complex, it is made simple and easy by the use of computer technology available to you on my Internet Web site, **www.burnratediet.com**. You will be able to use the site to calculate your Body Burn Rate, determine your ideal weight, and create your individualized Burn Rate Diet. You simply enter in the variables and let the computer do the work. It will enable you for the first time to have a nutritional plan that is an exact fit for *your* body and *your* lifestyle. It is a diet for you and about you. It is as unique as you are.

If you are not familiar with the use of the Internet or do not have access to it, the calculations are available in Appendix II at the back of the book.

THE DIETING DILEMMA

Before I explain the Burn Rate Test Diet in more detail, there is a note of caution I want to raise about the use of structured diets in weight control. The Burn Rate Test Diet and your personalized Burn Rate Diet represent the best solution I can find to a basic dilemma in weight control: Is a rigidly structured diet helpful or harmful? Many of my patients want me just to give them a meal plan to follow. They claim it is easier for them not to have to think about food. The structure seems to put their minds at ease and reduces the anxiety about trusting their own judgment. However, I have mixed feelings about recommending structured diets. When I began my work in weight control, I was exposed to the use of highly structured diets—the high protein, very low calorie diets. I saw many patients lose 50 to 100 pounds. Over the next two years, I watched those same patients gain back all the weight they lost plus more.

As I tried to understand what had caused the weight cycling, I began to believe that the structured diet was a main culprit. Many of my patients loved the ease of the structured diet. "Just tell me what to eat," they often said, "and I will be fine." More often than not, they did not end up fine. The very structure they craved became the yardstick to measure their failure. After a while, natural eating habits and preferences took over, leaving the people feeling ashamed that they were not able to conquer their particular food cravings.

In response to my patients' experiences, I started preaching flexibility and the importance of having a natural relationship to food to avoid the experience of failure and deepening shame. I asked my patients to write down what they ate each day on food records. They could eat whatever they wanted as long as they recorded the calories. Many of my patients found this work tedious. Many complained that I did not give them enough structure in their diet. But experience showed me that if I gave them the structure they wanted, I would be giving them the means to hurt themselves psychologically with the next failure.

With the Burn Rate Diet, I have struck a compromise. I create structure yet add flexibility in several ways. First, I use multiple menu plans that can satisfy different food preferences. I have found that people do better when they can eat the things they like. Consistently having to resist temptation leads to feelings of deprivation, and the person is worse off than before. To add variety and to minimize the frustration of cutting back on calories, I include many options in my Burn Rate Meal Plans. Second, I allow people to eat a certain amount of fat, which means that foods like French fries, cheese, milk, beef, and potato chips all have a reasonable place in the Burn Rate Diet.

The Burn Rate Diet is based on the idea that success at weight control requires the maintenance of a natural relationship to food. What exactly is natural eating? The first phrase that comes to mind is "eating in moderation." But does moderation mean eating only two pieces of pizza instead of four? Does it mean one scoop of ice cream instead of the whole hot fudge sundae? I believe that moderation means *sometimes a lot and sometimes a little.* Sometimes it is important to eat the four pieces of pizza or the entire sundae to keep your frustration from getting too high. The trick is to account for these indulgences by accounting for the calories. Knowledge of your burn rate gives you the ability to flex your intake to average the calorie level that your burn rate requires. Nothing is wrong or bad to eat as long as you account for it.

A natural relationship to food balances calorie control with eating for pleasure. It allows for eating a lot and eating a little, high fat and low fat, junk food and health food, chocolate as well as carrots. It supports the idea that food is essential to human life. The urge to eat is as natural as the urges associated with any other bodily function and is critical to survival.

The Burn Rate Diet is a way of eating that you will choose to follow in your own way. Some days, you will be exact with creating the menus and following the plan to the letter. Other days, you will be less exact, and will apply the principles in a general way. On yet another day, you won't even want to think about it. You will just want to eat whatever you want and not even be reasonable.

All of the above is human and okay. Don't force the choices. Trust your desire to live healthier and thinner. You will balance the more structured days with the more variable days. It is the best way to prevent the build-up of frustration that can destroy any weight control effort.

HOW DOES THE BURN RATE TEST DIET WORK?

With the caution in place about structured diets, I can now feel comfortable introducing to you the diet structure of the Burn Rate Test Diet. Keep in mind that this diet is not designed for weight loss, although the vast majority of you will lose weight during the two weeks on the Test Diet. The purpose of the Burn Rate Test Diet is to determine your Body Burn Rate. Once you know your Body Burn Rate, you can construct your own Burn Rate Diet, the highly individualized nutritional plan that you will follow for weight loss and long-term weight maintenance.

The Burn Rate Test Diet is a series of menu plans for breakfast, lunch, afternoon snack, and dinner that you should follow closely for fourteen days. I have provided seven different options for each meal. You can select any one you like, or even eat the same one every day. Each option is designed to achieve the same nutritional goals, so the selections are interchangeable as long as you don't substitute one meal for another—for example, eat a breakfast option for dinner. Instructions for viewing the Burn Rate Test Diet on the Web site are given on the next page. (The menu plans are also available in Appendix I at the back of this book.)

Portion control is important because the Burn Rate Test Diet is based on the minimum reasonable calorie levels for women (1,500 calories/day) and men (1,800 calories/day). After two weeks on this regimen, your weight loss or gain will be measured against the calorie level of the Test Diet. If you gain weight, then your Body Burn Rate is very efficient. You will need to eat less than 1,500 or 1,800 calories/day to lose weight. However, if you lose weight, the opposite is true.

Here is how it works. Each pound of body fat contains 3,500 calories. If you eat 3,500 calories more than you require, you will gain 1 pound. If you eat 3,500 calories less than you need, then you will lose 1 pound. Your weight loss or gain tells us how much your Body Burn Rate is above or below the calorie level of the Test Diet. For each pound per week that you gain or lose, your Body Burn Rate will be 500 calories per day above or below the Test Diet. For example, if you lose 2.2 pounds in the two weeks on the Test Diet, then your loss averaged 1.1 pounds per week, or your current needs are 550 calories per day above the Test Diet. If you are a woman, then the figure would be 1,500 + 550 = 2,050

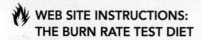 WEB SITE INSTRUCTIONS:
THE BURN RATE TEST DIET

Viewing the Burn Rate Test Diet

1. Web site address: **www.burnratediet.com**

2. Home page: Click on "Burn Rate Diet Interactives"

3. Click on section "Burn Rate Test Diet"

4. Screen will show: *Burn Rate Test Diet: Men* and *Burn Rate Test Diet: Women.* Click on the appropriate section.

5. Scroll through menu options for breakfast, lunch, snack, and dinner. Click on the brackets in orange to move to the menu plans for those meals. Print out the menus for later review.

calories. Since scale changes are due to loss of both body fat and water, a 20 percent adjustment is made to that figure to allow for water loss. In this example, the calculated Body Burn Rate would be 1,640 calories per day.

There is an additional benefit to following the Burn Rate Test Diet. Burn Rate principles offer a unique way to organize your food intake, and they take some getting used to. For example, the recommended foods for breakfast are probably different from what you're used to, and the fat intakes for all the meals may be higher. The Test Diet will help you adjust to a new way of eating based on Burn Rate concepts. As noted earlier, eventually you will create an individualized nutritional plan called your Burn Rate Diet that will be based on these organizing principles. The Test Diet gives you the chance to become familiar with this new way of eating.

GETTING STARTED

The Burn Rate Test Diet is an eating plan designed to measure your Body Burn Rate, or the total energy requirements of basal metabolism, muscular activity of daily living, and digestion. It does not include the energy expenditure from exercise or programmed activity. You will be asked to record the calorie expenditure of your exercise or programmed activities during the two weeks of the Test Diet. There will be a separate entry for this factor called "Exercise Calories" on the Web site or in the manual calculations in Appendix II when you use the results of the Test Diet to calculate your Body Burn Rate. You can refer to chapter 8 to determine the energy expenditure of your exercise or sport activity and to develop your own exercise plan. Athletes in particular will want to read this chapter.

As noted above, the menu plans of the Burn Rate Test Diet give you seven different options for breakfast, lunch, an afternoon snack, and dinner. Each option is identical in the amount of energy it provides and in its carbohydrate, protein, and fat content. The seven options are interchangeable, and each one can be used as many times as you want. Note also that you can make certain substitutions to suit your personal food preferences without altering the calorie content of your meals. Simply select one of the options at each meal, closely following the portion sizes to ensure calorie control. Vegetarian options are included in a separate section.

A two-week diet is hard to follow, but all is not lost if you "blow the diet" once you have begun. Continue to make the lowest calorie choices that are possible under the circumstances and record the total calories eaten for the day. Simply restart the structured diet on the following day. On any day that you "fell off the diet," record the total calories that you ate on that day. Subtract 1,800 calories from your total daily calories if you are a man and 1,500 calories from the total if you are a woman. This difference will be called "extra eating." Record each instance that you exceed the calorie level of the Test Diet. Then find the total over the fourteen days of the Test Diet, and enter this sum in the "extra eating" box on the Web site or in Appendix II if you do the calculations manually. This correction provides the flexibility needed to correct for the difficulty of being perfect for the full two weeks of the Test Diet without sacrificing the accuracy of the calculation of Body Burn Rate.

Pick a starting day when you are confident you will be able to follow the diet. Women should follow the diet for the first two weeks of their menstrual cycle. To begin the diet, weigh yourself undressed upon awakening and after urinating. This weight will be called your Start Weight. Record this weight in the box labeled Burn Rate Test Diet: Results.

Basic Instructions

1. *Fluids.* Drink at least six 8-ounce glasses (6 cups) per day of fluid. Limit caloric or alcoholic beverages as much as possible during the two weeks of the diet. Coffee, tea, soda water, or plain water are the best choices. If you drink alcohol or soda, consider the calories under Carbohydrate Calories.

2. *Spices/Sauces.* Spices do not add calories and are recommended to enhance the flavor of the food. Sauces with a wine base are low in calories, as the calories from the alcohol are lost in evaporation. Other sauces, such as soy sauce, may be

used, but use only the low-sodium brands to prevent water retention that can interfere with the accuracy of the Test Diet results.

3. *Free foods.* The following is a list of foods that may be added to the diet in reasonable amounts due to the negligible amount of calories:

Food	Amount	Calories	Total Calories from Carbohydrate	Protein	Fat
Mustard	1 tsp	12	4	0	8
Ketchup	1 tbsp	16	16	0	0
Salsa	1 oz	12	12	0	0
Garlic	1 clove	4	4	0	0
Celery	1 stalk	6	6	0	0
Cucumber	¼	9	9	0	0

Note: While foods like sauerkraut and dill pickles are low in calories, the high levels of sodium in these foods may increase water retention and limit the accuracy of the Test Diet results.

4. *Calorie values.* The calorie values for the foods listed are taken from the book *Complete Guide to Food Counts* by Corinne Netzer, 3rd Edition, Dell/Bantam, 1994. Make your portion sizes as accurate as you can. You may want to weigh and measure your foods for the first several days to become familiar with portion sizes. Later on, when you are following your own individual Burn Rate Diet, you will have more flexibility. For now, it's important to count calories.

5. *Substitutions.* Follow each option as closely as possible to provide a good measure of your Body Burn Rate. However, there are substitutions that can be made without significantly altering the results. Listed below are foods that have equivalent caloric values and can be used as substitutes for the foods listed on the Test Diet:

Vegetable equivalents: green beans, broccoli, cauliflower, carrots, spinach, tomatoes, squash, or any vegetables that contain less than 50 calories per cup after cooking

Fruit equivalents: Apple, orange, pear, plum, tangerine, or any fruits that contain less than 75 calories per piece

Carbohydrate equivalents: 1 medium potato = 1 cup rice or pasta

---

BURN RATE TEST DIET RESULTS:

Start Weight: _____lbs. Date: _____

Note: Due to the increased water retention from hormone changes, it is best for women to follow this diet in the first two weeks of their menstrual cycle.

On the morning of the fifteenth day, repeat the weigh-in and record below:

Final Weight: _____lbs. Date: _____

Subtract Final Weight from Start Weight and record below:

Weight Change: _____lbs lost / gained / neither

Extra Calories: _____cals over 14 days

Exercise Calories Expended in Exercise over 14 days: _____

WHAT IS YOUR MOST REASONABLE GOAL WEIGHT?

Before taking your results on the Burn Rate Test Diet to the Web site, there is one other important issue to discuss. The programs on the Web site will calculate not only your current Body Burn Rate, but also your predicted Body Burn Rate when you reach your goal weight. A drop in Body Burn Rate follows any reduction in body size because the body tries to defend its own weight set point by becoming more efficient and requiring fewer calories. You will have a value for your present Body Burn Rate that is calculated from the response to the Burn Rate Test Diet, and a pre-dicted *new* Body Burn Rate that is matched to your most reason-able goal weight. The computer will create a graph for you that will visually illustrate how your Body Burn Rate changes with changes in body weight. You will then be able to select your most reasonable goal weight, one that enables you to eat at least the rec-ommended minimum daily calorie intake (1,500 calories per day for women and 1,800 calories per day for men). Setting a goal weight that would require a lower level of food intake would be very hard to maintain. I don't encourage you to go for a drastic weight loss because I want you to achieve long-term success.

Change in Body Burn Rate is a major and largely unrecog-nized factor that contributes to the regain of weight. The hard, cold facts about energy regulation are that the less you weigh, the less you need to eat. I have observed this phenomenon over and over, and have documented this drop in metabolism in my patients by measuring it. My results were similar to those reported by other researchers (see chapter 2). I found through my study of individual patients that the ratio of change in body weight to change in Body Burn Rate appears on average to be about 10:1. For every 10 pounds that you lose, you lose 100 calories off your Body Burn Rate. This figure may vary from patient to patient, and may not even be consistent for the same patient throughout the course of his or her weight loss. For example, the initial weight loss may trigger a less significant drop in Body Burn Rate than the last 10 pounds of a 50-pound loss. The good news is that we don't have to speculate any longer about how this phenomenon applies to you. Now, with the Burn Rate Test Diet, you can remeasure your Body Burn Rate any time you like. Simply redo the Test Diet for fourteen days and calculate your new Body Burn Rate. You can record and watch how your Body Burn Rate varies with your weight change.

The bad news is that an extremely efficient Body Burn Rate makes it harder to lose weight. Moreover, if you begin with a slow-burning metabolism, it will drop even further as the weight comes off. At some point, it becomes unrealistic for you to fight nature. As I noted earlier, the minimum requirement I recommend for weight maintenance is 1,500 calories per day for women and 1,800 for men. People can get by on less intake. However, as time goes on, the inevitable demands of the natural relationship with food win out.

I want you to be thinner only if your Body Burn Rate enables you to do that. In most cases, you will be able to be thinner than you are, but you may never be as thin as you want to be. Let your Body Burn Rate dictate your ideal weight and truly live thinner for the rest of your life.

 WEB SITE INSTRUCTIONS:
CALCULATING BODY BURN RATE

1. Web site address: **www.burnratediet.com**
2. Click on section "Burn Rate Diet Interactives"
3. On this page, click on "Body Burn Rate and Burn Rate Diet Guidelines"
4. On this page, follow the easy steps to determine your Body Burn Rate

---

ADJUSTING FOR EXERCISE

If you choose to exercise during the fourteen days of the Test Diet, there is an adjustment that needs to be made. The total energy expenditure over the fourteen days will be affected by the energy expenditure of any activity outside the activities of daily living, from a competitive sport to taking a walk.

Adjusting for activity or exercise is easy. Using the caloric expenditure charts in chapter 8, simply keep track of the calories you burn during any of the activities. Add the total calories together for the fourteen days and enter this number into the "exercise calories" section in Step 2 on the Web site.

Here's an example. While on the Test Diet, Joan maintained her walking program of 3 miles per week. At her weight of 175 pounds, she burned over 100 calories per mile, totaling 600 calories for the 6 miles she walked in the fourteen days. On a daily basis, Joan would need to adjust by 43 calories to account for her exercise. That is, Joan's exercise program used up an average of 43 calories per day over the two weeks she was on the Test Diet. To calculate her Body Burn Rate accurately, she needed to take this caloric expenditure into account.

YOUR INDIVIDUALIZED BURN RATE DIET

Now that you have followed the Burn Rate Test Diet for two weeks and calculated your Body Burn Rate, you are ready to create your individualized Burn Rate Diet that offers you the most effective appetite control. The Burn Rate Diet is so valuable because you get the complexity that is needed for success, yet it's easy to use because of the technology available at my Web site. The Burn Rate Diet, the first cyberdiet in a diet book, makes all previous diets obsolete.

SELECTING THE COMPOSITION OF YOUR BURN RATE DIET

The standard diet recommended by leading health authorities and the medical community, including the American Medical Association and the American Dietetic Association, consists of 55 percent carbohydrate, 15 percent protein, and 30 percent fat. These percentages stay the same even if your total calorie intake changes. In your Burn Rate Diet, these percentages will be applied to your predicted Body Burn Rate to achieve your individual calorie levels of each food component. Many of my patients are surprised by these guidelines. They expect a higher protein intake and a lower fat intake. Truth is, most people eat too much protein. We need only 15 percent protein to have the necessary amount of amino acids to build muscle tissue. Also, as I've mentioned earlier, the truth is that dietary fat is needed for many body functions as well as for appetite control. It's your total calorie intake, not the amount of fat in your diet, that will determine your body size.

I recommend that the vast majority of people follow the Standard diet composition given above. However, some patients have medical conditions that require a reduced fat intake. I recommend a reduction to 25 percent fat for patients with heart disease, high cholesterol, or other medical conditions requiring a fat restriction, such as gall bladder disease. I call this the Medical diet composition. It includes 60 percent carbohydrate, 15 percent protein, and 25 percent fat. For athletes who have increased their muscle mass through intensive weight training, I recommend the Athletic diet composition of 50 percent carbohydrate, 20 percent protein, and 30 percent fat. These individuals require a slightly higher protein intake to maintain their increased muscle mass. On the Web site, select one of these options—Standard, Medical, or Athletic—when constructing your personalized Burn Rate Diet.

CALCULATING THE GUIDELINES OF YOUR BURN RATE DIET

Before making food choices, you need to determine exactly what your body needs from day to day and meal to meal. Now it is time for you to discover what your daily calorie level will be, how these calories will be distributed across your meals, and how many calories will be assigned to each food component—carbohydrate, protein, and fat—for each meal. If you have Internet access, simply follow the instructions listed on page 74 to complete this procedure using my Web site.

For those of you who do not yet own a computer, or who prefer to do things on your own, you can calculate your Body Burn Rate and determine the guidelines of your Burn Rate Diet manually. I have included the instructions for the manual calculations in Appendix II at the end of the book.

FOLLOWING THE BURN RATE DIET

Now that you know your Body Burn Rate, you are ready to follow your personalized nutritional plan to living thinner and healthier. In the following chapters, I will show you how to time your meals, to calculate how many calories per hour your Body Burn Rate requires, and to plan your meals to prevent hunger. I will also

---

🔥 WEB SITE INSTRUCTIONS: BURN RATE DIET GUIDELINES

1. Web site address: **www.burnratediet.com**

2. Home page: Click on section "Burn Rate Diet Interactives"

3. On this page, click on section "Body Burn Rate and Burn Rate Diet Guidelines"

4. Follow the easy steps to determine your personalized Burn Rate Diet Guidelines.

5. Your individualized Burn Rate Diet Guidelines will be displayed on the screen. This diet is listed by total calorie amounts needed for each meal, and further broken down into the individual amounts of carbohydrate, protein, and fat calories to suit your Body Burn Rate and diet composition.

---

show you how to plan your food intake around your exercise so that you can maximize your energy while you work out. To follow the Burn Rate Diet, you will need to match your Body Burn Rate to the burn rate of food. The burn rates of different foods will be covered in the next chapter.

5

Food Burn Rates

If I think back to the information about nutrition that I learned
from my parents, the first thing I was taught was, "Eat enough
protein." As a child, I never knew exactly what protein was, but I
knew it meant that you ate your meat to get it. The second idea
that I remember is, "You need to eat vegetables for vitamins." To
my mother, brussels sprouts were the epitome of a vegetable that
gave you lots of these things called vitamins. I was lucky because I
liked them, but my brother hid his in his napkin or pushed them
on the floor so he wouldn't have to eat them. From a child's perspective, I figured vitamins had to be important because I saw my
mom and dad taking lots of them in pill form, and telling me that I
needed to take my vitamin tablet every day to stay healthy. The
other foods, like potatoes and corn, just filled me up and made my
hunger go away.

   From talking to many of my patients, I learned that my experience of nutrition was similar to that of other children raised in the
1950s and 1960s. It is little wonder that this generation has
accepted the idea that protein needs to be the basis of a good
weight loss diet. You have been told, since you were a small child,
that protein protects you from harm by keeping you healthy. Is it

any wonder that you are ready to accept that it needs to be the central element in weight loss?

My knowledge of nutrition increased with my exposure to the Basic Four Food Groups posters in school. Food now consisted of four groups of things that you had to make sure you ate. Bread, grains, and cereals were in one group, fruits and vegetables in another, dairy products in a third, and meat, fish, and fowl in the fourth. My first reaction to the poster was "So where is the protein group and where are the vitamins?" I subsequently found out that protein is in both the meat group and the dairy group, and some is even sprinkled throughout the other groups. That was confusing to me, because I could not just eat meat anymore and be healthy.

The Basic Four Food Groups has given way to the Food Pyramid as the way to organize a healthy diet. Food is still broken down into groups, but now it is listed according to percentage of intake. Fat is at the top of the pyramid to emphasize that it should be the lowest intake of any food. Breads, grains, and cereals are on the bottom, and the largest component of food intake, with vegetables and fruits and proteins rounding out the groups that form the pyramid.

Nowhere in any of these models is food organized as energy. We have been trained to see food as different groups, like bread or vegetables, or parts, like protein and vitamins. Nobody told us that, in terms of energy, bread is the same as a vegetable, or that a glass of milk is the same as a few bites of chicken. Again in energy terms, did you know that the sugar in fruit is the same as the sugar in a lollipop? Though this concept may sound different or unusual to you, in fact, the only difference is that it is based on classifying food according to the burn rate of the energy sources contained in the food.

BURN RATES OF FOOD

In chapter 3 I described how food is used as fuel. The three fuel sources in food (carbohydrate, protein, and fat) are each absorbed into the body at different speeds and broken down into different component parts. The composition of a food and its rate of conversion into glucose units determine the rate at which the glucose made is available in the bloodstream. Simple sugars contained in everything from table sugar to fruit to soda don't need to be converted at all. They are directly absorbed within minutes and either used or stored within twenty minutes. More complex sugars are linked together in chains and are available as complex carbohydrates in foods such as bread, rice, potato, pasta, vegetables, and fruit. The chains of glucose units need to be broken down into easily absorbed units. It takes up to 2 hours to have all the carbohydrate from a meal or snack absorbed, used, or stored as fat in a fat cell.

Protein (see, mom wasn't all wrong!) provides amino acids, the building blocks for many different body parts like nails, hair, cartilage, and many others. As with any foodstuff, any excess amino acids are used for energy. We only need so many building blocks. A slab of steak as big as a plate is far more protein than we need in a day. Extra protein is converted into the basic energy molecule of the body, glucose. Converting excess protein into glucose takes much longer than breaking down carbohydrate.

There is an extensive conversion with multiple pathways that results in turning protein into glucose. That process takes up to four hours to complete. Fat needs to go through an even more complex transformation than protein to be turned into glucose, which can take up to six hours.

The rate at which foods are made available to the body in the form of dissolved sugar in the blood is called the food's *burn rate*.

NEW FOOD CLASSIFICATION SYSTEM: BURN RATES OF FOOD

In the Burn Rate Diet, you will learn to match your diet to your energy requirements. *Energy regulation is the key to weight control.* In this way, not only will you be controlling the process that determines the amount of fat in your body, but you will also have a steady supply of glucose to control your appetite.

The total amount of energy in any given food depends on the composition of that food. Foods can contain different amounts of carbohydrate, protein, and fat. Each component has its own burn rate. I call foods that contain over 80 percent of one component—

carbohydrate, protein, or fat—*pure* foods. Many carbohydrate foods, like vegetables, fruit, bread, and grains, fall into this category. Some protein foods, such as egg whites and certain fish and some shellfish, meet this definition of purity. Much fat, such as butter, margarine, mayonnaise, and oils, likewise are considered pure fat.

Other foods are a mixture of energy sources. Some contain significant amounts of two food components. I call these *dual mix* foods. The mix can be protein and fat, protein and carbohydrate, or carbohydrate and fat. Examples of protein/fat dual mix foods are turkey, ham, beef, and cheese. Examples of protein/carbohydrate dual mix foods are nonfat yogurt, skim milk, and low-fat cottage cheese. Examples of carbohydrate/fat dual mix foods are avocado, olives, potato chips, and chocolate. Some foods are a triple mix of all three food components. Whole milk, for example, includes significant amounts of fat, protein, and carbohydrate.

The Burn Rate Meal Plans are based on selecting foods by their principal components or energy source. (Burn Rate Meal Plans are described in the following chapter.) You don't need to be an expert on food composition to follow the Burn Rate Diet because your personal Burn Rate Meal Plans, which build in this information, can be generated at my Web site. If one day you aren't following a specific Burn Rate Meal Plan, you can still use Burn Rate Principles to improvise your meals and snacks if you know the composition of different foods.

Some of my patients enjoy putting together their own Burn Rate Meal Plans, while others find it tedious. Take a look at the lists in Appendix III. These lists organize foods into categories by the amount of protein, carbohydrate, and fat in each food. Pure Foods that contain only one food element are listed as Pure Carbohydrate, Pure Protein, and Pure Fat. As I explained above, a Pure Food is defined as a food that contains more than 80 percent of one food element. For example, bread is placed on the Pure Carbohydrate list despite the fact that a slice of bread contains several calories of protein and fat. A 75-calorie slice of bread may actually contain 6 calories of protein, 4 calories of fat, and 65 calories of carbohydrate. The 10 combined calories from fat and protein are 13 percent of the total 75 calories, making this slice of bread 87 percent carbohydrate, which exceeds the requirement of 80 percent or greater used to define a Pure Food. Bread is considered a pure carbohydrate, and the full 75 calories are listed as only carbohydrate on the Pure Carbohydrate list in Appendix III.

Foods that are mixtures of two or more of the three elements are classified as Dual Mix and Triple Mix. Dual Mix foods contain two elements and have three categories: Carbohydrate/Protein, Carbohydrate/Fat, and Protein/Fat. The same 80:20 rule applies with Dual Foods. If the two elements constitute more than 80 percent of the calories, the trace amounts of the third element are added equally to the calories of the two primary elements. For example, a food like potato chips contains two elements, carbohydrate and fat, and is called a Dual Mix Food. One ounce of chips contains 150 total calories. There are 73 calories of carbohydrate, 73 calories of fat, and 4 calories of protein. Protein contributes only 3 percent of the total calories. As a result, potato chips are listed as a Dual Mix Food in the Carbohydrate/Fat section, with 75 calories from carbohydrate, 75 calories from fat, and 0 calories from protein.

A food like milk is an example of a Triple Mix Food. Each food element is represented significantly and there is no need to combine any of the calorie groups. Four ounces of 2% milk contains 60 total calories: 20 calories of carbohydrate, 20 calories of protein, and 20 calories of fat. Each element is listed under its respective category.

In Appendix III, the food lists are organized in increasing amounts of calories. This organization will be helpful when you select the amounts of foods you need to meet the individual calorie requirements on your Burn Rate Diet. Both Pure and Mixed Foods are listed in small calorie increments so that you can fine-tune the amounts to suit your meal plans.

FUEL ADDITIVES: VITAMINS AND MINERALS

In the nineteenth century, it was discovered that vitamin C, or ascorbic acid, found in many fruits and vegetables, could cure scurvy of men at sea Ever since then, vitamins have assumed magical properties.

However, there is a huge difference between correcting a vitamin deficiency and taking more vitamins than you need. There are many diseases that do respond to vitamin therapy because of the existence of a deficit. However, many people unnecessarily take huge amounts of vitamins that serve no purpose other than to change the color of their urine. The fact is that eating a healthy diet will provide all the vitamins and minerals that your body needs. Five servings of various fruits and vegetables per day should provide the necessary amount of these elements.

That said, under certain circumstances, there is a need for vitamin supplementation. When you have significant changes in body fluid due to excessive sweating, urination, vomiting, or diarrhea, the fluid loss will create excessive loss of water-soluble vitamins and minerals. That is why you should supplement for at least thirty days after being sick. Another time to use a vitamin supplement is during an extended period of high stress, when your food intake is probably unplanned and haphazard and you are not eating as you should. Also, after the age of fifty-five, vitamin supplementation is needed as the body's need for vitamins increases. However, megadoses of vitamins should be avoided under any circumstances.

Vitamins that are fat soluble, including vitamins D, E, A, and K, are stored by the body. They are not lost with changes in body fluid so are not as susceptible to variations created by changes in fluid levels in the body. If taken in large quantities, they can build up to toxic levels in the body and cause significant organ and tissue damages and, in extreme cases, even death. The best way to ensure against vitamin toxicity is to take supplements when needed, but not when you are eating a normal and healthy diet.

ANTIOXIDANTS

Cancer research has spawned a renewed interest in the role of nutrition in the prevention and treatment of this disease. Recent research has focused on the role of chemical compounds called antioxidants, whose function in the body is to combine with active compounds called free radicals that can cause biochemical reactions resulting in cellular damage. Free radicals are caused in the body by carcinogenic compounds that are in the food we eat, the water we drink, and the air we breathe. Antioxidants help prevent cellular damage by combining with, and thereby neutralizing, the free radicals before they can do their harm.

There are many sources of these antioxidant compounds. Multivitamins and antioxidant supplements do not take the place of healthy foods. There are many substances present in food that are not included in commercial supplements. Foods like lemons, tomatoes, garlic, red wine, and many others contain compounds called riboflavins that neutralize free radicals. I have listed below some foods and their respective antioxidant compounds. The best strategy for disease prevention is to ingest the greatest variety of antioxidant compounds as possible. This can be accomplished by eating the widest variety possible of fruits and vegetables in the five daily servings included in your Burn Rate Meal Plan. Add garlic, which has been shown to promote good health, to taste whenever possible. Adding sauces made from a wide variety of spices and fruits (like the Burn Rate Sauces described in the Meal Plans) to your meat, fish, or fowl provides another means increasing the amount of antioxidants that you take in.

EXAMPLES OF ANTIOXIDANTS IN FOODS

Food	Antioxidant	Action in Body
Tomatoes	Lycopene	Cancer prevention
Garlic	Allium compounds	Stimulates immune cells
Grapes	Phenols	Slows tumor growth
Oranges/lemons	Limonene	Slows tumor growth
Green tea	Polyphenols	Protection of DNA
Hot peppers	Capsaicin	Inhibits toxic nitrosamines
Broccoli/cabbage	B-carotene/vit C	Protection of DNA

SUMMARY

Now that you know the burn rates of food and your Body Burn Rate, you are ready to apply this knowledge to build your own personal Burn Rate Diet. This food plan is ideally suited for your own burn rate, food preferences, and the timing of your meals. It is as unique as you are. In the next chapter, I will show you how to match your tastes in food to the calorie levels of your individualized Burn Rate Diet.

6

Principles of Meal Planning

By now, you have learned several things about your body and weight control. In chapter 4, you followed the Burn Rate Test Diet, entered your results on the Web site, and calculated your Body Burn Rate, your goal weight, and the guidelines for your individualized Burn Rate Diet. As a result, you now know the energy that your body needs at your current weight, and the amount of food (calories) you need to achieve and to maintain your goal weight. You have also read about how foods can be organized according to their burn rate and composition. You are now ready to match your burn rate to the burn rates of foods—the key to appetite control, weight management, and peak performance.

A NOTE OF CAUTION

Before I begin to show you how to build your own Burn Rate Diet, I want to sound the same note of caution that I mentioned back in chapter 4 when I introduced the Burn Rate Test Diet. I don't believe in structured diets as the answer to weight control. I believe that in order to be successful, you must maintain a natural relationship with food that is based on flexibility. You'll have high days and low days, meals when you eat a lot, meals when you eat a little. However, I have come to believe that there is a place for structure in meal plans. It helps you to organize your thinking around food. The structure does not have to interfere with your natural relationship to food as long you see it as information to help you plan rather than as something to adhere to rigidly. So be flexible, and trust your appetite and your desire to be thinner.

BURN RATE MEAL PLANS: FROM SIMPLE TO DETAILED

You can build your own Burn Rate Meal Plans in a variety of ways. You can do it simply or you can do it with a high level of detail and personalization. You can adopt Burn Rate Meal Plans that are generated at my Web site, or you can create your own meal plans from the tables in this book. On the days that you will be casual with your diet, you will use several general principles to guide your food choices. In this chapter, I will discuss these general principles, then move on to more detail and show you how to create detailed food plans that match the exact specifications of your own Burn Rate Diet. Even if you are happy with the Burn Rate Meal Plans you print out at my Web site, I'd like you to know how to plan your own Burn Rate Diet, since this is the diet you should be following well into the future, not only for weight loss, but also for weight maintenance. There will be occasions when you will need to improvise, and your knowledge of Burn Rate Principles will keep you on track.

There is a critical assumption made in the planning of the Burn Rate Meal Plans. The assumption is that the diet composition that is ideal for you is not just a daily composition but an hour-to-hour requirement for the body. If you need 55 percent carbohydrate as the total daily carbohydrate intake, you ideally would want 55 percent of your energy supply to come from carbohydrate each hour. The same is true of protein and fat. If you need 15 percent and 30 percent intakes each day, then you would want that same percentage to be the basis for the fuel supplied each hour. The Burn Rate Meal Plans are designed to supply this composition throughout the intervals between meals on an hour-to-hour basis.

There are several principles that will help you mix the right foods for the best energy supply between meals, based on the rate at which you burn food. Failure to follow these principles will cause an interruption in energy supply and a surge in appetite. Following are several simple principles to follow throughout the day.

 Meal Planning Principle 1:
Plan the Time Intervals Between Meals

The time intervals between meals determine the level of energy to be supplied from food at each meal. Because the longest-burning fuel, fat, is fully processed by the body in six hours, plan to have no more than six-hour intervals between your meals. That means that if you eat breakfast at 7:00 A.M., make sure you eat lunch no later than 1:00 P.M. and dinner no later than 7:00 P.M.

Based on how your body responds to breaking the fast that occurs during sleep, some of you may choose to eat only two meals per day plus the afternoon snack. Your time intervals will not be the same as those of the person who needs to eat breakfast to prevent energy lapses in the morning. The Burn Rate Diet is not organized to accommodate skipping breakfast, but I know from experience that some people prefer to skip the morning meal, so I will discuss how to construct a two-meal diet (with a night snack) on page 99.

In planning your Burn Rate Diet, you will also need to account for the additional energy required for any exercise that you do. Chapter 8 tells in more detail how to plan your food intake for exercise.

 Meal Planning Principle 2:
Calorie Control Each Meal

Weight control is based on calorie control. If you eat more by the end of the day than your Body Burn Rate, you will gain weight. If you eat less, you will lose weight. Eat the same and you will stay the same. What's unique about the Burn Rate Diet is the way in which meals are planned to meet your individual energy needs over the course of your day. Within the day, from meal to meal, calorie distribution is essential to appetite control. The calorie levels assigned to each meal in your Burn Rate Diet are designed to supply the energy needs of your personal Body Burn Rate over the time intervals between meals. Know the calorie level that you need at each meal, and make sure that you eat the necessary calories to supply a consistent stream of glucose to your muscles and brain each hour. This distribution of calories is ideally suited for your individual Body Burn Rate and will maximize your appetite control. Control of food urges will enable you to reach and maintain the most reasonable weight for you.

 Meal Planning Principle 3:
Control Carbohydrate at Breakfast

The idea behind this principle is illustrated in the name of the first meal that we eat, *breakfast*. You are breaking the fast imposed by sleep. The length of your sleep will determine the length of time that you have gone without food. Remember that six hours is the maximum interval that energy can be supplied to the body from any given meal. Even if you ate your last meal before you went to bed, and if you slept for eight hours, there would be at least two hours when you were fasting—that is, all the food you ate would already be stored or used. No matter when you last ate, your body needs to supply fuel for the Body Burn Rate during sleep. After the food you last ate has been processed, your body uses stored body fat broken down into ketone molecules for this purpose.

Breakfast is the time when the body needs to make a transition in fuel sources. When glucose is reintroduced back into the system, say, as a glass of orange juice, the body shuts off ketone production and converts to its preferred fuel, glucose. The rate of this conversion depends on how quickly your blood sugar levels rise. Fast fuels like carbohydrate (toast) and simple sugars (frosted cereal) quickly shut down ketone production. Slower-burning fuel, like protein or fat, allows for a more gradual reduction in ketone supply, so the oxidation of fat progresses even more slowly, gradually introducing the glucose. The proper mix of foods allows ketones and glucose to be used simultaneously.

If you choose to eliminate breakfast entirely from your diet, you will rely on ketones as your sole fuel source in the early portion of the day. Some people tolerate this well. Others feel nausea almost immediately upon rising, while others develop a "food headache" by midmorning if they skip breakfast. Some will feel no hunger, while others will be ravenous by lunchtime. Unless you are certain you feel your best without eating in the morning, I encourage you to eat breakfast. For most people, breakfast plays a critical role in appetite control.

Don't be confused by all the discussion about burning body fat to make you thinner. Energy is in a dynamic flux throughout the day. There are times when body fat is being used to supply energy. There are other times when excess glucose from meals will be stored in the fat cells. The occasional times when body fat is being used will cause you to be thinner only if the total amount of energy consumed and stored by the end of the day is less than the total amount of energy used.

Prolonging the use of ketones as long as possible in the morning ensures that the body will have two energy sources available, glucose and ketones. Managing carbohydrate intake is the key to controlling the rate at which ketones continue to be available. Remember that carbohydrate is a fast-burning fuel. It supplies a quick and ready supply of glucose. As glucose is the preferred fuel of the body, a quick rise in the glucose levels terminates the burning of body fat immediately. If carbohydrate intake is controlled at breakfast and mixed with protein and fat, a slow but steady supply of glucose is ensured throughout the morning. This consistent level of glucose causes the ketone production to be reduced gradually.

Each of you will have a different optimal level of carbohydrate at breakfast. It is calculated for you at my Web site and incorporated into your Burn Rate Diet Guidelines. Commit this number to your memory. Examine the food lists in Appendix III to determine the different combinations of carbohydrate foods that will fulfill this calorie level. For example, some of you may be able to eat a piece of bread and a piece of fruit or glass of juice at breakfast as your carbohydrate allotment. Others will have to make a choice of bread *or* juice/fruit. If you have low Body Burn Rate, you may have to substitute low-calorie bread for regular bread to avoid overshooting your carbohydrate requirement. Know these food choices, because planning them into your diet will be essential to maintain the steady stream of energy from breakfast to lunch.

Eating a Burn Rate Breakfast also means including more protein and fat than you may be accustomed to. Eggs, meat, cheese, peanut butter, cottage cheese, and other protein/fat combinations are all appropriate. A small amount of carbohydrate, such as a piece of fruit or single slice of bread is needed for the quick start, but protein and fat are needed for sustained energy throughout the morning.

Meal Planning Principle 4:
Eat Fat and Protein at Every Meal

We are used to believing that carbohydrate foods are the most important, and we plan our meals accordingly. We eat cereal for breakfast and bread and salad at lunch and use pasta, potato, or rice as the staple of dinner. We have come to think of pretzels as a better snack food than potato chips or peanuts. We have forgotten along the way that all the components of food are important. Protein not only supplies essential amino acids to build the tissues of the body, but it also is a medium-range fuel that needs to be included to balance the energy supply. That dreaded component, fat, also has a role in providing a steady stream of calories, especially at the end of a typical six-hour interval between meals. After all the energy from carbohydrate and protein is gone, the energy from fat remains. Without it, we can't last and keep our appetite under control.

To maintain a steady supply of glucose to the body throughout the day, protein and fat need to be included in each meal. It is best to think of these two elements as combined because nearly all protein foods contain an element of fat. (As you can see in Appendix III, list of pure protein foods is very short.) When planning your protein and fat intake for a day, combine the calorie amounts of the two and distribute them across your meals. The calories from protein and fat should be the same at breakfast and lunch. This is because the intervals between breakfast and lunch and between lunch and dinner should be the same: six hours.

Meal Planning Principle 5: Include an Afternoon Snack

The carbohydrate eaten at lunch will create a high dose of glucose. This replenishes the energy taken from the body fat stores and used as ketones from breakfast to lunch. If this energy is not replenished at lunch, the body increases the strength of the appetite signal as the day moves along. The body knows it is operating at an energy deficit, and its requests for food will become increasingly demanding. You want to create a surge in glucose at lunch so that some of it is stored as body fat. This does not mean that eating lunch will make you fat. It simply means that the rate at which body fat is burned needs to be carefully controlled to prevent a surge in appetite. Fat cells want to be full, and resist shrinkage by calling for increased energy to refill them. You want to slow down the rate of fat loss from cells so the appetite strength will not increase throughout the day, resulting in excess snacking and increased calorie intake.

As the lunch calories from protein and fat are used up, you will begin to run out of energy about four hours after lunch. You still have some of the energy available from the fat intake at lunch, but this amount alone is not sufficient to fuel the Body Burn Rate per hour for the last two hours of the typical six-hour interval between lunch and dinner. An afternoon snack can offset this potential drop in energy. The calorie level of that snack is calculated for you in your Body Burn Rate Diet Guidelines. The recommended composition of the snack is carbohydrate. This is based on the assumption that most people plan six-hour intervals between meals. Our bodies and our appetite systems are geared to the six-hour interval of fat oxidation. If we exceed that time frame, we begin to place ourselves into the fasting state, and begin the shift to ketones as the fuel supply.

If the six-hour time interval is consistent with your habits, eat carbohydrate for your afternoon snack. This food will be burned in two hours and not interfere with your appetite at dinner. If you eat dinner much later in the day, for example at 8:00 or 9:00 P.M., use the percentages of the Diet Composition you selected for your Burn Rate Diet to determine the calories from carbohydrate, protein, and fat for the afternoon snack. This could mean that instead of a handful of pretzels for your snack, you have half a handful of pretzels and a glass of milk. Or you put peanut butter or a piece of cheese on your crackers instead of eating only the crackers.

THE ENERGY CUBE

The Energy Cube on the next page illustrates Burn Rate Diet Principles in a visual way. The Energy Cube is a four-sided figure with four bands on each side. The sides of the Energy Cube represent the passage of time throughout the day. Each side represents six hours. As long as your meals are six hours apart, your breakfast, lunch, and dinner can be placed at three of the corners of the Energy Cube. Typical eating times are indicated along the bands.

Each band of the Energy Cube represents a fuel source. Carbohydrate, protein, and fat are represented in the first three bands. The innermost band indicates the level of ketones in the bloodstream from the burning of body fat. Each of the different fuels is illustrated by a different pattern based on its respective burn rate. *Spotted* is the fast burning fuel, carbohydrate, that is burned or stored within two hours. Protein, the medium fuel that requires four hours to burn, is *checked*. Fat, the longest-burning fuel, is shown *striped*. As the body consumes each fuel, its band loses its pattern and eventually is shown as white. White on a band indicates that there is a complete absence of fuel from that fuel source. White signals that the tank is on E for empty.

Periods of low fuel cause appetite to rise. The strength of appetite can be inferred from the Energy Cube. The more patterns that exist at any one point across all four bands, the greater is the glucose and/or ketone supply in the blood. More white space means greater appetite. As fuel is used, more white appears, and the stronger will be the appetite. The strongest level of appetite will correspond to any period that shows white in all four bands of the Energy Cube.

As you can see from each side of the Energy Cube, the idea is

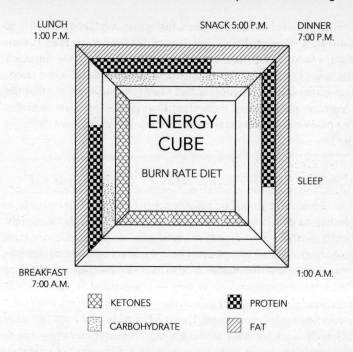

LUNCH
1:00 P.M.

SNACK 5:00 P.M.

DINNER
7:00 P.M.

ENERGY
CUBE

BURN RATE DIET

SLEEP

BREAKFAST
7:00 A.M.

1:00 A.M.

KETONES   PROTEIN

CARBOHYDRATE   FAT

This Energy Cube indicates the ideal use of carbohydrate, protein,
and fat to control appetite all day long.

to fill the intervals between your meals so there are no gaps in
your energy supply throughout your day. Disruptions in energy
supply can lead to a surge in appetite. There can be too little
energy available if you don't eat enough food. Interestingly, eating
too much of a fast-burning fuel, like carbohydrate, also leads to a
disruption in energy supply because there is a rush of energy followed by rapid storage. When the energy is stored, it is not immediately available for use in the blood stream, and we feel hungry.

The innermost band of the Energy Cube, in the *scaled* pattern, indicates the presence of ketones from the breakdown of
body fat. As sleep progresses, there are more ketones available.
This is caused by the increasing rate at which fat is oxidized once
the glucose from the dinner meal has been used.

The Energy Cube acts like a fuel gauge for the different fuel sources in the diet. Every variation of the Burn Rate Diet—Standard, Medical, and Athletic—fills out the Energy Cube in much the same way. Notice that on the diagram at least one of the bands is patterned at all periods on this Energy Cube, representing the ideal way to eat using Burn Rate Diet principles. This indicates the presence of some fuel source for energy at all times throughout the day.

USING THE ENERGY CUBE TO PLAN YOUR BREAKFAST

The Burn Rate Breakfast provides a slow but steady infusion of glucose to blend with the ketones produced from the overnight fast. The Burn Rate Breakfast consists of a moderate amount of carbohydrate, such as a piece of bread; and protein and fat, such as eggs, bacon, and margarine on the toast. By the time the spotted fuel (carbohydrate=bread) is used up in two hours, there is still checked (protein=egg white, meat of bacon), striped (fat=margarine, egg yolk), and scaled (body fat) fuel available to last until lunch. In contrast, look at the Energy Cube representing a high carbohydrate/low fat diet on the next page. The effects of eating a high-carbohydrate, low-fat breakfast, such as cereal with skim milk, can be clearly seen. Eating cereal at breakfast brings in glucose at such a rapid rate that it shuts down ketone production. After two hours, the absence of energy can be seen in the empty white space across all four bands of the Energy Cube.

USING THE ENERGY CUBE TO PLAN YOUR LUNCH

Let's go back to the Burn Rate Diet Energy Cube to examine the effects of lunch on the fuel supply. Recall that both fuels, glucose and ketones, fueled the interval between breakfast and lunch. Fat is the secondary storage system of the body, the spare tank. When you dip into the spare tank for energy, your body sounds an alarm in the form of increased hunger. This is the price to pay for using ketones as fuel. Unless the reserves are replenished at lunch, hunger will continue to build all day, and you may find yourself snacking too much in the afternoon, or overeating at dinner.

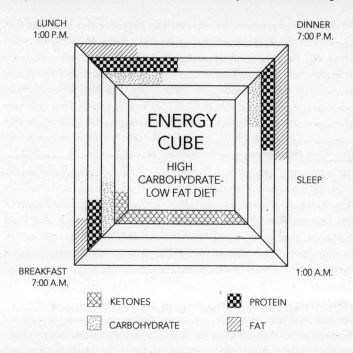

This Energy Cube represents a high carbohydrate/low fat diet. Each meal provides a surge of calories that are quickly expended, leading to an increase in appetite well in advance of the next meal.

The calories in your lunch meal can reduce the excessive hunger created by ketone depletion. Carbohydrate is quickly absorbed, and the subsequent rush of glucose into the system counteracts the body's hunger alarm. This is why a Burn Rate Lunch includes a bit more carbohydrate than breakfast.

USING THE ENERGY CUBE TO PLAN YOUR AFTERNOON SNACK

Lunch is illustrated in the patterns on the Burn Rate Energy Cube. The spotted fuel (carbohydrate) indicates the rush of glucose into the bloodstream, some of which is used to replace body fat used in the morning for energy. The checked fuel (protein) and the striped fuel (fat) continue to supply energy in the afternoon. However, because there is no energy boost from ketones, as there is in the morning, an afternoon snack is recommended to bolster the energy supply, preferably carbohydrate in the form of fruit, pretzels, popcorn, or the like. If you eat your snack in the late afternoon, there are only two hours remaining to dinner. Since the burn rate of carbohydrate is two hours, your snack does not interfere with the appropriate hunger for the dinner meal. If you'll be eating dinner late, then the composition of your snack should be adjusted to accommodate the increased time interval. A protein/fat snack would provide a longer-burning fuel to cover the increased interval. In the High Carbohydrate/Low Fat Diet Energy Cube, there is no late afternoon snack. The energy supply in the afternoon is low, as shown by presence of the white space across all four bands of that interval.

USING THE ENERGY CUBE TO PLAN YOUR DINNER

The purpose of the dinner meal is to complete your fuel requirements for the day. Breakfast and lunch were primarily protein and fat to provide energy for the full six-hour interval between meals. Carbohydrate was carefully controlled to prevent a strong insulin reaction. At dinner, however, the onset of an insulin reaction after a high-carbohydrate meal is beneficial. The lethargy induced by the insulin can help you sleep. So dinner will consist primarily of carbohydrate—such as potatoes, rice, pasta, bread, and vegetables—with a small amount of protein and fat, usually a portion of meat, fish, fowl, eggs, or cheese. Protein and fat are less important at dinner because most of us go to bed between ten o'clock and midnight, so we don't need a rich fuel mix to keep us going.

On the Burn Rate Diet Energy Cube, the spotted, checked, and striped bands indicate the energy supplied by a normal dinner. Notice that by one o'clock in the morning, glucose from each of the three bands is gone, and ketone production begins. The scaled band throughout the sleep period indicates the increasing availability of ketones for use during sleep.

USING THE ENERGY CUBE TO PLAN YOUR EVENING SNACK

If you prefer an after-dinner snack, the calories can be carved out from your dinner or afternoon snack allowance. After-dinner snacks should be planned based on the impact they will have on your ketone supply in the morning. High-carbohydrate snacks like pretzels, crackers, fruit, and so on at night will result in high ketone levels in the morning. The fuel will be burned or stored within two hours after eating. Ketone production will begin two hours after the onset of sleep. Ketones will be produced for six hours (assuming an eight-hour sleep). Snacks of protein and fat like cottage cheese, a glass of milk, nuts, eggs, or even a piece of chicken will result in a low ketone supply in the morning. These snacks require six hours to be burned. Ketone production will only occur for two hours, rather than the six following a carbohydrate snack.

As I've mentioned earlier, your choice of a late snack depends on how well you tolerate ketones and the level of ketone production that maximizes your energy level upon awakening. Some individuals can eat a light breakfast or even none at all and not be hungry until noon. Because they function well on ketones, their evening snack (if they want one) should consist of carbohydrate only. For others, high ketone levels may be associated with nausea in the morning. They need to reduce the amount of time their body spends burning body fat at night by eating a protein/fat snack before going to bed. The extended burn rate of these fuels will continue to provide energy throughout sleep and will prevent ketone production for nearly the entire sleep period.

PUTTING FOOD ON YOUR PLATE

Now that you know how to organize your Burn Rate Diet, you need to add the specific foods that meet the requirements of your individualized nutritional plan. In the next chapter, I will show you how to add the foods you like to your meal plans.

7

Your Burn Rate Diet

Now that you know the general principles of the Burn Rate Meal Plans and have studied the Energy Cubes, it is time to put food into your individualized Burn Rate Diet. My Web site makes this process as simple as possible, but you need to do some groundwork before you get started. Making your eating plans fit exactly what you need requires some thought. But then again, anything of value requires some effort. It is time to decide for yourself whether you are worth the work. A weight control problem requires time to manage. If you use simple solutions like structured diets that are not personalized to your needs, your appetite will not be controlled and you will struggle. Do the work now so you can avoid the problem of having to do the work over and over again.

If you do not have Internet access, you can use the Meal Charts in this chapter together with the food lists in Appendix III to design each meal. If you do have Internet access, my Web site allows you to let the wonder of high technology create Burn Rate Meal Plans for you with little time involved. Simply follow the instructions on the Web site (**www.burnratediet.com**) to plan your Burn Rate meals. Go to the Web site and click on "Support

Network." As a member of the Support Network, you will have access to the computerized Burn Rate Meal Plans. Follow the easy steps to determine the foods that fit the calorie amounts for your individualized Burn Rate Diet. (Each meal that you create will be stored for your reference in your own personal file for ready access or printing whenever you want.) However, whether or not you are online, I encourage you to familiarize yourself with the meal planning process that is described below for each meal. Knowledge is power. Once you become familiar with the process, you will have the power to supply your body with exactly the fuel it needs.

Before deciding whether to do the meal planning yourself, or leave it to modern technology with the Web site, I'd like you to do a little work the old-fashioned way. Write down on the Meal Charts the foods that you may want in a given meal. Figure out which foods are Pure and which ones are Mixed, using Appendix III. This exercise will give you practice selecting the food choices from the food lists and making adjustments in portion sizes to fit your individual needs.

For each of you, the Burn Rate Diet will have individualized calorie amounts for each meal, as well as individualized break-

♨ YOUR PERSONALIZED BURN RATE DIET GUIDELINES

Daily Calorie Level: _____ calories per day

	Breakfast calories	Lunch calories	Snack calories	Dinner calories
Carbohydrate	_____	_____	_____	_____
Protein	_____	_____	_____	_____
Fat	_____	_____	_____	_____
TOTAL	_____	_____	_____	_____

downs of carbohydrate, protein, and fat. The first step in creating your own Meal Plan is to return to your personalized Burn Rate Diet Guidelines calculated on the Web site or in Appendix III. You will need this information whether you plan to use the Web site or not.

START WITH MODIFYING THE TEST DIET

Some of you will have a good idea of the menus that you will want to create. Others may not know exactly what you want or know how to plan a meal. If you know what you like to eat and know how to plan meals, continue reading and you will apply your ideas to create your Burn Rate Meal Plans. For those of you who need more direction, go back to the Web site or Appendix I. Review the meals outlined in the Test Diet. By now, you have your own personalized Burn Rate Diet Guidelines that will be different than the calorie levels I used to create the Test Diet. Your first step in meal planning might be to select the meals that you used during the Test Diet, and refigure the amounts and calories to suit your own Burn Rate Diet Guidelines. This will give you seven breakfasts, lunches, and dinners to have as handy references to guide your food choices. You can later add more menus as your meal planning skills improve or as your tastes change.

BURN RATE BREAKFAST

Below are several ideas for you to consider for your Burn Rate Breakfast. Notice that the typical breakfast choice of hot or cold cereal is replaced by the foods of the old farmer's breakfast. Eggs, bacon, sausage, and the like all have their place in the Burn Rate Diet, with portion control being individualized. Remember that each person will have a different calorie level to fulfill to create his or her ideal breakfast, so constructing a variety of menus requires some thought. The good news is that you only have to do it once; then you can save the menus to be repeated over and over. After all, how many different breakfasts do you typically eat? Three? Four? It is not as many as you think, and the time you take to create your Burn Rate Breakfast will be well worth the effort.

Burn Rate Breakfast Examples:

Ham and cheese half-sandwich

Half a bagel with lox and cream cheese

Two eggs with bacon

Cheese omelet with bacon

Peanut butter on a rice cake

Egg and bacon sandwich

Chipped Beef on toast

Breakfast burrito

Cottage cheese and fruit

The Cereal Option

While the recommended Burn Rate Breakfast resembles the old farmer's breakfast, many of you may still want to have a breakfast of hot or cold cereal. You can do that and still follow the Burn Rate Diet, but you will need to resolve the problem of midmorning hunger that would result from the carbohydrate load of eating all your cereal all at once. Cut your total breakfast calories in half, and eat half as cereal in the morning and half as a midmorning snack. I recommend fruit or bread (bagel, toast, etc.) for the snack. While not ideal, this option can at least maintain the desired calorie control and help you to vary your breakfast options.

The No Breakfast Option

Some of my patients report that they skip breakfast entirely, feel fine throughout the morning, and do not overeat at lunch. If this is your experience, then you are an individual who can use ketones very effectively. The buildup overnight of ketones from the breakdown of body fat serves as your energy source in the morning. Eating breakfast may interfere with the supply of this energy source and may make you feel worse. If you followed the Burn Rate Test Diet faithfully, then you already know whether or not you are a breakfast person. If you skip breakfast, you have two choices to deal with the breakfast calories. You can eliminate them completely and revise your weight goals and Burn Rate Diet Guidelines. Or you can add half of the calories to lunch and half to dinner. Add the appropriate amounts to carbohydrate, protein, and fat at those two meals.

How you feel in the morning is influenced by the food you ate the night before. If you ate nothing after dinner, your ketone levels will be at their maximum in the morning. If you ate a carbohydrate snack after dinner, the levels will be less. If you ate protein or fat as an after-dinner snack, your ketone levels in the morning will be lowest. Experiment with different foods after dinner and examine their effects on your energy level in the morning up to lunch. You will find the right combination that will enable you to make the right decision about whether to eat breakfast or not.

TEN STEPS TO CREATING A PERSONALIZED BURN RATE BREAKFAST

In the next few pages you will fill out a Meal Chart for each meal in order to familiarize yourself with the correct way to create a personalized Burn Rate Diet breakfast, lunch, and dinner. I've provided examples of calculations for two typical breakfasts. Both breakfasts have the same calorie allowances, to show you how you can incorporate variety into your meals without changing your calorie totals. All of the calorie values are taken from the food lists in Appendix III.

Burn Rate Breakfast Example #1:
English Muffin with Bacon and Melted Cheese

Goal and Total Allowances

Step 1:   Use your Burn Rate Diet Guidelines to determine your calorie allowances for breakfast

Total allowance for Burn Rate Breakfast calories = 316

Enter this figure on your breakfast meal chart as "total allowance"

Breakdown: Carbohydrate calories = 124

Protein calories = 62

Fat calories = 130

Enter these figures on your breakfast meal chart as each "goal"

Filling the Carbohydrate Allowance

Step 2:   Select your first carbohydrate choice

Carbohydrate choice #1: English muffin

English muffin is a pure carbohydrate with 65 calories

Enter this number on your breakfast meal chart

Step 3:   Calculate your carbohydrate balance

Carbohydrate allowance   124

English muffin   - 65

Balance   59

Step 4:   Select your second carbohydrate choice

Carbohydrate choice #2: Apple juice

Apple juice is a pure carbohydrate with 60 calories in 4 ounces

Enter this number on your breakfast meal chart

Calculate your carbohydrate balance

Balance from Step 3   59 calories

Apple juice   - 65

Balance   -1, or 0

(Note: a one-calorie differential is meaningless. However, if the differential is over 10 calories, reconfigure your choices.)

Filling the Protein Allowance

Step 5:   Select your first protein choice

Protein choice #1: Bacon

Bacon is a dual mix food

3 slices of bacon contain:

> 24 protein calories and
>
> 66 fat calories

Enter these numbers on your breakfast meal chart

Step 6:　Calculate your protein balance

Protein allowance	62
Bacon	- 24
Balance	38

Step 7:　Select your second protein choice

Protein choice #2: Cheese

Cheese is a dual mix food

1 ounce of cheese contains:

> 37 protein calories and
>
> 74 fat calories

Enter these numbers on your breakfast meal chart

Calculate your protein balance

Balance from Step 6	38 calories
Cheese	- 37
Balance	1, or 0

Filling the Fat Allowance

Step 8:　Calculate your fat balance

Fat allowance	130
Fat from bacon	- 66
Fat from cheese	- 74
Fat balance	- 10

Step 9:　Select your fat choice

(Note: a negative balance means you have overrun your total allowance.)

Step 10:　Recalculate your fat balance

> No further choices are available to you

🔥 BURN RATE DIET: BREAKFAST MEAL CHART

Total calorie allowance for breakfast   __316__

	CALORIES		
FOOD / AMOUNTS	**CARBOHYDRATE**	**PROTEIN**	**FAT**
Carbohydrate GOAL:	124		
1. English muffin	65	___	___
2. Apple juice	60	___	___
3. _____	___	___	___
TOTAL:	125		
BALANCE:	-1(0)		
Protein GOAL:		62	
1. Bacon		24	66
2. Cheese		37	74
3. _____		___	___
TOTAL:		61	
BALANCE:		1(0)	
Fat GOAL:			130
1. _____			___
2. _____			___
3. _____			___
TOTAL:			140
BALANCE:			-10(0)

Burn Rate Breakfast Example #2:
Fried Eggs, Toast, and Juice

Goal and Total Allowances

Step 1: Use your Burn Rate Diet Guidelines to determine your calorie allowances for breakfast

Total allowance for Burn Rate Breakfast calories = 316

Enter this figure on your breakfast meal chart as "total allowance"

Breakdown: Carbohydrate calories = 124

Protein calories = 62

Fat calories = 130

Enter these figures on your breakfast meal chart as each "goal"

Filling the Carbohydrate Allowance

Step 2: Select your first carbohydrate choice

Carbohydrate choice #1: Toast

Toast is a pure carbohydrate with 72 calories

Enter this number on your breakfast meal chart

Step 3: Calculate your carbohydrate balance

Carbohydrate allowance 124

Toast - 72

Balance 52 calories

Step 4: Select your second carbohydrate choice

Carbohydrate choice #2: 8 ounces skim milk

Skim milk is a dual mix food

8 ounces contain:

43 carbohydrate calories and

43 protein calories

Enter these numbers on your breakfast meal chart

Recalculate your carbohydrate balance

Current balance	52 calories
8 oz. skim milk	- 43
New balance	9, or 0

(Note: a 9-calorie differential is meaningless. However, if the differential is over 10 calories, reconfigure your choices.)

Filling the Protein Allowance

Step 5: Recalculate your protein balance

Protein allowance	62 calories
8 oz. skim milk	- 43
Current balance	19

Step 6: Select your second protein choice

Protein choice #2: 1 egg

Egg is a dual mix food

1 egg contains:

> 27 protein calories and
> 48 fat calories

Enter these numbers on your breakfast meal chart

Step 7: Recalculate your protein balance

Current balance	19 calories
Egg	- 27
Balance	- 8, or 0

(Note: an 8-calorie differential is meaningless. However, if the differential is over 10 calories, reconfigure your choices.)

Filling the Fat Allowance

Step 8: Calculate your fat balance

Fat allowance	130 calories
Egg	- 48
Current balance	82

Step 9:   Select fat choice

Fat choice #2: 1 ounce regular cream cheese

Cream cheese is a pure fat food with 90 calories

Enter this number on your breakfast meal chart

Step 10:   Recalculate fat balance

Balance remaining   82 calories

Cream cheese   - 90

Balance   - 8, or 0

(Note: an 8-calorie differential is meaningless. However, if the differential is over 10 calories, reconfigure your choices.)

🔥 BURN RATE DIET: BREAKFAST MEAL CHART

Total calorie allowance for breakfast ___316___

	CALORIES		
	CARBOHYDRATE	PROTEIN	FAT
FOOD / AMOUNTS			
Carbohydrate GOAL:	124		
1. Toast, 1 slice	72		
2. Skim milk 8 oz.	43	43	
3.			
TOTAL:	115		
BALANCE:	9(0)		
Protein GOAL:		62	
1. Egg, 1 whole		27	48
2.			
3.			
TOTAL:		70	
BALANCE:		-8(0)	
Fat GOAL:			130
1. Cream cheese, 1 oz.			90
2.			
3.			
TOTAL:			138
BALANCE:			-8(0)

Build Your Own Breakfast

Remember that all these calculations can be done for you on the Web site. If you want to learn how to do it yourself, follow the ten steps below to build your own Burn Rate Breakfast that matches the specific calorie levels of your Burn Rate Diet Guidelines. Fill out the practice meal chart on page 112 as you go along. Remember to enter all the calories from each component of a mixed food on your meal chart. Keep in mind that you may need to keep reconfiguring your choices or adjusting your portions until you get the calorie totals to come out right. If there is a differential of over 10 calories, rework your selections.

Goals and Total Allowances

Step 1:   Use your Burn Rate Diet Guidelines to determine your calorie allowances for breakfast

Total allowance for Burn Rate Breakfast
calories = _____

Enter this figure on your breakfast meal chart as "total allowance"

Breakdown: Carbohydrate calories = _____

Protein calories = _____

Fat calories = _____

Enter these figures on your breakfast meal chart as each "goal"

Filling the Carbohydrate Allowance

Step 2:   Select your first carbohydrate choice from the following food lists:

Pure Foods:

Pure Carbohydrate

Mixed Foods:

Carbohydrate/Protein

Carbohydrate/Fat

Carbohydrate/Protein/Fat

Carbohydrate choice #1: _____

Enter this number on your breakfast meal chart

If your choice of carbohydrate is a mixed food, enter the calories of its different components on your meal chart.

Step 3:   Calculate your carbohydrate balance

Carbohydrate allowance _____ calories

Carbohydrate choice #1 _____

Current balance _____

Step 4:   Select additional carbohydrate choices from the food lists containing carbohydrates until the carbohydrate allowance is filled

Carbohydrate choice #2 _____

Enter this number on your breakfast meal chart

If your choice of carbohydrate is a mixed food, enter the calories of its different components on your meal chart.

Recalculate your carbohydrate balance

Current balance _____ calories

Carbohydrate choice #2 _____

New balance _____

Continue to make carbohydrate choices and recalculate the balance until the carbohydrate allowance is filled.

Enter these numbers on your breakfast meal chart

Filling the Protein Allowance

Step 5:   Select your first protein choice from the following food lists:

Pure Foods:

Protein

Mixed Foods:

Carbohydrate/Protein

Protein/Fat

Carbohydrate/Protein/Fat

Protein choice #1: _____

Enter this number on your breakfast meal chart

> *If your choice of protein is a mixed food, enter the calories of its different components on your meal chart.*

Step 6:   Calculate your protein balance

Protein allowance   _____

Protein choice #1   _____

Current balance   _____

Step 7:   Select additional protein choices from the food lists containing protein until the protein allowance is filled

Protein choice #2 _____

Enter this number on your breakfast meal chart

> *If your choice of protein is a mixed food, enter the calories of its different components on your meal chart.*

Recalculate your protein balance

Current balance   _____

Protein choice #2   _____

New balance   _____

Continue to make protein choices and recalculate the balance until the protein allowance is filled

Enter these numbers on your breakfast meal chart

Filling the Fat Allowance

Step 8:   If mixed foods have been used in any choices above, compute the fat balance before making a fat choice

Calculate your fat balance

Fat allowance   _____ calories

Total fat from Steps 2–6   _____

Current balance   _____

Step 9:   Select your fat choice from the Pure Fat food list:

Fat choice #1: _____

Enter this number on your breakfast meal chart

Step 10: Recalculate your fat balance

Current balance _____

Fat choice #1 _____

New balance _____

Continue to make fat choices and recalculate the balance until the fat allowance is filled

Enter these numbers on your breakfast meal chart

BURN RATE DIET: BREAKFAST MEAL CHART

Total calorie allowance for breakfast _____

	CALORIES		
	CARBOHYDRATE	**PROTEIN**	**FAT**
FOOD / AMOUNTS			
Carbohydrate	GOAL: _____		
1._____	_____	_____	_____
2._____	_____	_____	_____
3._____	_____	_____	_____
	TOTAL: _____		
	BALANCE: _____		
Protein		GOAL: _____	
1._____		_____	_____
2._____		_____	_____
3._____		_____	_____
		TOTAL: _____	
		BALANCE: _____	
Fat			GOAL: _____
1._____			_____
2._____			_____
3._____			_____
			TOTAL: _____
			BALANCE: _____

BURN RATE LUNCH

The key to planning the Burn Rate lunch is the replacement of the body fat stores that were depleted during the nighttime fast. Recall that the body converts fat into ketone fuel during a fast and makes ketones available for energy. Upon awakening, this ketone fuel is a fuel boost for the morning energy needs. However, recall also that there is a price to pay for the burning of body fat for energy. Reduction in body fat stores creates a surge in appetite. If some of the fat stores are not replaced, the resulting appetite will be strong and will cause you to overeat at some point in the day.

Lunch involves a trade-off. While you want your body fat stores to be reduced, the speed of this reduction needs to be carefully controlled or your appetite will surge. Carbohydrate gives you the fastest fuel to serve this purpose. Unlike breakfast, where the control of carbohydrate was emphasized, lunch involves eating enough carbohydrate to control appetite plus enough calories to fuel the Body Burn Rate for the six-hour interval from lunch to dinner. A serving or two of fruit and other foods is added to fulfill the individual Burn Rate Diet lunch requirements.

Listed below are examples of several Burn Rate lunches:

Tuna sandwich

Pizza, two slices

Soup and salad

Grilled cheese sandwich

Macaroni and cheese

Cottage cheese and fruit plate

TEN STEPS TO CREATING A PERSONALIZED BURN RATE LUNCH

Now you will learn how to fill out a Meal Chart for lunch. First, let me show you how I do the calculations for two typical lunches. Both have the same calorie allowances, to show how you can incorporate variety into your meals without changing your calorie totals. All of the calorie values are taken from the food lists in Appendix III.

Burn Rate Lunch Example #1:
Tuna Fish Sandwich

Goal and Total Allowances

Step 1:   Use your Burn Rate Diet Guidelines to determine your calorie allowances for lunch

Total allowance for Burn Rate lunch calories = 418

Enter this figure on your lunch meal chart as "total allowance"

Breakdown: Carbohydrate calories = 250

Protein calories = 42

Fat calories = 125

Enter these figures on your lunch meal chart as each "goal"

Filling the Carbohydrate Allowance

Step 2:   Select your first carbohydrate choice

Carbohydrate choice #1: Bread, two slices

Bread is a pure carbohydrate with 82 calories per slice

Enter 164 calories on your lunch meal chart

Step 3:   Calculate your carbohydrate balance

Carbohydrate allowance	250 calories
Bread, two slices	- 164
Balance	86

Step 4:   Select your second carbohydrate choice

Carbohydrate choice #2: Apple juice

Apple juice is a pure carbohydrate with 90 calories in 6 ounces

Enter this number on your lunch meal chart

Recalculate your carbohydrate balance

Current balance from Step 3	86
Apple juice	- 90
Balance	- 4, or 0

(Note: if the differential is over 10 calories, reconfigure your choices.)

Filling the Protein Allowance

Step 5:   Select your first protein choice

Protein choice #1: Tuna fish (canned, in water)

Tuna fish is a pure protein with 45 calories in 1.5 ounces

Enter this number on your lunch meal chart

Step 6:   Calculate your protein balance

Protein allowance	42 calories
Tuna fish	- 45
Balance	- 3, or 0

Step 7:   You have used up your protein allowance, so no further protein choices are open to you

Filling the Fat Allowance

Step 8:   Calculate your fat balance

Fat allowance	125 calories
Fat from Steps 3–7	0
Current balance	125

Step 9:   Select your first fat choice

Fat choice #1: Lite mayonnaise

Lite mayonnaise is a pure fat food with 120 calories per 6 teaspoons

Enter this number on your lunch meal chart

Step 10: This uses up your fat allowance, so no more fat choices are open to you.

🔥 BURN RATE DIET: LUNCH MEAL CHART

Total calorie allowance for lunch ___418___

	CALORIES		
	CARBOHYDRATE	PROTEIN	FAT
FOOD / AMOUNTS			
Carbohydrate GOAL:	250		
1. Bread, 2 slices	164	___	___
2. Apple juice, 6 oz.	90	___	___
3. _____	___	___	___
TOTAL:	254		
BALANCE:	-4(0)		
Protein GOAL:		42	
1. Tuna fish, 1.5 oz.		45	___
2. _____		___	___
3. _____		___	___
TOTAL:		45	
BALANCE:		-3(0)	
Fat GOAL:			125
1. Lite mayonnaise, 6 tsp.			120
2. _____			___
3. _____			___
TOTAL:			120
BALANCE:			5(0)

Burn Rate Lunch Example #2:
Soup and Salad

Goal and Total Allowances

Step 1:   Use your Burn Rate Diet Guidelines to determine your
           calorie allowances for lunch

           Total allowance for Burn Rate lunch calories = 418

           Enter this figure on your lunch meal chart as
           "total allowance"

           Breakdown: Carbohydrate calories = 250

                      Protein calories = 42

                      Fat calories = 125

           Enter these figures on your lunch meal chart as
           each "goal"

Filling the Carbohydrate Allowance

Step 2:   Select your first carbohydrate choice

           Carbohydrate choice #1: Broth soup

           Broth soup is a triple mix food with:

           Carbohydrate   44 calories

           Protein   9

           Fat   10

           Enter these numbers on your lunch meal chart

Step 3:   Calculate your carbohydrate balance

           Carbohydrate allowance   250

           Soup   - 44

           Current balance   206

Step 4:   Select your second carbohydrate choice

           Carbohydrate choice #2: Tossed salad

           Tossed salad has 28 calories of carbohydrate in 4 cups

           Enter this number on your lunch meal chart

           Calculate your carbohydrate balance

Current balance from Step 3   206 calories

Tossed salad   - 28

New balance   178

You still have 178 calories to apply to your choice of fruits that are pure carbohydrate.

Carbohydrate choice #3:
Apple   82 calories

Carbohydrate choice #4:
Cantaloupe   92

                                     174

This fills the carbohydrate allowance.

Filling the Protein Allowance

Step 5:   Select your first protein choice

Protein choice #1: Chicken, 1 ounce

Chicken is a dual mix food that contains:

Protein   32 calories

Fat   16

Enter these numbers on your lunch meal chart

Step 6:   Calculate your protein balance

Protein allowance   42 calories

Chicken   - 32

Balance   10, or 0

Step 7:   You have used up your protein allowance, so no further protein choices are available to you.

Filling the Fat Allowance

Step 8:   Calculate your fat balance

Fat allowance   125 calories

Fat calories from broth soup   - 10

Fat calories from chicken   - 16

Current balance   99

Step 9:   Select your next fat choice

Fat choice #1: Lite salad dressing, 4 teaspoons

Lite salad dressing is a pure fat food with 100 calories per 4 teaspoons

Enter this number on your lunch meal chart

Step 10: You have used up your fat allowance, so no further fat choices are available to you.

🔥 BURN RATE DIET: LUNCH MEAL CHART

Total calorie allowance for lunch ___418___

		CALORIES	
	CARBOHYDRATE	PROTEIN	FAT
FOOD / AMOUNTS			
Carbohydrate GOAL:	250		
1. Broth soup, 1 cup	44	9	10
2. Salad, 4 cups	28		
3. Fruit (apple/ cantaloupe)	174		
TOTAL:	246		
BALANCE:	4(0)		
Protein GOAL:		42	
1. Chicken, 1 oz.		32	16
2.			
3.			
TOTAL:		41	
BALANCE:		1(0)	
Fat GOAL:			125
1. Lite salad dressing, 4 tsp.			100
2.			
3.			
TOTAL:			126
BALANCE:			-1(0)

Build Your Own Lunch

Follow the ten steps below to build your own Burn Rate lunch that matches the specific calorie levels of your Burn Rate Diet Guidelines. Fill out the practice meal chart on page 124 as you go along. Remember to enter all the calories from each component of a mixed food on your meal chart. Keep in mind that you may need to keep reconfiguring your choices or adjusting your portions until you get the calorie totals to come out right. If there is a differential of over 10 calories, rework your selections.

Goal and Total Allowances

Step 1:   Use your Burn Rate Diet Guidelines to determine your calorie allowances for lunch

Total allowance for Burn Rate lunch calories = _____

Enter this figure on your lunch meal chart as "total allowance"

Breakdown: Carbohydrate calories = _____

Protein calories = _____

Fat calories = _____

Enter each figure on your lunch meal chart as the appropriate "goal"

Filling the Carbohydrate Allowance

Step 2:   Select your carbohydrate choice from the following food lists:

Pure Food:

Pure Carbohydrate

Mixed Food:

Carbohydrate/Protein

Carbohydrate/Fat

Carbohydrate/Protein/Fat

Carbohydrate choice #1: _____

Enter this number on your lunch meal chart

If your choice of carbohydrate is a mixed food, enter the calories of its different components on your meal chart.

Step 3:   Calculate your carbohydrate balance

Carbohydrate allowance   _____ calories

Carbohydrate choice #1   _____

Current balance   _____

Select your second carbohydrate choice from the food lists in Step 2

Carbohydrate choice #2: _____

Enter this number on your lunch meal chart

If your choice of carbohydrate is a mixed food, enter the calories of its different components on your meal chart.

Step 4:   Recalculate your carbohydrate balance

Current balance from Step 3   _____ calories

Carbohydrate choice #2   _____

New balance   _____

If necessary, rework your choices until you meet your allowance.

Filling the Protein Allowance

Step 5:   Select your first protein choice from the following food lists:

Pure Food

Pure Protein

Mixed Food

Carbohydrate/Protein

Protein/Fat

Carbohydrate/Protein/Fat

Protein choice #1: _____

Enter this number on your lunch meal chart

If your choice of protein is a mixed food, enter the calories of its different components on your meal chart.

Step 6:   Calculate your protein balance

Protein allowance   _____ calories

Protein choice #1   _____

Current balance   _____

Select your second protein choice from the food lists in Step 5

Protein choice #2: _____

Enter this number on your lunch meal chart

If your choice of protein is a mixed food, enter the calories of its different components on your meal chart.

Step 7:   Recalculate your protein balance

Current balance from
Step 3   _____ calories

Protein choice #2   _____

New balance   _____

If necessary, rework your choices until you meet your allowance.

Filling Your Fat Allowance

Step 8:   Calculate your fat balance

Fat allowance   _____ calories

Total fat calories from
previous choices: _____

Current balance   _____

Step 9:   Select your first fat choice from the Pure Fat food list

Fat choice #1: _____

Enter this number on your lunch meal chart

Step 10:   Recalculate your fat balance

Current balance   _____ calories

Fat choice #1   _____

New balance   _____

If necessary, rework your choices until you meet your allowance.

🔥 BURN RATE DIET: LUNCH MEAL CHART

Total calorie allowance for lunch _____

		CALORIES		
		CARBOHYDRATE	PROTEIN	FAT
FOOD / AMOUNTS				
Carbohydrate	GOAL: _____			
1._____		_____	_____	_____
2._____		_____	_____	_____
3._____		_____	_____	_____
	TOTAL: _____			
	BALANCE: _____			
Protein	GOAL: _____			
1._____			_____	_____
2._____			_____	_____
3._____			_____	_____
	TOTAL: _____			
	BALANCE: _____			
Fat	GOAL: _____			
1._____				_____
2._____				_____
3._____				_____
	TOTAL: _____			
	BALANCE: _____			

BURN RATE AFTERNOON SNACK

Remember that the purpose of an afternoon snack is to provide the same energy boost that is provided by the ketones in the morning. Since ketone production has been shut off by lunch, a supplement to the energy supply is needed by late afternoon. This is especially true after the protein gauge is nearing empty, and only the calories from the slow, steady burning of fat that you ate at lunch are available. The snack needs to serve as a quick "pick me up" that is burned fast and does not provide so much fuel that you will not want to eat dinner. Carbohydrate is the perfect fuel for that purpose. It provides a two-hour supply of fuel that keeps appetite low and energy high until dinner.

Many of my patients tell me that they feel they don't need the afternoon snack, and that they would prefer to eat a late-night snack instead. I believe that you should listen to your body, and if a late-night snack works best for you, then plan it that way. What you need to watch out for is the surge of appetite at dinner that may make you overeat your calorie amount. If you are able to skip the afternoon snack and not overeat at dinner, then transferring the calories into a late-night snack may work for you. As I mentioned in the prior discussion on night snacks, different snacks will change the ketone load in the morning. No snack gives you the highest ketone level. A carbohydrate snack will yield a higher level than an similar calorie protein or fat snack at night. Since this is ideal for most people, the recommendation to eat carbohydrate snacks in the afternoon holds true for a different reason in the late-night snack. In both cases, you want a fast-burning fuel. In the afternoon, you don't want to interfere with natural appetite at dinner. In the evening, you want to have the body begin to build the ketone supply as soon as possible. Carbohydrate is the ideal fuel in both situations.

Listed below are several options for the Burn Rate Afternoon Snack:

All carbohydrate:

Pretzels

Popcorn

Fruit

Juice

Bread

Cereal

Pancakes

Waffles

Mixed food:

Milk

Cheese

Chocolate

Potato chips

Yogurt

Cottage cheese

Bagel with cream cheese

CREATING A PERSONALIZED BURN RATE AFTERNOON SNACK

Obviously, planning your afternoon snack is not as complex as planning your other meals, but it's still important to do the job right. Your afternoon snack (if you choose to have one) will keep your energy up until dinner but not spoil your appetite for dinner. Let me show you how I plan an afternoon snack. All of the calorie values are taken from the food lists in Appendix III.

Burn Rate Afternoon Snack Example #1: All Carbohydrate

Step 1:   Use your Burn Rate Diet Guidelines to determine your calorie allowance for your afternoon snack.

Total allowance for Burn Rate afternoon snack: 260 calories

Enter this number on your afternoon snack meal chart.

Step 2:   Select your first carbohydrate

            Carbohydrate choice #1: Banana

            Banana is a pure carbohydrate with 100 calories

            Enter this number on your afternoon snack meal chart

Step 3:   Calculate your carbohydrate balance.

Carbohydrate allowance	260 calories
Banana	- 100
Balance	160

Step 4:   Select your second carbohydrate

            Carbohydrate choice #2: Pretzels

            Pretzels are a pure carbohydrate with 165 calories in 1.5 ounces

            Enter this number on your afternoon snack meal chart.

            Recalculate your carbohydrate balance

Current balance	160 calories
Pretzels	- 165
New balance	- 5, or 0

🔥 BURN RATE DIET: AFTERNOON SNACK CHART

Total calorie allowance for afternoon snack ___260___

	CALORIES		
	CARBOHYDRATE	PROTEIN	FAT
FOOD / AMOUNTS			
Carbohydrate GOAL:	260		
1. Banana	100	___	___
2. Pretzels	165	___	___
3._____	___	___	___
TOTAL:	265		
BALANCE:	-5(0)		
Protein GOAL: ___			
1._____		___	___
2._____		___	___
3._____		___	___
TOTAL: ___			
BALANCE: ___			
Fat GOAL: ___			
1._____			___
2._____			___
3._____			___
TOTAL: ___			
BALANCE: ___			

Burn Rate Afternoon Snack Example #2: Mixed Foods

Goal and Total Allowances

Step 1:   Use your Burn Rate Diet Guidelines to determine your calorie allowances for your afternoon snack

Total allowance for Burn Rate snack calories = 260

Enter this figure on your snack meal chart as "total allowance"

Breakdown: Carbohydrate calories = 143

Protein calories = 39

Fat calories = 78

Enter these figures on your snack meal chart as each "goal"

Filling the Carbohydrate Allowance

Step 2:   Select your first carbohydrate choice

Carbohydrate choice #1: Whole milk, 6 ounces

Whole milk is a triple mix food with:

Carbohydrate	37 calories
Protein	38
Fat	37

Enter these numbers on your snack meal chart

Step 3:   Calculate your carbohydrate balance

Carbohydrate allowance	143
Milk	- 37
Current balance	106

Step 4:   Select your second carbohydrate choice

Carbohydrate choice #2: Cookies, 2 chocolate chip

Chocolate chip cookies (2) are a dual mix food with:

Carbohydrate	60 calories
Fat	40

Enter this number on your snack meal chart

Calculate your carbohydrate balance

Current balance from Step 3   106 calories

Chocolate chip cookies   - 60

New balance   46

You still have 46 calories to apply to your choice of foods that are pure carbohydrate.

Carbohydrate choice #3: Nectarine, 45 calories

This fills the carbohydrate allowance.

Filling the Protein Allowance

Step 5:   Calculate your protein balance

Protein allowance   39 calories

Milk   - 38

Balance   1, or 0

You have used up your protein allowance, so no further protein choices are available to you.

Filling the Fat Allowance

Step 6:   Calculate your fat balance

Fat allowance   78 calories

Fat calories from milk   - 37

Fat calories from cookies   - 40

Current balance   1, or 0

You have used up your fat allowance, so no further fat choices are available to you.

BURN RATE DIET: AFTERNOON SNACK CHART

Total calorie allowance for afternoon snack __260__

CALORIES

	CARBOHYDRATE	PROTEIN	FAT
FOOD / AMOUNTS			
Carbohydrate GOAL:	143		
1. Whole milk	37	38	37
2. Choc. chip cookies, 2	60	0	40
3. Nectarine	45	0	0
TOTAL:	142		
BALANCE:	1(0)		
Protein GOAL:	39		
1.			
2.			
3.			
TOTAL:		38	
BALANCE:		1(0)	
Fat GOAL:			78
1.			
2.			
3.			
TOTAL:			77
BALANCE:			1(0)

BURN RATE MEAL PLANS: DINNER

Dinner is the meal that is the easiest to plan. You do not need to worry about the interval till the next meal because you will most likely be asleep in four to six hours. Our activity pattern is different in the evening, with most people relaxing and winding down from a busy day. Energy distribution is therefore not as critical to this interval. At dinner, you should eat the balance of all your unused fuel. Dinner enables you to fulfill the requirements of the composition of the diet that you initially selected when planning your Burn Rate Diet. (Most of you will have selected the Standard option of 55 percent carbohydrate, 15 percent protein, and 30 percent fat. Some of you with other nutritional needs have selected the Medical or Athletic option.) Dinner is the meal that is designed to complete the plan and to supply whatever is needed to fulfill your nutritional and energy needs for the day.

Listed below are examples of several Burn Rate dinners:

Chicken Parmigiana

Turkey Casserole

Pasta with Shrimp

Spaghetti and Meatballs

Steak and Potatoes

Pork Fried Rice

Fish Dinner

TEN STEPS TO CREATING A PERSONALIZED BURN RATE DINNER

Following are my calculations for two Burn Rate dinners, chicken parmigiana and baked codfish. Note that these meals have different calorie allowances. All of the calorie values for the foods are taken from the food lists in Appendix III.

Burn Rate Dinner Example #1: Chicken Parmigiana

Goal and Total Allowances

Step 1:   Use your Burn Rate Diet Guidelines to determine your calorie allowances for dinner

Total allowance for Burn Rate dinner calories = 663

Enter this figure on your dinner meal chart as "total allowance"

Breakdown: Carbohydrate calories = 323

Protein calories = 141

Fat calories = 199

Enter these figures on your dinner meal chart as each "goal"

Filling the Carbohydrate Allowance

Step 2:   Select your first carbohydrate choice

Carbohydrate choice #1: Pasta

Pasta is a pure carbohydrate with 197 calories per cup

Enter 197 calories on your dinner meal chart

Step 3:   Calculate your carbohydrate balance

Carbohydrate allowance   323 calories

Pasta   - 197

Current balance   126

Step 4:   Select your second carbohydrate choice

Carbohydrate choice #2: Tomato sauce

Tomato sauce is a pure carbohydrate with 40 calories in 2 ounces

Enter this number on your dinner meal chart

Recalculate your carbohydrate balance

Current balance   126

Tomato sauce   -40

New balance   86

You still have 86 calories of carbohydrate to use up.

Carbohydrate choice #3: Cauliflower (1 cup), 28 calories

Carbohydrate choice #4: Peas (½ cup), 58 calories

Recalculate your carbohydrate balance

Current balance	86
Cauliflower	- 28
Peas	-58
New balance	0

Filling the Protein Allowance

Step 5:   Select your first protein choice

Protein choice #1: Chicken

Chicken is a dual mix food. Three ounces of chicken contain:

Protein	102 calories
Fat	60

Enter this number on your dinner meal chart

Step 6:   Calculate your protein balance

Protein allowance	141 calories
Chicken	- 102
Current balance	39

Step 7:   Select your second protein choice

Protein choice #2: Lite cheese

Lite cheese is a dual mix food. One ounce contains:

Protein	40 calories
Fat	40

Enter these numbers on your dinner meal chart

Recalculate your protein balance

Current balance	39
Cheese	- 40
New balance	- 1, or 0

Filling the Fat Allowance

Step 8:   Calculate your fat balance

Fat allowance	199 calories
Fat from Steps 3-7	- 100
Current balance	99

Step 9:   Select your first fat choice

Fat choice #1: Margarine, 3 teaspoons

Margarine is a pure fat food with 100 calories per 3 teaspoons

Enter this number on your dinner meal chart

Step 10:   Recalculate your fat balance

Current balance	99
Margarine	- 100
New balance	- 1, or 0

This uses up your fat allowance, so no more fat choices are open to you.

🔥 BURN RATE DIET: DINNER MEAL CHART

Total calorie allowance for dinner   _663_

		CALORIES		
		CARBOHYDRATE	PROTEIN	FAT
FOOD / AMOUNTS				
Carbohydrate	GOAL: _323_			
1. Pasta, 1 cup		197	___	___
2. Tomato sauce, 2 oz.		40	___	___
3. Cauliflower, 1 cup		28, 58	___	___
Peas, 1/2 cup	TOTAL:	323		
	BALANCE:	0		
Protein	GOAL:		141	
1. Chicken, 3 oz.			102	60
2. Lite cheese			40	40
3.			___	___
	TOTAL:		142	
	BALANCE:		-1(0)	
Fat	GOAL:			199
1. Margarine, 3 tsp.				100
2.				___
3.				___
	TOTAL:			200
	BALANCE:			-1(0)

Burn Rate Dinner Example #2:
Fish Dinner

Goal and Total Allowances

Step 1: Use your Burn Rate Diet Guidelines to determine your calorie allowances for dinner

Total allowance for Burn Rate dinner calories = 796

Enter this figure on your dinner meal chart as "total allowance"

Breakdown: Carbohydrate calories = 388

Protein calories = 170

Fat calories = 239

Enter these figures on your dinner meal chart as each "goal"

Filling the Carbohydrate Allowance

Step 2: Select your first carbohydrate choice

Carbohydrate choice #1: Rice

Rice is a pure carbohydrate with 180 calories per cup

Enter 180 calories on your dinner meal chart

Step 3: Calculate your carbohydrate balance

Carbohydrate allowance	388 calories
Rice	- 180
Current balance	208

Step4: Select your second carbohydrate choice

Carbohydrate choice #2: Broccoli

Broccoli is a pure carbohydrate with 28 calories in 1 cup

Enter this number on your dinner meal chart

Recalculate your carbohydrate balance

Current balance	208
Broccoli	- 28
New balance	180

You still have 180 calories of carbohydrate to use up.

Carbohydrate choice #3: Applesauce (1 cup), 120

Carbohydrate choice #4: Grapes (1 cup), 60

Recalculate your carbohydrate balance

Current balance	180
Applesauce	- 120
Grapes	- 60
New balance	0

Filling the Protein Allowance

Step 5:   Select your first protein choice

Protein choice #1: Cod

Cod is a pure protein food with 180 protein calories in six ounces.

Enter this number on your dinner meal chart

Step 6:   Calculate your protein balance

Protein allowance	170 calories
Cod	- 180
Current balance	- 10, or 0

Step 7:   You have used up your protein allowance, so no other protein choices are open to you.

Filling the Fat Allowance

Step 8:   Select your first fat choice

Fat choice #1: Tartar sauce, 5 teaspoons

Tartar sauce is a pure fat food with 165 calories in 5 teaspoons.

Enter this number on your dinner meal chart

Step 9:   Calculate your fat balance

Fat allowance	239
Tartar sauce	- 165
Balance	74

Step 10:   Select your second fat choice

Fat choice #2: Margarine, 2 teaspoons

Margarine is a pure fat food with 67 fat calories in 2 teaspoons

Enter this number on your dinner meal chart

Recalculate your fat balance

Current balance   74

Margarine   - 67

New balance   7, or 0

This uses up your fat allowance, so no more fat choices are open to you.

🔥 BURN RATE DIET: DINNER MEAL CHART

Total calorie allowance for dinner   _796_

	CALORIES		
	CARBOHYDRATE	**PROTEIN**	**FAT**
FOOD / AMOUNTS			
Carbohydrate GOAL: _388_			
1. _Rice, 1 cup_	_180_	___	___
2. _Broccoli, 1 cup_	_28_	___	___
3. _Applesauce, 1 cup_	_120, 60_	___	___
Grapes, 1 cup TOTAL:	_388_		
BALANCE:	_0_		
Protein GOAL: _170_			
1. _Baked Cod, 6 oz._		_180_	___
2. _____		___	___
3. _____		___	___
TOTAL:		_180_	
BALANCE:		_-10(0)_	
Fat GOAL: _239_			
1. _Tartar sauce, 5 tsp._			_165_
2. _Margarine, 2 tsp._			_67_
3. _____			___
TOTAL:			_232_
BALANCE:			_7(0)_

Build Your Own Dinner

Follow the ten steps below to build your own Burn Rate dinner that matches the specific calorie levels of your Burn Rate Diet Guidelines. Fill out the practice meal chart on page 144 as you go along. Remember to enter all the calories from each component of a mixed food on your meal chart. Keep in mind that you may need to keep reconfiguring your choices or adjusting your portions until you get the calorie totals to come out right. If there is a differential of over 10 calories, rework your selections.

Goal and Total Allowances

Step 1:   Use your Burn Rate Diet Guidelines to determine your calorie allowances for dinner

Total allowance for Burn Rate dinner calories = _____

Enter this figure on your dinner meal chart as "total allowance"

Breakdown: Carbohydrate calories = _____

Protein calories = _____

Fat calories = _____

Enter these figures on your dinner meal chart as each "goal"

Filling the Carbohydrate Allowance

Step 2:   Select your carbohydrate choice from the following food lists:

Pure Food:

Pure Carbohydrate

Mixed Food:

Carbohydrate/Protein

Carbohydrate/Fat

Carbohydrate/Protein/Fat

Carbohydrate choice #1: _____

Enter this number on your dinner meal chart

If your choice of carbohydrate is a mixed food, enter the calories of its different components on your meal chart.

Step 3:   Calculate your carbohydrate balance

Carbohydrate allowance   _____ calories

Carbohydrate choice #1   _____

Current balance   _____

Select your second carbohydrate choice from the food
lists in Step 3

Carbohydrate choice #2: _____

Enter this number on your dinner meal chart

*If your choice of carbohydrate is a mixed food, enter the
calories of its different components on your meal chart.*

Step 4:   Recalculate your carbohydrate balance

Current balance from Step 3   _____ calories

Choice #2   _____

New balance   _____

If necessary, rework your choices until you meet your
allowance.

Filling the Protein Allowance

Step 5:   Select your first protein choice from the following food
lists:

Pure Food

Pure Protein

Mixed Food

Carbohydrate/Protein

Protein/Fat

Carbohydrate/Protein/Fat

Protein choice #1: _____

Enter this number on your dinner meal chart

*If your choice of protein is a mixed food, enter the
calories of its different components on your meal chart.*

Step 6:   Calculate your protein balance

Protein allowance   _____ calories

Protein choice #1   _____

Current balance   _____

Select your second protein choice from the food lists in Step 5

Protein choice #2: _____

Enter this number on your dinner meal chart

If your choice of protein is a mixed food, enter the calories of its different components on your meal chart.

Step 7:   Recalculate your protein balance

Current balance from
Step 3   _____ calories

Choice #2   _____

New balance   _____

If necessary, rework your choices until you meet your allowance.

Filling the Fat Allowance

Step 8:   Calculate your fat balance

Fat allowance   _____ calories

Total fat calories from
previous choices   _____

Current balance   _____

Step 9:   Select your first fat choice from the Pure Fat food list

Fat choice #1: _____

Enter this number on your dinner meal chart

Step 10: Recalculate your fat balance

Current balance   _____ calories

Choice #1   _____

New balance   _____

If necessary, rework your choices until you meet your allowance.

🔥 BURN RATE DIET: DINNER MEAL CHART

Total calorie allowance for dinner   _____

	CALORIES		
	CARBOHYDRATE	PROTEIN	FAT
FOOD / AMOUNTS			
Carbohydrate	GOAL: _____		
1._____	_____	_____	_____
2._____	_____	_____	_____
3._____	_____	_____	_____
	TOTAL: _____		
	BALANCE: _____		
Protein		GOAL: _____	
1._____		_____	_____
2._____		_____	_____
3._____		_____	_____
		TOTAL: _____	
		BALANCE: _____	
Fat			GOAL: _____
1._____			_____
2._____			_____
3._____			_____
			TOTAL: _____
			BALANCE: _____

SPICING UP YOUR BURN RATE MEAL PLANS

Spices are among the greatest discoveries in the history of mankind. It is no wonder that many daring adventures, wars, and colonizations were fueled by the need to feed the human taste for the exotic. The sugar trade in the Caribbean, the travels to the Far East in the Middle Ages, and the modern day variety of spices and condiments available in a grocery store, are all testimony to the strength of the influence of the human palate. Taste and pleasure need to be included in your diet or you will find inappropriate ways to add this factor into your eating.

In the Burn Rate Diet, variety, taste, and pleasure can all be included simply by the use of spices and sauces. One of the greatest things about spices is that they have no calories! Salt, pepper, rosemary, thyme, fennel, curry, and any other spice that you enjoy can satisfy your palate. Use them to your heart's content.

Sauces add another dimension to taste and pleasure. You can take the simplest meal, like a breast of chicken, and make it taste completely different by the use of different sauces. The trick to sauces is to have them contain very little calories. Using fruits and vegetables as the base, or bouillon cubes, or wine (whose calories diminish when the alcohol in the wine evaporates) can do this. A salsa made from tomato, pepper, mango, onion, and cilantro has less than 10 calories for several tablespoons but can add tremendous flavor to a breast of chicken or piece of fish.

My wife, Diane, has generously granted me permission to provide you with several of the sauces she has created for this very purpose. I have included them below for your use as Burn Rate Sauces. Use them to fill your Burn Rate Diet with taste and pleasure. Enjoy the sauces, change them to suit your own tastes, and above all, enjoy your food!

BURN RATE SAUCES

GINGER SAUCE

Ingredients:

½ cup soy sauce

1 cup water or vegetable stock

1 teaspoon minced fresh ginger

1 teaspoon minced fresh garlic

1 tablespoon brown sugar

Instructions:

Put all ingredients in a saucepan and bring to a boil. Remove from the heat and let sit for 20 minutes to blend flavors.

Total amount: 25 tablespoons

Calories per tablespoon: 5 calories

TOMATO FIESTA SAUCE

Ingredients:

1 cup minced cilantro

1 teaspoon minced fresh garlic

4 tablespoons freshly squeezed orange juice (juice of ½ orange)

3 tablespoons freshly squeezed lime juice (juice of whole lime)

1 teaspoon salt

¼ teaspoon pepper

1 teaspoon chili powder

1 teaspoon olive oil

½ cup water or vegetable stock

1 cup chopped tomatoes

Instructions:

Put all ingredients except tomatoes in a saucepan. Bring to a boil. Cook for 5 minutes. Add tomatoes. Cook for another 5 minutes over medium heat. Let sit for 20 minutes to blend flavors.

Total amount: 40 tablespoons

Calories per tablespoon: 3 calories

TANGY BARBECUE SAUCE

Ingredients:

⅓ cup ketchup

1 cup (8 ounces) orange juice

⅛ teaspoon orange zest (peel)

½ teaspoon chili powder

1 tablespoon brown sugar

1 teaspoon Worcestershire sauce

Instructions:

Place all ingredients in a saucepan and bring to a boil. Simmer over low heat until sauce is thickened.

Total amount: 20 tablespoons

Calories per tablespoon: 9 calories

SUMMARY: BURN RATE MEAL PLANNING

You now know how to add food to your Burn Rate Diet, and how to add taste to it as well. Your Burn Rate Diet Meal Plans will enable you to maintain a constant stream of energy throughout the entire day, bring your weight to its healthiest level, and restore your natural relationship to food. In the next chapter, I will explain the role of exercise. I will show you how to adjust your eating for the energy requirements of exercise, and help you develop a realistic plan to reduce stress and body weight with exercise.

8

Exercise

People who use the gym in the hospital where I work come up to me and say, "Doc, I don't understand what's going on. I've been coming to this gym for three months now and have barely lost a pound. I feel better. I am stronger and don't huff and puff when I go up the stairs, but I haven't lost any weight. You would think after all this work that something would come off! What is going on?"

I hate to respond to this question because I am afraid of their emotional response to the answer. The answer that they may not want to hear is that exercise alone is a really hard way to lose weight. The average calorie expenditure of most one-hour work-outs, including lifting weights and thirty minutes of aerobic conditioning with a bike or treadmill, is about 400 calories. If you go to the gym three times per week, you'll burn three times 400 calories per week, or 1,200 calories. There are 3,500 calories in a pound of body fat. You need to expend 3,500 calories to burn off one pound of body fat. At the rate of 1,200 calories a week, you'll lose about one pound every three weeks, assuming that the increase in activity level hasn't affected your appetite. If you eat an extra 100 calories each time you work out, you will lose one pound every four weeks. If you drink a sport drink when you train, you can very easily take in as many calories as you burn and never lose a pound, even after several months!

THE REACTION

After I tell people these facts, a reaction sets in that resembles a slow-burning fire that increases in intensity the longer it burns. Typically the initial reaction is satisfaction because they now have an answer that makes sense. They will say things like, "Oh, no wonder that I haven't lost any weight." Then I wait for the Reaction. It may take minutes or days. When it hits, the response sounds something like, "Hey, wait a minute. Why am I doing all this work, when nothing is going to come of it?" If I am around when the Reaction hits, then I get the chance to tell people what I am about to tell you. If it occurs when they get home, or percolates in their brains for a couple of days, I will probably never see them in the gym again. The power of the truth never ceases to amaze me. Of course, the power of myth is mighty, too.

The problem with the Reaction is that it reveals the problems created by believing in false hope. Most likely, the exerciser was led to believe that it's possible to spot reduce and lose weight with exercise. The exerciser also may believe that there is an increase in metabolism with exercise, so it should be possible to lose weight by eating the same and working out. Some people believe that all this work is increasing the size of their muscles and increasing their metabolic rate. They firmly believe that the increased metabolic effect of exercise will cause fat to be burned up, and all in the right places.

When the expected effects don't occur, false hope gives way to no hope. Over 80 percent of people stop exercising in the first twelve weeks of an exercise program. If you exercise only to lose weight, the numbers say that you will be sorry that you tried. This is not to say that *extensive* aerobic activity can't cause changes in body weight. Running 5 miles per day or sport training for three hours per day will give you the caloric expenditure numbers that you are looking to attain. The runner who logs 35 miles per week will lose one pound per week, 52 pounds per year, provided that his or her food intake stays constant, and his or her Body Burn Rate doesn't lower too dramatically with the loss of weight. The young athlete who is training for a sport, and who spends three hours per day running or doing agility drills may drop a pound or more each week.

But most of us don't have the time to devote to exercise that a young athlete can give. Most of us with spouses, maybe children, and demanding jobs find it difficult to find three times a week to work out. We may find our workout schedule interrupted by a child's illness, or a new work project that the boss needed yesterday.

THE RIGHT REASONS TO EXERCISE

There is real hope. You don't have to quit exercising when it doesn't produce weight loss, because you shouldn't be looking for weight loss from your exercise plan. There is little research to support the idea that metabolism is elevated by aerobic activity in any significant way to alter the biology of weight regulation. Real hope with exercise comes in a different form. I believe that there are three other good reasons to exercise. The first, and most important, is stress relief. Working muscles provides relief of tension. The second is calorie expenditure. The more calories you burn, the less restriction you have on your calorie intake. The third good reason is general health. Cardiovascular training helps to strengthen the heart to carry whatever body weight is healthy for you. If you have the time and can maintain the commitment, resistance weight training can tone and/or increase muscle mass that in turn will increase your Body Burn Rate.

Stress Management

There are two types of stress that exercise can alleviate. The first is the stress from daily living. We all cope with people who don't listen, schedules that overlap, breakdowns in communication, transportation glitches, things and people that don't make sense, and millions of other annoyances. Each episode of distress is imprinted in our muscles. What we call tension is actually muscular tension. As stress events accumulate, muscular tension builds. Repetitive movement can reduce muscular tension by tiring muscles and reducing the tension within them.

So what does this have to do with your eating? Many people eat when they are under stress. The reason is frustration. You become more frustrated as your stress increases. You may feel that someone or something is taking things away from you, like time, or burdening you with problems that they should be solving themselves. In that case, the last thing you will want to do is to restrict your eating in any way. It is the one thing that nobody can take away from you. When you get frustrated, you will protect your right to eat at all costs. Letting off the pressure by exercise will increase your ability to cope with frustration and enable you to eat with more control.

The second type of stress is the stress of weight management itself. Managing your weight takes time. I often tell my patients that time management is more important in weight control than food management. It is not what you eat at any given meal that matters. It is the accounting and adjustment at subsequent meals that determines whether weight goes up or down. It is so easy to deny yourself the time that your weight control requires—work, children, doctor's visits, pets, parents, friends. The list is endless. Giving weight control the time it deserves becomes a burden. Your time can always be spent doing something else. Weight control becomes a stressor just by itself.

Exercise can relieve this stress just as it can relieve the stress of external events. If you give exercise the time it requires, you will be more efficient with all your other tasks. The simple act of having the time alone to think while you exercise allows you to review your priorities and put your efforts where they will have the greatest reward. You will organize your time better and feel more in control of your life. If you give yourself time and use it to exercise, it will give you back more than it takes.

Calorie Expenditure

The second good reason to exercise is to burn calories. Increased calorie expenditure can offset a lowered Body Burn Rate. The more calories you can burn with exercise, the higher your average daily caloric intake can be. Better yet, the calories burned in exercise can be used to compensate for the occasions where your intake is higher than normal. As I said earlier, the average one-hour workout expends about 400 calories. Even at 300 calories, working out three times per week for an hour, you can burn 900 calories. These 900 calories can go a long way at a party. You don't have to watch and worry about the extra glasses of wine, hors d'oeuvres, or dessert that you will most likely eat. The exercise calories give you the freedom to let loose, be normal, and most of all, not worry. They reduce the distress of watching and being aware. You can earn your freedom with the calories from exercise.

The temptation exists to use these calories to further reduce your weight. I have some patients who say to me, "Doc, if I work out faithfully for a year, then even if I only lose one pound per month for the next twelve months, I will be 12 pounds lighter at the end of a year!" While this all sounds good in theory, it rarely happens that way. I want you to put your faith in what I see happen with the majority of people. I want you to have real hope instead of false hope with exercise. I believe that many people can use exercise to lose a moderate amount of weight (10 to 15 pounds), but that most need the exercise calories to eat more freely at social events. You can make that decision for yourself. Just be realistic about the pressures that weight control brings and don't expect yourself to do the impossible.

General Health

The third good reason to exercise is general health. Cardiovascular exercise improves your heart and circulation. Any intensive activity is a stressor on the body. It prepares the body to handle the stresses of everyday life. This is why exercise has such a positive effect on all the body systems, from keeping the heart and muscles strong to helping the hormone and autoimmune systems function. Exercise is a form of stress inoculation that prepares the body to defend itself from life stress. Muscular movement and stretching keeps the body limber and able to function and prevents the muscle and ligament pulls that are the curse of the weekend athlete. Even gentle exercise, like yoga and walking, contribute to overall health and well being.

MUSCLE MASS AND BURN RATE

Muscle is an active tissue that requires energy to move. The larger the muscle, the greater is the energy used in each movement. The more muscles, or the greater the muscle mass in the body, the greater will be the energy requirements of the body.

Take two people who have the same Body Burn Rate. If one starts weight lifting, chances are his or her muscle mass will increase. As this individual gains more muscle mass in response to the workouts, his or her Body Burn Rate will increase. This sounds almost too good to be true. If you could add more muscle mass to someone with a low Body Burn Rate, you could theoretically increase that person's energy requirements and enable him or her to eat a higher level of calories without gaining weight. You could "cure" a weight problem through resistance weight training.

There are several problems with this thinking. For one, few women, especially postmenopausal women, have the hormones to significantly increase their muscle mass. Some women with higher testosterone levels can respond well to weight training and alter their Body Burn Rate. Most cannot, and end up quitting a weight training program for lack of results.

On the other hand, many men, especially young men, can weight train and significantly increase muscle mass. So why don't more people use this approach? The problem goes back to time and effort. It is extremely hard work to weight train. It requires discipline and commitment that often interfere with the balance among work, love, and play. It is also a temporary fix that goes away once you stop training. Muscles reduce in size when they are not used. Resistance weight training needs to be a life-long commitment in order to maintain the effects on metabolism and muscle size.

Weight training can be beneficial for reasons other than increasing muscle mass. Done correctly, weight training can maintain your existing muscle mass, shape, and tone and increase the strength of your muscles. It can help prevent the loss of muscle tissue through aging and inactivity. In that way, it can protect your current Body Burn Rate from the effects of aging. Psychologically, weight training can have a positive effect on your self-esteem.

Increasing the amount of weight that you can lift gives an increasing sense of power and mastery over your body. It can make you feel stronger and more powerful, a tangible reward that can improve your self-worth.

Whether you decide to weight train or not, the real issue is to find for yourself the source of real hope with your exercise program. False hope is offered so readily and so easy to sell. Look at the magazine ads and exercise equipment that feature so-called spot reducing. You can't pick up a magazine or newspaper today that doesn't feature exercise equipment or nutritional supplements to reduce your thighs, waist, stomach, buttocks, or whatever else bothers you. Using sit-ups and exercise equipment that helps you do stomach crunches will tighten the muscles in that area but will not reduce the fat around the abdomen. Genetic factors alone determine where your fat will be stored.

Calorie control, not nutritional supplements for increasing metabolic rate, is the key to reducing your fat stores and your source of real hope. Truth is, nobody can predict where the weight will come off. It appears that genetics play a role not only in where the fat is stored, but also what sites will get reduced at what time in the course of weight loss. You will most likely reduce your fat stores first in the area that you last created. For example, if your arms were the last place you noticed getting bigger, your arms may be the first place that gets thinner. As your weight loss continues, your eventual natural shape will emerge. It is unique to you. We are not all made to be the same size and shape. Don't let some unhealthy image of the ideal person become the yardstick by which you judge your body. Be the healthiest that you can be, and let that serve as the measure of the best that you can be. If you find this thinking hard to adopt, read the next several chapters on the psychology of weight control. It's important for you to change your approach so you do not hate your body for some reason beyond your control.

BURN RATE EXERCISE PLAN

Now that you know you should exercise for stress management and calorie expenditure, I will help you design a program to achieve those goals. Later in this chapter, I will present the Burn Rate Walking Program. There are multiple levels to the program, each of which is designed to achieve a different exercise goal. To understand how the program was designed, it is important to understand the trade-off that had to be made in designing the program.

The first problem that we need to resolve is the potential conflict among the goals of exercise. Should you walk for thirty minutes or jog for ten minutes? Is it better to do fifteen minutes of stretching and calisthenics than to walk for fifteen minutes? The answer depends on your goals. Stress relief is best served either by intensive aerobic activity or by increasing the length of time of a moderate activity. Calorie expenditure is maximized by duration. The longer you go, the more calories are burned. General health is served by either approach. Since duration serves all three goals, I have designed a program for you that increases your calorie expenditure by increasing the duration of your exercise.

PLANNING YOUR EXERCISE PROGRAM

It's always easier to reach a goal when you have a plan. Implementing an exercise regimen goes more smoothly when you know exactly what you need to do, why you need to do it, and when.

Step 1: Check With Your Physician

If you are unclear whether you have any exercise restrictions, consult with your doctor before undertaking any exercise program. For people with a known medical condition, such as heart disease, orthopedic injuries, etc., it is best to determine your exercise tolerance before beginning any exercise program. Contact your physician if you have any questions about your ability to exercise.

Step 2: Determine Your Fitness Level

There are several ways to determine your tolerance for exercise. One is a formal stress test that your physician can prescribe. A medical technician under the supervision of a medical doctor monitors your heart's response to increased physical output on a treadmill. If you are over forty years old and have never had a stress test as part of your annual physical, discuss the possibility with your doctor.

A second method to check your exercise tolerance involves your lungs. As your demand for oxygen increases with exercise, the lungs need to provide more oxygen to the blood that carries it to the muscles with the increased pumping of the heart. The lungs' capacity to oxygenate the blood can be measured by an exercise tolerance test called a VO2 Max test. In this test, you breathe into a mouthpiece that collects samples of your breath and analyzes it for oxygen and carbon dioxide while you exercise. As the intensity of the exercise is increased, the change in content of your breath indicates what is going on in your muscles. When the demand for oxygen exceeds the lungs' ability to provide it, there is a steep rise in carbon dioxide output. This is called your anaerobic threshold. To maximize calorie expenditure, you want to exercise just below your anaerobic threshold to prevent yourself from becoming too tired.

The VO2 Max test does not require a medical prescription if you have no medical conditions and do not smoke. As you get older, or if you have any medical problems, medical supervision is required. If no medical review is needed, the test is typically available at most health clubs in an oversimplified version that involves a workout on an exercycle and that relies on mathematical equations to approximate the VO2 Max results. If you want a true reading, you can get tested at a medical facility that has a metabolic cart, a device to measure gas exchange in your breathing. The test is referred to as an Exercise Tolerance Test.

In the absence of either of those medical tests, there is a third general measure of fitness that you can use: your pulse, or resting heart rate. Resting heart rate indicates the number of times your heart beats per minute. The higher your cardiovascular fitness level, the stronger your heart becomes. More blood is pumped per heart stroke, allowing the heart to reduce the number of beats per minute to provide the same amount of oxygen. In this manner, the resting pulse rate can be seen as a general measure of cardiovascular fitness.

To take your pulse and determine your fitness level, locate

your pulse in either your wrist or your neck. Count the number of beats in a 10-second period and multiply by six to calculate the beats per minute. Compare your result to the chart below:

Fitness Level	Resting Pulse Rate (beats/minute)
Excellent	<55 or lower
Above average	55–69
Average	70–84
Below average	>85 or higher

If your fitness level is below average, start at the lowest level, Level A, of the Walking Program that is described below. If your fitness level is average or above, start at Level D of the Walking Program. Continue to take your resting pulse before exercising once every ten weeks. It will provide you with a measure of your progress toward health improvement and show you the positive impact of your Walking Program on your heart / lung fitness.

Step 3: Know Your Body Through Your Pulse Rate

When you exercise, it is important to know the difference between pushing yourself and overdoing it. The body is a machine that adapts itself to the conditions that it experiences. If you exert yourself on a regular basis, your body will attempt to accommodate this pressure by increasing the size of your muscles, the size of your heart, and the efficiency of your lungs. Similarly, if you are inactive, the body adjusts by decreasing the muscle mass, including that of the heart, and altering the lung capacity.

When you initially increase the stress on your body, it goes into a transition phase. Your body becomes sore from the muscle strain but responds by laying more muscle tissue. The stress on the heart makes the heart stronger in the long term. But how much stress is too much? How do you tell the difference between pushing yourself and pushing too hard?

One method is to monitor your pulse rate while you exercise. There is a safety zone for exertion, called the Training Heart Rate

Zone. In this zone, which takes into account your current fitness level and your age, the body is subjected to enough stress to promote strengthening, but not enough to overwhelm its current capacity. Your Training Heart Rate (THR) should always fall within the Training Heart Rate Zone.

🔥 HOW TO DETERMINE YOUR TRAINING HEART RATE (THR)

To determine your optimal training heart rate (THR), you first need to establish your work capacity, the amount of effort that your body can tolerate:

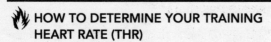

	Fitness Level			
	Excellent	Above Average	Average	Below Average
Work Capacity	.70	.60	.50	.40

You will need all of the following information:

Age _____ years   Work Capacity (WC) _____

Pulse Rate _____ beats / minute (resting heart rate, or RHR)

The formula for determining your THR is as follows:

WC x ([220 minus your age minus your RHR] + your RHR)

Here is an example: Age: 40 Pulse Rate (RHR): 78 Work Capacity: .50

THR = WC (.50) x ([220 - your age (40) - your RHR(78)]) + your RHR [78] = .50 x (102 + 78) = 90 beats/minute

Check your pulse rate as you exercise. If your pulse rate exceeds the THR value you obtained above, you are exceeding your body's ability to provide oxygen. You are huffing and puffing because you are trying to provide the oxygen by accelerating your rate of breathing. Your body is telling you that you are out of oxygen; you need to slow down to let it catch up.

BURN RATE WALKING PROGRAM

The Burn Rate Walking Program is designed to gradually increase your weekly calorie expenditure to eventually burn 800 to 1000 calories per week. The chart below will help you figure your own calorie expenditure for your weight. Multiply the time you walk by the calories per minute listed below to compute the actual calories you expend.

Here is something important to know. If you walk a mile in fifteen or twenty minutes, you will burn the same number of calories. You may huff and puff more, but you burn few calories huffing and puffing. Calorie expenditure is linked to distance more than rate. If you want to burn more calories, exercise longer, not harder. I'd rather see you walk twice around the block and burn 200 calories than burn 110 by running at top speed.

 CALORIES PER MINUTE EXPENDED IN WALKING

This table is based on a walking rate of 3 miles per hour, or a mile in 20 minutes. For example, at this rate a 200-pound person uses seven calories per minute, or 140 calories in 20 minutes.

Body Weight in Pounds

	150	175	200	225	250	275	300	325	350	375	400
Calories burned per minute	5	6	7	8	9	10	11	12	13	14	15
Calories burned in 20 minutes	100	120	140	160	180	200	220	240	260	280	300

Don't be confused by the figures in the table on page 159. The first line is calories per *minute*. The calories per *mile* are listed in the last line since the person walks one mile in 20 minutes. They stay relatively the same (within 10 percent) regardless of how fast you go.

The Burn Rate Walking Program starts at a very low level of activity designed for the person who has been inactive. The walking time is gradually lengthened, then the frequency of the walks is increased, to reach the goal of 800 to 1000 calories per week (see page 161). After Level J, the next goal is to increase stress relief by increasing the cardiovascular demand of the walking. Levels K through M keep the same distance, two miles, but cut down on time. Levels N through P use two and a half miles, with a gradual increase in speed. The rate of calorie expenditure is not significantly altered, but the same amount of exercise takes less time. Notice that by Level J, you are walking a total of 8 miles per week. The goal of the subsequent levels from Levels K through P is to do the 8 miles more quickly and improve the cardiovascular benefit to your body. However, if you choose to stop at Level J, you will still achieve the level necessary to meet your calorie expenditure goals.

BURN RATE WALKING PROGRAM

The Burn Rate Walking Program has sixteen levels, A through P. These calculations are based on a 200-pound person walking at a rate of 1 mile in 20 minutes. The individual calories expended need to be calculated based on the your individual body weight and the speed that you walk. Refer back to the previous chart to determine your calories burned per week.

Level	Calories Burned	Weekly Program
A	140	Walk 10 minutes, 2X per week
B	210	Walk 15 minutes, 2X per week
C	280	Walk 20 minutes, 2X per week
D	420	Walk 20 minutes, 3X per week.
E	525	Walk 25 minutes, 3X per week
F	630	Walk 30 minutes, 3X per week
G	840	Walk 30 minutes, 4X per week
H	980	Walk 35 minutes, 4X per week
I	1,120	Walk 40 minutes, 4X per week
J	1,260	Walk 45 minutes, 4X per week
K	1,260	Walk 2.0 miles in 30 minutes (4.0 MPH) 4X per week
L	1,260	Walk 2.0 miles in 27 minutes (4.5 MPH) 4X per week
M	1,260	Walk 2.0 miles in 24 minutes (5.0 MPH) 4X per week
N	1,260	Walk 2.5 miles in 30 minutes (5.0 MPH) 4X per week
O	1,260	Walk 2.5 miles in 27 minutes (5.5 MPH) 4X per week
P	1,260	Walk 2.5 miles in 24 minutes (6.0 MPH) 4X per week

LIFESTYLE ACTIVITIES: BURNING EXTRA CALORIES

There are many hidden ways that you can burn extra calories. Our modern way of life has eliminated many of the activities that once contributed to the number of calories burned per day. Wood no longer needs to be chopped, stacked, or carted into the house; a mere flip of the thermostat takes care of the heat. The food processor eliminates chopping recipe ingredients by hand. Bread no longer needs to be kneaded. Elevators eliminate the need to climb stairs. Riding lawn mowers cut down on our walking.

All these devices save time that we can use to do other important functions, but there is a price: how much we get to eat. To get a little more exertion out of life, park the car the farthest spot away in a parking lot next time you go grocery shopping or to a mall. Take the trash out one container at a time. Walk to any store that is within a mile of your home. Take items upstairs one at a time. Answer the phone that is farthest away. The extra 100 calories per day that you expend can give you 700 extra calories per week to eat the little things that you want without having to worry about the impact on your weight. Another perspective is that the 100 calories per day can change your body weight by 10 pounds in a year. It certainly seems a better alternative to live a life of planned inconvenience than to have to diet for ten weeks to lose that 10 pounds.

EXERCISE AND ENERGY REGULATION

The Burn Rate Walking Program is ideal for weight control purposes because it does not stimulate appetite. The calories expended can be used to provide more flexibility in your eating and help you to live at the level of calorie restriction that you have selected. However, the relationship of appetite to exercise changes when your level of activity intensifies. Activities such as mountain climbing, long hikes, mountain biking, running 5K races, tennis matches, rounds of golf carrying your own clubs, playing basketball for an hour, or playing a softball game require an extensive expenditure of energy over an extended period of time and thus require an increased energy supply. Maintaining the appetite control that is central to the Burn Rate Diet presents a different challenge if you pursue such activities than it does with the moderate activity of the walking program.

Later in this chapter, I'll address the issue of supplying the food you need to sustain your energy level throughout the duration of a recreational activity. By knowing what to eat before or after extended exercise, you won't end up feeling tired and hungry and vulnerable to snack attacks.

In determining your personalized Burn Rate Diet, only activities of daily living were included. Body Burn Rate is made up of basal metabolic rate plus the energy of digestion and the muscular activity of daily living. This does not include the energy requirements of an exercise activity, like playing tennis, taking an hour-long aerobics class, etc. In addition, there are special considerations that need to be addressed, such as the timing of your eating, the water needs of your muscles during exercise, and supplying the energy over the entire duration of the activity.

SPORT NUTRITION: HYDRATION

The first consideration in planning to provide the energy you need for exercise is the water balance in the body. Water balance refers not only to the *amount* of fluid in the body that may be needed for cooling by sweating, but also to the *location* of that fluid in the body, that is, whether it is available to the muscles or located in the stomach. Digestion requires that fluid be present in the stomach. If your body is trying to digest food while you exercise, the absence of fluid at the muscular level can cause muscle cramping. You must drink water regularly and in sufficient quantity to allow for normal muscle functioning. Body water is in constant flux. It moves within the body, exiting the body in elimination as fluid in the bowel, urine, and sweat. Failure to replace water lost from the body causes dehydration. Thirst is the signal that the fluid levels are too low. However, by the time you feel thirsty, your body is already approaching dehydration. This is why you must start drinking water before you work out to prevent even the appearance of thirst.

Your body needs more water during exertion because of fluid

losses from sweating and increased breathing. These losses can be significant. A pint of water weighs one pound. In three hours of intense activity, your body weight can change by 10 to 15 pounds! This means that 10 to 15 pints of fluid—or 5 to 7 quarts, more than a gallon of liquid—can be lost in these three hours.

Supplying water to the body is complicated by the need to also supply the energy for the activity. Most of the energy will be supplied by your last meal. However, during periods of increased activity you may require quicker access to fuel. The trick is to combine the two needs—to supply the right amount of water for hydrating and the right concentration of sugars/carbohydrates for refueling. Fortunately, water is quickly absorbed into the body from an empty stomach. It takes to to fifteen minutes for a cup of water to enter your system. However, if sugar is added to the water, it can take up to three times longer, thrty to forty-five minutes, to clear the stomach. If the sugar concentration is too high, the body needs to shift water away from the muscles to dilute the concentration of sugar in the stomach. The end result is a double whammy. The new liquid not only fails to enter your system, but also relocates the water already in the system to the wrong place. Undiluted fruit juices, soda, and certain energy replacement drinks can become detriments to performance because their carbohydrate content can be too high. However, various researchers have determined that a solution with a sugar concentration of 2.5 percent or less will empty from the stomach almost as quickly as plain water. At the same time, it will allow the resupply of glucose to the muscles to prevent drops in energy during performance.

A new approach to the water/sugar combinations has led to the use of glucose polymers in some drinks. Glucose polymers are chains of glucose linked together that may be absorbed at the same rate as single glucose units. Concentration levels are still important. A 7 percent solution of glucose polymers is the maximum concentration that will not interfere with the absorption of water. For example, compare two sport drinks: Exceed, which contains 7.2 percent carbohydrate from glucose polymers, and Gatorade, which contains 5.9 percent carbohydrate in the form of sugars. Both supply almost the same amount of calories per serving. However, the Exceed formulation at 7.2 percent is more consistent with the recommended guideline of 7 percent polymer concentration, while the Gatorade at 5.9 percent is twice the recommended level of 2.5 percent simple sugar. This means that Gatorade may affect the rate of clearing of water from the stomach more than Exceed.

Minerals called electrolytes are depleted when you sweat because they are water-soluble. As you lose water, you lose essential electrolytes needed for muscle function, such as potassium, sodium, calcium, magnesium, and others. The issue is whether you need to replenish these minerals during the course of your activity or afterwards. The ingestion of the minerals may come at the expense of the delivery of water to the body. Since the store of electrolytes is usually maintained by a healthy diet, and is easily replenished in the next meal after you exercise, it is not necessary to take in these minerals as you exercise. Electrolyte drinks taken during exercise can lead to muscle fatigue by affecting the availability of fluid to the muscles.

Use these rules to guide your fluid intake during recreational and sport activities:

1. Drink only water if the duration is less than two hours. Drink a cup of fluid for every fifteen minutes of activity. That means one pint for thirty minutes and one quart for each hour. Bring a water bottle and drink at this ratio throughout your activity.

2. If your workout lasts longer than two hours, dilute a glucose polymer drink to about 7 parts water to 1 part drink. If you want to be very precise, calculate how many calories you expect to burn during your activity, factor in how long you'll be exercising, and make sure your fluid allowance contains an appropriate number of calories.

SPORT NUTRITION: ENERGY SUPPLY

The amount of energy you'll need during an athletic activity includes your Body Burn Rate plus the calories expended in your activity or sport. As with hydration, your first consideration should be the length of time required for digestion. Movement of food out of the stomach into the intestines typically requires one hour. Fast-burning foods like carbohydrate only burn for two hours.

This means that for the first of those two hours the energy will be spent digesting your food rather than in the activity. If you eat only carbohydrate, this leaves only half the calories eaten for the first hour of your activity. If your activity will last no longer than one hour, then you will be able to eat one hour prior to your exercise, and still have the energy of a carbohydrate meal available for the second hour. If your exercise is longer than one hour, then you will need to rely on the longer-burning fuels, like fat and protein. These should also eaten at least one hour prior to exercise to allow for digestion, but the energy can now last from two to six hours after a meal. Since fat and protein take longer to digest, plan to eat two hours before the activity.

How much to eat before exercise will depend on the amount of work required for the activity. Work is measured in calories. Information in the chart below will allow you to calculate the caloric expenditure of a wide variety of activities. Caloric expenditure of any exercise is based on moving a mass through a distance. The bigger the muscles, the more energy is required.

🔥 CALORIES SPENT PER MINUTE OF PHYSICAL ACTIVITY

Activity	Body Weight (pounds)					
	150	200	250	300	350	400
Walking, mile/15 min	6	8	10	12	14	16
Walking, mile/20 min	5	7	9	11	13	15
Walking mile/30 min	3	5	7	9	11	13
Jogging, mile/7 min	16	20	24	28	32	36
Jogging, mile/9 min	13	17	21	25	29	33
Bike riding, 5 miles/hr	5	7	9	11	13	15
Bike riding, 10 miles/hr	7	9	11	13	15	17
Swimming, 25 yds in 75 sec	6	8	10	12	14	16
Aerobic dancing, moderate	4	6	8	10	12	14
Aerobic dancing, vigorous	6	8	10	12	14	16
Basketball	7	9	11	13	15	17

SPORT SNACKS

Your first step in constructing an appropriate sport snack that will be eaten one hour before an activity is to determine the number of calories you'll be expending. You can determine the calories expended by multiplying the minutes of your activity by the calories expended per minute from the chart. Some sports are more difficult to calculate. Golf, for example, involves walking and swinging the clubs. The average person will walk about 3 or 4 miles playing eighteen holes of golf, and burn 300 to 400 calories per round. Tennis is another example that is hard to calculate. Per minute of activity, it is the same as basketball. However, there is so much stop and start to the game that the expenditure is only 50 percent of the energy of basketball. Use 50 percent of the calories per minute of basketball applied to the total time that you are on the court as the energy expended. In a similar way, you can estimate the calories of various activities like in-line or ice-skating by using the figures for moderate aerobic dancing.

Once you have determined the caloric requirements per hour of your activity, and how many hours will be required for that activity, you can determine the amount of energy you need. I call the food eaten specifically for exercise a Sport Snack. The Sport Snack must be eaten at least one hour before you exercise to prevent water from accumulating in your stomach for digestion. Your choice of food for a Sport Snack depends on the length of time for your activity added to the hour you need for digestion. If the activity requires less than one hour, a carbohydrate snack will satisfy this energy need. However, if the activity is longer than one hour, then you will need to add fuels like protein and fat, which supply energy over a longer period of time. The composition of Sport Snacks with multiple fuels should follow the basic recommendation for ideal human intake: 55 percent carbohydrate, 15 percent protein, and 30 percent fat.

Calculating a Sport Snack

Information Needed:

Activity: _____ Duration: _____ hrs

Calories Burned per Hour: _____ cals

Total Calories You Will Burn: _____ cals

If the duration of your exercise will be less than one hour, choose a carbohydrate snack that corresponds to the number of calories you will burn. For example, swimming laps uses 10 calories per lap for a 250-pound person. If you swim 20 laps, you will burn 200 calories and it will take you about twenty-five minutes to complete. You should eat a carbohydrate snack of 200 calories one hour before you begin or add the calories to any meal eaten at least one hour prior to the activity. Carbohydrate snack choices include foods like fruit, pretzels, bread, popcorn, vegetables, rice, and potato. Refer to the carbohydrate lists in Appendix III for many other options. If the duration of your exercise will be longer than one hour, you need to add the extra calories to your meal or construct a more complex snack. Eat two hours before you exercise to allow for the longer period of time needed to digest protein and fat.

CREATING A PERSONALIZED BURN RATE SPORT SNACK

Planning a sport snack is not as complex as planning your other meals, but it's still important to do the job right. Your snack will keep your energy up as you exercise and prevent a surge of appetite after you finish. Let me show you how I plan sport snacks. All of the calorie values are taken from the food lists in Appendix III.

Burn Rate Sport Snack Example #1:
Mountain Hiking for One Hour

Step 1:   Determine how many calories you will expend, based on the type of activity and how long you'll be doing it.

Activity: Hiking

Duration: 60 minutes

Calories you will burn: 200

Total calorie allotment for Burn Rate sport snack: 200

Enter this number on your sport snack meal chart

Breakdown:

Carbohydrate	200
Protein	0
Fat	0

Enter this number on your sport snack meal chart

Step 2: Select your first carbohydrate

Carbohydrate choice #1: Banana

Banana is a pure carbohydrate food with 100 calories

Enter this number on your sport snack meal chart

Step 3: Calculate your carbohydrate balance

Carbohydrate allowance   200 calories

Banana   - 100

                                  100

Step 4: Select your second carbohydrate

Carbohydrate choice #2: Pretzels

1 ounce of pretzels has 110 calories

Enter this number on your sport snack meal chart

Step 5: Calculate your total carbohydrate balance

Balance from Step 3   100 calories

Pretzels   - 110

                           - 10, or zero

This uses up your carbohydrate allowance, so no more carbohydrate choices are open to you.

🔥 BURN RATE DIET: SPORT SNACK CHART

Total calorie allowance for sport snack _____200_____

	CALORIES		
	CARBOHYDRATE	**PROTEIN**	**FAT**
FOOD / AMOUNTS			
Carbohydrate GOAL:	200		
1. Banana	100	_____	_____
2. Pretzels	110	_____	_____
3._____	_____	_____	_____
TOTAL:	210		
BALANCE:	-10(0)		
Protein GOAL: _____			
1._____		_____	_____
2._____		_____	_____
3._____		_____	_____
TOTAL: _____			
BALANCE: _____			
Fat GOAL: _____			
1._____			_____
2._____			_____
3._____			_____
TOTAL: _____			
BALANCE: _____			

Burn Rate Sport Snack Example #2: 18 Holes of Golf, 5 Hours

Step 1: Determine how many calories you will expend, based on the type of activity and how long you'll be doing it.

    Activity: Golf

    Duration: 5 hours

    Calories that you will burn: 450

    Total calorie allowance for Burn Rate sport snack: 450

    Enter this number on your sport snack meal chart

    Breakdown:

      Carbohydrate (55 percent) 248

      Protein (15 percent)   68

      Fat (30 percent)   134

    Enter these numbers on your sport snack meal chart

Filling Your Carbohydrate Allowance

Step 2: Select your first carbohydrate choice

    Carbohydrate choice #1: Banana

    Banana is a pure carbohydrate with 100 calories

    Enter 100 calories on your sport snack meal chart

Step 3: Calculate your carbohydrate balance

    Carbohydrate allowance 248 calories

    Banana   - 100

    Balance   148

Step 4: Select your second carbohydrate choice

    Carbohydrate choice #2: Cheerios

    Cheerios are a pure carbohydrate with 110 calories per cup

    Enter this number on your sport snack meal chart

Calculate your carbohydrate balance

Balance from Step 3	148 calories
Cheerios	- 110
Balance	38

You still have 38 calories of carbohydrate to use up

Carbohydrate choice #3: Milk, 1 cup, 2%

Milk is a triple mix food:

Carbohydrate	40 calories
Protein	40
Fat	40

Enter these numbers on your sport snack meal chart

Recalculate your carbohydrate balance again

Balance from Step 5	38 calories
Milk	- 40
Balance	- 2, or 0

Filling the Protein Allowance

Step 5:   Select your first protein choice

Protein choice #1: Bacon

Bacon is a dual mix food. Four slices of bacon have:

Protein	32 calories
Fat	88

Enter these numbers on your sport snack meal chart

Step 6:   Calculate your protein balance

Protein allowance	68 calories
Milk	- 40
Bacon	- 32
Balance	- 4, or 0

Step 7:   You have used up your protein allowance, so no further protein choices are open to you.

Filling Your Fat Allowance

Step 8:   Calculate your fat balance

Fat allowance	134
Fat from milk	- 40
Fat from bacon	<u>- 88</u>
Balance	6, or 0

This uses up your fat allowance, so no more fat choices are open
to you.

🔥 BURN RATE DIET: SPORT SNACK CHART

Total calorie allowance for sport snack __450__

	CALORIES		
	CARBOHYDRATE	**PROTEIN**	**FAT**
FOOD / AMOUNTS			
Carbohydrate GOAL:	248		
1. Banana	100		
2. Cheerios, 1 cup	110		
3. Milk, 2%, 1 cup	40	40	40
TOTAL:	250		
BALANCE:	-2(0)		
Protein GOAL:		68	
1. Bacon, 4 slices		32	88
2.			
3.			
TOTAL:		72	
BALANCE:		-4(0)	
Fat GOAL:			134
1.			
2.			
3.			
TOTAL:			128
BALANCE:			6(0)

A QUICK NOTE: KETONES AND ATHLETIC PERFORMANCE

As you recall, ketones result from the breakdown of body fat for energy. They supply energy whenever the body has been deprived of glucose for over six hours. In our current discussion of Sport Snacks, I have not included the use of ketones. Ketones can come into play as an energy source for working out or competing under several different scenarios. The first is if you work out or train in the morning. Upon arising, your body is producing ketones. This energy is available for use. If you eat a carbohydrate sport snack an hour prior to an activity, any ketone production occurring at that point will terminate. If you do not eat at all and continue your fast, you may use ketones solely as your fuel source. How well that works will depend on how effectively your body uses ketones. You can find that out through trial and error. Do not eat after waking up and do your workout. If you get tired and can't complete the workout, you will need to rely on your sport snacks for energy. If your energy levels remain high throughout your workout, then you should not eat any sport snack before working out.

If you train in the morning, another alternative is to add the calorie requirement of your training to your Burn Rate Breakfast in the form of protein and fat. As with all Burn Rate Breakfasts, your carbohydrate level will still need to be kept low to prevent the abrupt loss of ketones.

The other potential use of ketones in athletic performance involves competitions that require endurance, like marathons and triathlons. These activities require the fueling of the body for high-energy output over an extended period of time, as much as six to eight hours in the case of a triathlon. The issue here is how to use ketones if you are involved in an activity greater than two hours in duration.

Similar to the combining of fuels in a Burn Rate Breakfast, the goal would be to maximize the use of both glucose and ketones so that you will have more fuel available throughout that long time interval. Maintaining the fasting state upon awakening could do this, and eating a pre-event meal that is low in carbohydrate and consistent with the calorie levels of your Burn Rate Breakfast. Knowing your Body Burn Rate and the hourly energy requirements of the event would enable the you to supplement with the right amount of carbohydrate in the water bottle. Maximum energy availability can then be achieved by matching the Body Burn Rate to both the burn rates of the foods in the pre-event meal and the intake of sugar in the water bottle throughout the event.

9

Self-Esteem
and Burn Rate

As you follow the Burn Rate Diet, you will encounter many challenges to succeed at living thinner. Whether it is finding the time to pay attention to your food intake or to exercise, there will be tests of your motivation to keep going with your weight control. Each test will tell you something about yourself. Each will be a potential learning experience about how you feel about your weight and yourself. Knowledge of yourself will give you the ability to stick with your plan to live thinner for life.

DEBBIE'S STORY: MAD AT MOM, MAD AT MYSELF

Debbie is a patient who illustrates how powerful the emotions are that influence the ability to control body size. When she was eighteen years old, her mother brought her to see me because she was 25 pounds overweight. Mom was concerned about her daughter's health and had been advised by the family doctor to see a specialist in weight control. At the first interview, it was apparent that Debbie did not want to be there. She was sullen, answered questions with one-word answers, and was generally noncooperative. Her mother did all the explaining about Debbie's eating habits and weight history, with Debbie rolling her eyes or correcting her mother whenever she disagreed.

I was able to convince Debbie to meet with me for two visits by promising to continue treatment only if she wanted to. She denied that she had any problems with her weight, and said she just wanted to be left alone. She stated that she didn't eat any differently than her friends, and certainly did not need any help in managing her weight. After two sessions, she said that she did not want to continue.

After she left, I wondered what would be in store for her. Her behavior clearly signaled a problem. I wondered if she was subjected to a lot of subtle pressure at home about her weight. Her mother appeared far more concerned than Debbie did. Her extra weight was not medically significant, and would not cause her any health problems at this time. Since their family doctor hadn't spoken to me directly, I wasn't certain if the doctor had truly advised the mother to seek help, or if he had just mentioned it and the mother had used this as an excuse to push her daughter to lose weight.

I got the answer several years later when Debbie returned to see me. Now at the age of thirty, Debbie was married with two young children. She came to see me because her 25-pound weight problem had now doubled to 50 pounds. She described her eating as "totally out of control" and said she had no time for herself in which to do anything about it. In addition to eating the regular three meals per day, she would nibble on food while she cooked or made the children's lunches. When I asked her about exercise, she just looked at me and said, "You've got to be kidding. I'm lucky if I get to be sick by myself."

Her marriage was also showing signs of strain. Her husband made cruel remarks to her about her weight, and showed little interest in sex. They fought constantly about money or managing the children. Her mother did not like her husband, and did not feel comfortable coming over to the house to see the children. There was constant pressure from Mom to bring the children to her, so she could avoid contact with Debbie's husband.

When I asked Debbie to identify her most significant problem, she replied, "My weight." I was surprised by her statement. Here was a woman who was overwhelmed by her life. She was overrun by the demands of her children and had an unsupportive spouse, and her mother didn't accept her choice in marriage. Despite all this, she felt her weight was her biggest problem. I shared my surprise with her and asked her to explain. She said, "I've let myself go. I have nobody to blame for that. I can blame my husband or mother for not treating me right. I certainly can't blame my children for just being children. But who else is to blame for my weight problem?"

Debbie's comment was remarkable to me because of the depth of shame it revealed. Having met her previously, I suspected that her parents had been ashamed of Debbie as a teenager. Though never stated directly to her, their own shame was more obvious to Debbie than she had originally admitted to me when I had first seen her. She knew that Mom had overreacted to the doctor's discussion about her weight, and had used it as an excuse to try to put Debbie on a diet. The fact that Mom would never admit her feelings about Debbie's weight only infuriated her more.

Debbie's husband gave her further doses of shame. He had fallen in love with her despite the fact that she was never a thin girl. He later admitted that he had hoped that marriage would make her happy enough to finally lose the weight, and he was angry that she had never tried hard enough. He was embarrassed to do normal things with her. He didn't like to jog with her because of the way her fat jiggled. He didn't want her to wear a bathing suit. He blamed their poor sexual relationship on her weight, and said that he didn't feel attracted to her since she had gotten so fat. When they had sex, he wanted to have the lights turned out. While she could never bring herself to ask, she wondered if it was to hide her fat.

As if this wasn't enough, everywhere Debbie looked there were pictures of thin models, athletes, and actresses. At least once a week some newscaster reported a new study that described the health risks of obesity. There were always advertisements on the radio and in the newspaper about somebody who had just lost 50 pounds on a new magical weight loss plan.

At work, Debbie was subjected to "helpful" remarks from her

co-workers. When donuts or bagels were brought into the office, invariably some co-worker would say, "Do you need that?" They were clueless to the fact that their comments were demeaning, and that they might not have the right to comment on Debbie's eating simply because they were thin and she was not. Their comments communicated the assumption that fat people were lazy, weak, and had no self-control, and needed to have others intervene to help them control themselves.

It's no wonder that Debbie didn't trust me in those initial sessions years before. She was convinced by the way she had been treated by the world that I wouldn't understand. As another patient once told me, I was a "civilian" and couldn't be trusted.

The messages were clear and consistent from all corners. Debbie's weight problem was her fault. If others could be thin, then why couldn't she? If others could succeed on a diet, then why not her? The collective shame became her personal shame and humiliation.

THE EMOTIONS

Debbie's story shows you what can happen when you don't understand the emotions that drive your behavior. Emotions are significant and confusing reactions inside of us. They tell us what events are important and alert us to problems. You may not be able to recall whether it was sunny three days ago, but you can probably remember the weather on your wedding day. The emotion of the day tagged the memory as significant.

Some emotions signal the presence of problems. Guilt tells us that we may have done something wrong, broken some rule, or harmed someone. Anger lets us know that something important may have been lost, that a problem exists in our relationship with another significant person, or that we are threatened by something. The bigger the reaction, whether experienced at the time or later, the bigger the problem. Since effectively controlling anger is so critical to weight management, it will be discussed in greater detail in the next chapter.

Of all our emotions, shame is the one that provides the most confusing information. Shame is a destructive emotion that tells us we are inadequate and worthless. It originates in the inadequacies of others that have been passed on to us. Parents' insecurities are imprinted in the shameful feelings of a child. Society's preoccupation with thinness reflects society's own problems, but it becomes internalized by fat people, who feel ashamed for failing to live up to the standard. It is not experienced as another's shame. It feels like their own, something they have done to themselves.

THE SHAME-GUILT CYCLE

Debbie's sense of shame is common among the many patients that I have treated. The shame comes in many forms. It can be seen in the eating of snack foods in private or the avoidance of the scale. It is visible in the excuses for not wanting to go swimming or to the beach. It is evident in the attempts to be in the back of pictures or seated on a couch holding a pillow. It is apparent in the anxiety of being in a gym or the need to find out if you are the fattest person in the room at a party.

The more shame is hidden, the more it grows. The bigger it gets, the more avoidance behavior it causes. These attempts to reduce shame set in motion a series of events that I have called the Shame-Guilt Cycle. There are four steps in the cycle. Shame is the beginning, or Step One. It is followed by attempts to compensate or Overcontrol, which is Step Two. Step Three is Impulsivity that follows the excessive control. Guilt is the emotional response to acting impulsively. Step Four, Guilt, only feeds the sense of shame, and the cycle renews.

I want to discuss each step of Shame-Guilt Cycle in more detail because it is such a common experience for nearly all my patients. This vicious cycle must be interrupted for you to be successful at weight management. The cycle begins with a deep sense of *shame,* not just an embarrassment kind of shame, but a deep sense of humiliation and inadequacy that is hard even to admit to oneself. Choices based on shame, especially on the deepest shame, are bound to be unhealthy because they are attempts to compensate for or to overcome the shame. However, nothing can ever truly overcome this shame because it is based on the inadequacies of others. It is a prescription for failure. Shame can only cause you to be unreasonable and a confirmed perfectionist.

The unreasonable actions used to overcome shame are called overcontrol, the second step in the Shame-Guilt Cycle. *Overcontrol* is an attempt to avoid the shame of potential failure. Overcontrol can take many forms. I recall one patient who followed a highly structured diet for six months without one single episode of cheating. He would get angry with me because I encouraged him to be flexible with the diet. He used to say to me, "You're the only diet doctor I've ever seen who wants me to cheat!" I was concerned that he was trying too hard, and I feared a catastrophic reaction to any failure. He had lost the natural relationship to food that is based on flexibility. I knew that for him, eating anything outside his structured diet was bound to evoke a strong sense of shame.

My worst fears were confirmed. When he finally started to flex the diet, he experienced every dieter's nightmare. He lost control and overate. That seemed reasonable to me. He hadn't eaten any foods for pleasure for over six months. It was about time that he broke down and ate something good. He didn't see it that way. He saw his "cheating" as evidence of his lack of self-control. The shame was too great for him, and he never recovered. He very quickly regained all his weight.

There are many examples of overcontrol. They include setting unrealistic weight goals, exercising to excess, being too rigid with a diet, dieting during vacation or holidays, not adjusting expectations during times of increased stress, and many more.

JOAN'S STORY: NOBODY'S PERFECT

A good example of overcontrol can be seen in the way one of my patients, Joan, approached her weight management before I knew her. She had followed a highly structured diet for several weeks and had been thrilled with her weight loss. She felt on top of the world, but was concerned about how she was going to manage the diet with a dinner party she was planning. She was a gourmet cook, well known among her friends for her desserts. She knew she had to make one of her famous desserts that were loaded with calories. She also knew that she had a habit of tasting food while she was cooking, especially if chocolate was required in the recipe!

Joan decided to handle the problem by relying on her newly discovered self-control. She told herself that since she had done so well on the diet so far, she could certainly handle a dinner party. She vowed she would watch herself closely, eat nothing while she cooked, and avoid the dessert.

The dinner party came and went. Joan stuck faithfully to her plan. She didn't nibble while she cooked, and didn't eat a morsel of the dessert. However, after all the guests had left and she was cleaning up in the kitchen, she found herself nibbling at the leftovers. Before long, she had made herself a whole plate and had eaten every bite. Then she helped herself to a serving of the dessert. She was racked with guilt ten minutes later and was very upset with herself. She wondered how and where her self-control had fallen.

The third step in the Shame-Guilt Cycle is *impulsivity*. The overcontrol of Step Two leads directly to the loss of control in Step Three. Suppression of natural instincts can only work short term. Eventually, the frustration builds and overwhelms the ability to hold it back. If Joan had let herself enjoy the party and had eaten normally, she would not have overeaten later that evening. The problem wasn't with the eating. It was with her attempt to force a perpetually unnatural relationship to food.

Guilt is the usual reaction we feel when we have acted impulsively. Guilt signals that we have broken some set of rules that we are supposed to keep. Joan's reaction is typical in nearly all my patients. Like her, most of my patients would have believed it was themselves, and not the plan that was the source of the problem. Their guilt renews their feelings of inadequacy about their lack of self-control, which deepens their sense of shame, and the cycle renews.

SHAME, GUILT, AND SELF-ESTEEM

As you might imagine, each pass through the Shame-Guilt Cycle takes another chunk out of people's belief in themselves. Each time around makes them distrust their natural reaction to food, and deepens their guilt. Soon, they begin to distrust any act of eating. Their opinion of their relationship to food becomes distorted, and their opinion of themselves becomes warped.

Loss of self-esteem is evident in many reactions that my patients have described to me. For example, many patients love the idea of weight loss programs that seem to offer a simple solution. My patients want magic because they do not believe that they are capable of exercising self-control. They do not trust their own motivation to lose weight, and believe that the solution lies in some diet pill, special food, or herb.

I recognize the fear of failure in many of my patients' reactions. They hold onto their larger size clothes "just in case. . . ." They thrive on compliments from others rather than build on a solid sense of self and their continuous improvement. Their psychological highs from early successes insulate them from their own fears. I become concerned when I see this high develop. Even worse is preaching. When I hear another patient telling a friend about how successful he or she has been on a given plan, and telling the friend that he or she needs to try it, I get worried. The patient seems to be reacting to the temporary relief of their own fears of failure, and is projecting success before it is realized. I see firsthand the unrealistic approach that these dieters are taking. As good athletes advocate, when you deal with pressure, the best approach is "never too high, never too low." Intense reactions to small steps can only indicate the presence of fear that will surface when the inevitable setbacks occur.

SARAH'S STORY: ONLY WINNERS NEED APPLY

Sarah came to see me on the advice of a friend. Sarah and her friend had joined a local behavior modification group. Two features of this group were attractive to these two women. It was free, and it claimed to have the highest success rate of any program in the country. Participants met in weekly groups and were assigned weight goals that had to be met each week. If they did not meet their goals, they were terminated from the group.

Sarah was forty-eight years old and had only recently experienced problems with her weight. In the past five years, she had slowly gained 40 pounds—8 to 10 pounds per year. She would lose each 10 pounds she gained, only to gain it back each time plus more. She came to see me because she had been dismissed from the program. She had been successful losing 35 pounds in a year and was only 5 pounds from her goal weight. She was especially upset by the fact that her friend remained in the program, and she was cut off from the circle of friends they had built together in the group.

At her first visit, Sarah said, "I feel so badly because I let my friends down. I felt so great for so long with that program. I enjoyed seeing the group each week and really felt connected to them. They were all pulling for me to lose the weight when I ran into trouble, and I just couldn't do it. I even tried not eating for several days before the weigh-in, but nothing worked. I just can't understand what is wrong with me."

In her words, Sarah is describing a process of internalizing a problem that has nothing to do with her. In this case, the program failed the dieter, not the other way around. This program was designed to use the shame that dieters feel as a weapon against them. The threat of being kicked out of the group created motivation by fear of rejection. To make matters worse, the weight goals were not individualized for each patient's Body Burn Rate. In the end, Sarah was trying to accomplish a goal that was unrealistic for her. She had believed in the program because this program had the highest success rate in the country. She did not believe in her own hard work, and the program had done nothing to foster her self-esteem. As I told her, of course the program had an apparently high success rate. They threw out anybody who was unsuccessful, and didn't count the dropouts in their success rate. The program markets magic and leaves the failures to the patients.

A more realistic approach for Sarah was the one I presented to her based on burn rate principles. Her Body Burn Rate had changed because she had dropped some weight. In addition, she was approaching menopause. She now had to make some realistic decisions about how much restriction in her eating she could tolerate and how much exercise could realistically be added to her lifestyle. Whatever body weight was associated with these lifestyle changes would be the most reasonable weight for her. After determining her Body Burn Rate, Sarah was able to establish what weight was right for her and succeed on her own terms. She did not need the group after all.

THE SELF IN SELF-ESTEEM

Our self-esteem or self-worth reflects how we have organized our many life experiences and categorized them. There are two levels to the organization of the self. We have a "Good Self" and a "Bad Self." We rate experiences as good or bad based on the rules that we have internalized from our parents. When we are children, our parents' rules predominate. Our sense of self is based on how well we follow mom and dad's rules. If we are able to please our parents most of the time, we feel content. When our actions meet with disapproval, we feel guilt and shame. These emotions signal that the Bad Self has broken the rules, and the jolt of emotional current serves as a reminder to get back in line.

This organization of the self makes sense. There is good and bad, right and wrong: You follow the rules, you please others, and you feel good. Break the rules, you displease others, and you feel bad. However, there is another level, a third level, that I call the "Ugly Self." It is created from experiences that don't make sense and is associated with levels of emotional current that can interfere with our ability to function.

The collection of experiences that don't make sense and contribute to the dominance of the Ugly Self involve mixed messages. Mixed messages are given whenever there is a difference between someone's word and his or her behavior. An example is when a parent says that she loves all her children the same yet favors one child. Another is when a parent hits a child and then tells the child that it is for his own good, or that it hurts the parent more than the child. A third example is when the parent teases a child but denies the anger that is masked by the joke. The individual with a weight problem has encountered this problem numerous times. Over-weight teenagers are told to stop eating so much. When they get angry and tell their parents to leave them alone, the parents retort that they intervene because they only want to help. A husband will comment on a wife's eating a dessert but then deny that her weight bothers him at all. A boss will state that a person's weight has nothing to do with success at a particular job but then reject overweight applicants for any new position.

The emotional reactions to this confusion are severe and over-whelming. There are dread, terror, panic, high doses of guilt, and immeasurable shame. The feelings are so intense that overweight people either avoid situations that make them feel that bad or accept conflicting and confusing situations without critical review. Overweight individuals exercise a high level of control in order to avoid any situation that can serve as a reminder. For example, they won't wear shorts. They say to themselves, "I could never do that. That is just not me. I can't explain why I feel this way. I just couldn't do that."

The organization of the psychological self, with the Good, the Bad, and the Ugly, determines the level of emotional reaction to any experience. If you have had many damaging experiences, like many trips through the Shame-Guilt Cycle, the Bad Self predomi-nates over the Good Self. While this is not a good situation, it can be changed. The level of emotion that you feel is reasonable. You can work with it, learn over time to erase or ignore it, and eventu-ally free your options to act as you prefer. You can choose to play by the rules you establish for yourself; you don't have to adopt the rules handed down by your parents. For example, you may feel bad if you fail to eat in the way you had planned or if you drop off your exercise plan for several weeks. You can ignore this level of shame and guilt as you realize the stress load in your life and make adjustments based on reasonable choices. You can recover from failure, learn from the experience, and continue to develop a healthier lifestyle.

This capacity to work with the emotions of the Good Self and Bad Self does not apply to the emotional levels associated with the Ugly Self. The Ugly Self's emotional reactions freeze people in their tracks and make them avoid difficult situations. Unfortunately, however, we cannot always avoid the situations that activate the extreme reactions of the Ugly Self. For the dieter, some failure is inevitable. Perfect adherence to an exercise program is difficult to sustain. Calorie restrictions are hard to live with short term, let alone for the rest of your life. If any perceived failure causes the extreme shame of the Ugly Self to erupt, then we experience massive, overwhelming anxiety and panic. We run away from the experience, deny it happened, and distort even the memory of it. Most important, we cannot learn from the experience. The amount of guilt and shame is so large that we avoid or distort our recollections in order to cope. There is no room for learning by trial and error with the Ugly Self. The emotions are too big and too strong and can only be managed through avoidance.

For many of my patients, weight issues have created an overdeveloped Ugly Self. These are people who have been told that they are weak, lazy, and have no self-control. Many of them believe this description and even embrace it. When the Ugly Self is so large, denial, distortion, and avoidance are always present. The presence of these defenses signals trouble because they indicate that the person is running away from his or her experiences and will not be able to learn from them.

I recognize the Ugly Self in my patients' reactions and behavior. One indication is the presence of something that one of my patients described as her "fat shield." This shield is a set of things that people do to compensate for their fatness, or to distract attention from it. The fat shield can take the form of working extra hard to please others in hope that they will overlook the apparent weakness that the dieter feels is so visible. Another giveaway is the adoption of the stereotypic fat, jolly attitude. Many of my patients hide their depression and fear of rejection even from themselves. They replace it with a false sense of acceptance, and become the center of social attention to compensate for being fat. Another example is what many of my patients have called "unconscious eating." They report that they often eat without accounting for it, like nibbling in the kitchen when cooking, eating some of the cold cuts when making the children's sandwiches for school, or eating a bit of leftovers while cleaning up the kitchen. With unconscious eating, we try to kid ourselves about the amount of calories we have eaten, rather than face the truth. This distortion reflects an unnatural relationship with food that does not allow eating for pleasure. People who diet try to suppress their need for taste and pleasure or, even worse, distort it to make it acceptable.

Other patients have a smaller Ugly Self. These patients recognize that something doesn't make sense about how others explain their weight problem. Some know that they don't eat more than their friends and some may even exercise more. I have many patients tell me, "I don't get it. I am an active person. Even if I don't exercise as regularly as I should, I am always doing something. I never just sit around. So how come I am fat?" These people are aware that things don't make sense, and they are looking for a different answer. While they may feel bad about their weight, they don't avoid or distort the situation. They challenge and confront the problem. They are struggling to put their experience in the Good or Bad portion of the self. Their Ugly Self is not in charge.

MOLLY'S STORY: I THINK I CAN'T

Molly is a good example of the Ugly Self in charge. Molly, age twenty-eight, came to see me one year after the birth of her first child, Joshua. She weighed 60 pounds more than her prepregnancy weight and was very scared. Molly never had a weight problem before, didn't know what to do or where to begin, and emotionally felt she had entered the "twilight zone." She kept repeating the same phrase over and over: "This just isn't me. It's not me." As it turns out, Molly never had to watch what she ate, and pregnancy became a good excuse to eat whatever she wanted. After all, she was now eating for two, and needed to eat to make sure the baby was healthy. It was great. She felt no guilt for eating several hot fudge sundaes two or three times a week, snacking on cookies or chips throughout the day, and having a sandwich before going to bed each night.

At first, her weight gain did not alarm her doctor. However, after she had gained 40 pounds by her sixth month, her doctor recommended that Molly curb her food intake. Molly tried, but couldn't bring herself to change her eating. Pregnancy was getting more uncomfortable every day, and food helped her feel better. She didn't want to feel worse than she already felt.

Much to her horror, Molly gained 25 more pounds in the last trimester of the pregnancy, a total of 65 pounds for the whole pregnancy. Molly hoped that the weight was mostly baby and water, but she was wrong. She was 40 pounds higher than her prepregnancy weight one week after Joshua's birth, and still 40 pounds heavier at her six-week checkup.

Molly came to see me one year later. She was now 60 pounds heavier and in a state of panic. When I asked Molly why she was overweight, she really didn't give me a clear answer. She mentioned that she had gotten pregnant and started eating more, but couldn't explain to me what typical days looked like, or describe what she usually ate. She said that she ate a lot without thinking about it, and really didn't know.

I asked Molly to keep a record of what she ate and drank for one week. The next visit, she showed me a napkin with some foods scribbled on it and some scraps of paper with other foods. She told me that she found it hard to remember to write down what she ate, and didn't like doing it. She asked me to put her on a structured diet and tell her what to eat.

Molly became visibly upset when I put pressure on her to keep her food records. She thought it was a stupid idea and didn't see the reason for it. I knew the source of Molly's resistance because I had seen it in other patients. She was ashamed that she had "let herself go" during her pregnancy and didn't want to face the emotion that would surface when she realized what she ate. Her Ugly Self was in charge and Molly was protecting herself from experiencing the powerful emotions of a reaction from the Ugly Self.

Molly decided to stay in treatment with me when I told her that we needed to focus on her emotional reactions before we tried to have her lose any weight. I told her my concerns about the Ugly Self, the strength of the reactions, and the senselessness of her shame. Molly felt relieved to discuss the problems she was having in her marriage and her family, and came to realize that her shame was less about her eating and more about feeling that she had disappointed others. Glad to say, treatment helped Molly to take the emotion out of her eating, and eventually she returned to her prepregnancy weight.

A STRONGER SELF: FROM UGLY TO BAD TO GOOD

Like Molly, all people have an Ugly Self. The size of yours will determine how functional you are as a person and how well you can learn from experience and solve life's problems. When the Ugly Self is in charge, it makes people dysfunctional and bound to repeat the same experiences over and over.

The basic goal of psychological treatment is to change the proportions of the Good, the Bad, and the Ugly. Burn Rate Principles help accomplish this task. When we apply biological principles to explain a weight control problem, they make sense. The body is the problem, not the person. The sense of self is protected.

The more you internalize Burn Rate Principles, the more your self heals. Ugly is replaced by merely Bad from each experience of failure. Shame is encountered, but the Burn Rate Principles enable damage control. They deflect shame by providing explanations that make sense and affirm self-control. Bad eventually becomes replaced by Good, as you encounter success at managing a reasonable weight.

JIM'S STORY: TOO MUCH OF A GOOD THING

Jim was a 58-year-old upper management executive. Always stocky but active, he began to have a weight problem in his twenties that he attributed to both lack of time to play sports and his new wife's good cooking. These explanations actually were well-disguised evidence of the Ugly Self. Jim saw himself as the problem, eating too much and not exercising as much as he should.

The first time Jim went on a diet, he was in his early thirties. The Ugly Self was in charge and wanted the quick fix. Jim's doctor prescribed diet pills for him and he lost 50 pounds. He regained 60 pounds within a year. Jim's Ugly Self described how he let himself go and lacked the willpower to stop eating.

He waited ten years to do another major diet. In between, he went numerous times to programs like Weight Watchers without much success. By his own admission, Jim went to these programs to get his wife off his back, but his heart really wasn't committed. By this time, he was nearly forty-five years old and was experiencing health problems caused by his weight. He was placed on blood pressure medication to control his hypertension. On his physician's advice, he joined one of the liquid protein diet programs at a local hospital. He lost over 80 pounds and looked fit and trim, weighing the same weight that he had when he was twenty-four years old.

In the end, this success only served to further develop the Ugly Self. Jim regained the 80 pounds plus more over the next two years. He tried valiantly to stem the tide. After regaining 40 pounds, he tried returning to the liquid diet, but he couldn't stick with it. He tried Weight Watchers again but only managed to lose 15 pounds before quitting. Five years later, he weighed more than when he started. He was embarrassed and humiliated. He changed doctors to avoid having to face that physician again. His blood pressure was controlled with medication, but the dose was now higher, and he experienced episodes of lightheadedness despite the medication.

Jim came to see me as a last resort on the urging of his wife. She badgered Jim to set up an appointment with me and he finally did. Here's how Jim described himself to me in the first interview:

"I have been bad with my weight all my life. I'm an Italian and I love to eat. What can I say? It's in the genes. We Italians love to eat, and we eat too much. My wife is such a great cook and I don't want to not eat her cooking. I was raised to eat everything on my plate. Hey, I don't want to insult the cook. It's just not polite."

You can see the size of Jim's Ugly Self from his description. His weight gain is totally his fault. The reference to his culture is a way for him to have an explanation that softens the sense of shame. He seemed to be saying that all Italians like to eat. He's Italian, so it's understandable that he likes to eat. When I asked Jim if he ever considered that his metabolism might have changed since he was a young man, he said, "I don't believe that stuff about metabolism. I think people who are fat just eat too damned much. Lots of Italians are overweight. There's nothing more to it."

The size of his Ugly Self dictated Jim's approach to the treatment plan that I developed. I wanted Jim to learn to be flexible with his eating within the range indicated by his Body Burn Rate. The goal was to maintain the natural relationship to food, with high and low days, sometimes carrots and sometimes chocolate. Jim had his own interpretation of what I wanted him to do. He rigidly controlled his calories, with his wife cooking all the low-fat meals that he demanded. He took vegetables to work for lunch, and had the same breakfast of cereal and skim milk each morning. He ate well below the calorie level that I recommended and was losing weight at a rate of 2 or 3 pounds per week.

Jim was ecstatic, and on a high. I was not. I was worried. The way he approached the dieting process told me that Jim's Ugly Self was still in charge. I knew that this treatment was doomed if we couldn't move Jim's perception about his self-control at least to the Bad Self, and ultimately to the Good Self. I wanted Jim to shrink the Ugly Self, but all Jim wanted to do was shrink his body size. We weren't on the same page, and weren't even treating the same problem.

These situations have a way of playing themselves out. Eventually, Jim ran out of gas with his approach, crashed, and burned. He had lost 30 pounds, and quickly started to regain his weight. He became depressed when he saw the return of his old eating habits. He was eating hoagies and potato chips for lunch and couldn't understand why he couldn't get back to doing what he had been doing before.

Fortunately, Jim admitted to me that he was depressed about his dieting failure. That admission opened the door to discuss the other failures he was experiencing at work and in his personal life. Our previous clash about his weight control already had communicated to Jim that I believed in him and his ability to exercise control. Understanding Burn Rate Principles enabled him to stay in treatment with me despite the exposure of his personal shame and humiliation. In fact, the exposure of his shame to me was Jim's first step in reducing the size of his Ugly Self and increasing the size of his Bad Self. Jim would still blame himself and argue with me about Burn Rate ideas. Each time he failed to restart his exercise program or to introduce any calorie restriction, he always was quick to see personal failure on his part. But at least he was talking about his failures and not running to the next quick fix program to lose the weight. He even began to argue with his wife to get off his back and trust his judgment with his food.

After two years in treatment, Jim was able to heal his self-esteem. While he was only 10 pounds lighter than when he first came in, and his new doctor was still demanding that he lose another 75 pounds, Jim knew that was an unrealistic goal. He knew that his Body Burn Rate was low, and that the level of caloric restriction he'd need to exercise in order to live at that weight was unrealistic. His weight was no longer an issue in his marriage, and he even began to convince his doctor that medication instead of weight loss was the right answer for him. His body size was not significantly different, but his Good Self certainly was. We had accomplished what I had hoped. We had reduced the burden of Jim's weight that was threatening to crush his self-esteem and replaced it with a means to feel good about himself and his weight control.

PROTECTING SELF-ESTEEM WITH BURN RATE

Jim is a good example of someone who successfully applied Burn Rate Principles to organize his weight control. Many choices contributed to the restoration of his self-esteem. For one, while he originally came to me to lose weight, he realized that there was more to his troubles than following a diet, and he didn't resist redefining his weight problem as a self-esteem issue. Secondly, he was willing to understand the emotions behind his diet failures, and to use bio-psychological principles to harness his emotional reactions. He learned to replace shame with science. Lastly, he never gave up, and today is still working toward a healthier self.

POINTS TO REMEMBER

- Denial is the hallmark of the Ugly Self. Examples of denial include avoiding the scale or the mirror, unconscious eating, hiding food, eating when others aren't around, resistance to keeping food records, and so on.

- Shame grows when it is hidden. Go to the beach and wear your bathing suit. Don't hide in sweat pants or baggy clothes. Eat what you want when you go out.

- Trust is the antidote for shame. Trust your instincts around food. Have the second helping if you really want it. You can adjust for it. Remember it is sometimes carrots or celery, sometimes junk food.

- Overcontrol breeds impulsivity. If you restrict too much, you will react impulsively. Examples of overcontrol include structured diets, avoidance of foods you want, dieting during vacations or holidays, dividing foods into good and bad foods, unrealistic goal weights for your Burn Rate, and expecting high rates of weight loss.

- If you lose control with food, it's a safe bet that you set yourself up by trying too hard. Self-blame will not help you discover what you need to change for the next time.

- Self-esteem is built through continuous improvement.

YOU ARE NOT ALONE

Struggling with these emotions can be difficult. Knowing that others understand, will listen, and help you learn is important to effectively coping with your weight. To assist with this problem, I have created a Support Network on the Web site for people who want to talk with others who use the Burn Rate Diet. You will have access to a bulletin board, newsletter, and chat room to exchange ideas with others and with me. Go to **www.burnratediet.com**, select the "Support Network" page, and follow the instructions to enroll. Support is only a click away, and I personally look forward to hearing from you.

10

Stress and Burn Rate

Controlling your weight can be stressful. Watching what you eat is
a stress all by itself. There are all the commitments to others that
interfere with time for yourself. Juggling all the balls can be frustrating and overwhelming. As a result, managing stress may be as
critical to the effectiveness of your Burn Rate Diet as what you
eat.

LYNN'S STORY: WHO'S GOT TIME?

Lynn, one of my patients, is forty-two years old and holds down
two jobs. One is as the mother of three children—two girls and a
boy. The second job is as an elementary school teacher. Lynn is
also 30 pounds overweight and can't understand why she has so
much trouble taking care of herself. She gained about 10 pounds
with each pregnancy and has never been able to return to her
prepregnancy weight. Let's examine a day in her life and see if we
can help her answer her own questions about why she can't manage her weight.

Lynn gets up at six in the morning and helps the older children
get ready for school before she must get herself off to work and

the baby to child care. In the afternoon, she is running one child to soccer practice and the other to dance lessons. In between, there is the baby to be fed and bathed before she has to pick up the other two. In the middle of all that, she is trying to prepare dinner and hoping that she has all the ingredients on the shelf.

Once the children have been picked up, dinner must be finished and put on the table before the children start acting up because they are hungry. While she finishes making dinner, she is trying to help one daughter with her homework. Maybe this is one of the days that her husband isn't traveling and he comes home by 6:30 P.M. and takes over with the child who needs the homework help. If not, she is left to fend for herself and hopes that the baby cooperates so that she can finish dinner and begin the nightly rituals of showering and bathing. In between, there might be an argument or two between the children about the video games or choice of TV show, or who gets to have the first shower. Once she finally gets the children into bed and quiet for the evening, she must grade some papers, or prepare a lesson plan for the next day before she can go to sleep herself. All the while, she is hoping that she can get five minutes to relax and unwind.

In the midst of all this, Lynn can't see why she is overweight. She has friends who have the same number of children and still look great. Some even hold down jobs that are more demanding than hers. At least as a teacher, she gets to be home almost at the same time as her children. After all, she doesn't have to worry about after-school day care as many of her friends do. So why can't she get the figure back that she had before having children?

Lynn's perspective is skewed by the comparison to her friends. She is comparing body size and is ignoring burn rate. She doesn't realize that her friends may have a higher Body Burn Rate than she does. She only knows to compare lifestyles and stresses. In her own mind, her stress seems less by comparison. She doesn't recognize that she is comparing apples to oranges, and does not appreciate the extra level of work that is required to manage a lower burn rate. She only knows to blame herself.

We know how damaging Lynn's self-blame can be. We can also see from her life experience what the stresses are doing to her ability to effectively manage her weight. In the next section, I will focus more specifically on these stresses and show you how to cope with both your weight and your life.

STRESS EATING AND BURN RATE

There are strong emotional reactions beyond shame and guilt that can also interfere with weight control. I will collectively refer to these emotional experiences as "stress." Stress is known to play a large role in a variety of medical disorders, including high blood pressure, heart disease, headaches, irritable bowel, and soft tissue injuries. These conditions illustrate the basic mind/body connection. Increased muscular tension and other biochemical changes created by a response to stress can actually create pain in specific areas like the head or back. Through muscle spasms, stress can exacerbate a condition like irritable bowel.

Obesity, whether it is mild, moderate, or severe, can be added to that list of medical conditions. There is a mind/body connection to eating, especially when it comes to emotions. The presence of emotions disrupts normal biological functions like sleeping, eating, and sex. When some people become emotionally upset, they eat.

The relationship between stress eating and body weight is not as clear as you may think. Eating serves as a stress management strategy for fat and thin people alike. When under stress, some people eat, regardless of their body size. Some say that they can't eat at all when under stress. Still others report that they eat a lot when mildly distressed but can't eat when the emotion turns into something more severe, such as depression. The increase in eating under stress doesn't necessarily increase body weight. It depends on your Body Burn Rate. As the burn rate drops, so too does the margin for error. It becomes that much harder to compensate for any episode of overeating. You put weight on faster and take it off slower. If your burn rate is higher, you don't gain as much weight for the same amount of overeating, and you lose it more quickly, too. You can recover more quickly by cutting back for one or two days rather than for the five or seven days it takes those whose burn rate is lower. Because of this narrower margin, people who have a low burn rate need to be more stress resilient. They need to recognize and resolve life's problems quicker than others before they pay a bigger price. Stress management becomes essential to their weight control.

WHAT IS STRESS?

Stress is a term that is familiar to all but not necessarily well understood. Stress is often confused with pressure. If a person feels pressure, they say that they are under stress. But not all stress is bad for you. There is a certain level of stress that helps us perform, pushes us to complete a task when we could occupy our time with other things. Studying in school is an example. Only a handful of students that I knew in college or graduate school kept up with all their assignments. There was always so much else to do, from jobs to spending time with friends and family to having fun. The deadline of an exam or a term paper due date would bring a strong sense of urgency or pressure to get the task done by the time required. Without this pressure, it was too easy to get lost in all the other things that could occupy your time.

All of us live under pressure. It is unavoidable in modern life, but it is a question of degree. As stress levels rise, the pressure no longer becomes helpful. You can't think straight, you forget things, become disorganized, and your ability to perform suffers. This level of pressure is what I will call stress in this discussion. It is pressure that is excessive and unproductive. It does not help solve a problem or get something accomplished. It creates chaos and disorganization. It causes people to adopt short-term strategies for its immediate relief at the expense of doing what they want or feel they should be doing. Stress changes our behavior because it is disruptive and needs to be reduced at all costs.

RECOGNIZING STRESS

One of the first steps in coping with stress is recognizing it when it occurs. It is often invisible to the person who is stressed. We continue to push ourselves, oblivious to the obvious signs of stress, like eating too much or not sleeping well. We don't understand what is going on and expect ourselves to keep going.

200 The Burn Rate Diet

Let's go back to Lynn, who is 30 pounds overweight due to burn rate changes that occurred with each of her three pregnancies. Only she doesn't know that, and feels that her body size is her fault for eating more and exercising too little. Lynn has tried numerous diets, and had difficulty sticking to any one of them. On the last one, she was doing well for two weeks, and had dropped 4 pounds. Then, her son got one of those childhood viruses and she spent many sleepless nights caring for him. She tried keeping her diet, but found herself nibbling at leftovers at 4:00 A.M. while she was trying to entertain her screaming child. A week after his period of illness, Lynn was no longer on the diet. She didn't attribute the failure to her son's illness. She blamed her lack of willpower. After all, kids get sick all the time and that shouldn't be an excuse to eat.

Truth is, a sick child is stress. The mother is typically the one who has the responsibility to manage the illness, to know when to go to the doctor and what time to give the medication and in what dose. It is an awesome responsibility. If you run to the doctor for reassurance, you feel like a whining mother. If you wait too long to take your child, something serious could be going on and you'll feel guilty if you don't catch it quickly. There is no good choice for the mother. You're either a fool or wrong.

Notice that Lynn doesn't recognize this. To her, it comes with the job of being a mom. She expects herself to handle her son's illness, and makes no adjustment for the emotional toll that it takes. She sees breaking her diet as an over-reaction. If you were to talk to her, she would argue that life is full of stress and that you have to handle it. If you overate every time a child got sick, you would never stick to a diet.

Lynn does not recognize that there are periods when the sum total of life events can become overwhelming. There is a difference between a time in your life when you have lost your job, have no money, have a sick elderly parent to care for, and have a child home sick, and another time when life is otherwise going well and your child gets sick. Your emotions help you tell the difference between those two situations. Trusting your own emotional reactions will help you differentiate the two events. If you react strongly and therefore can't stop eating, believe the stress reaction. It is that big for you at that time. Your emotions and your body will tell you the level of stress. If you have physical symptoms like headaches, fatigue, stomach problems, blood pressure changes, and so on, then your body is trying to tell you something. If your eating is out of control, you can't sleep, and you become forgetful, irritable, and tempermental, watch out. You are in a high-stress time and are not in control of yourself.

You need to believe in your emotions during a high-stress period. Don't analyze yourself and your right to react. If you are that upset, even if your reaction appears small, give it importance. If you are responding, the problem is as big as the reaction. It is not a time for self-denial and high demand on yourself. It is a time to take stock of what is going on in your life, to find where the problem is, and to solve it. It is not a time to blame yourself or expect the impossible. When stress hits, it is easy to incorrectly focus on your eating and being out of control as if you can change the way you eat in response to stress. What you can do is fix problems as early as they start.

With emotional reactions, finding the problem is not as simple as it may seem. There is often much confusion about whether you are reacting to what is in front of you or to what you carry forward from what has been behind you.

KATHY'S STORY: BEATING BLAME

Finding the real problem is not as easy as it seems. Consider the case of Kathy, a fifty-four-year-old woman with a husband and two grown children. While she did struggle to control her weight in her thirties and forties, she was able to be successful following one diet or another, and even managed to keep the weight off for several years. Since menopause, she feels she has lost the "battle of the bulge." Her weight is the highest it has ever been. She is developing orthopedic problems with her knees and her physician wants her to lose 50 pounds before considering surgery.

Kathy tried different diet programs unsuccessfully before contacting me. When I asked her to describe the problem, she said, "I don't know what the problem is anymore. I can't understand what has happened to me. I used to be able to diet and even kept the weight off for many years. I don't understand how I could be so successful then, and can't do anything about it now. Plus, my knees are beginning to hurt and the doctor won't operate until I lose the weight."

Here was Kathy's definition of the problem. Somehow, somewhere, she had lost her willpower. She felt unable to stick to a diet the way she did before. To her, the problem was self-control. She had lost it and wanted me to give it back to her. She wanted a structured diet that she could follow until she got herself all the way down to where she had been when she was thirty. After all, if she could do it once before—and she was the same person as she was back then—she should be able to do it again.

Kathy was defining the problem as a psychological problem of self-control. I call this problem an internal problem because it seems to be a problem that Kathy has with herself. Nobody is doing anything to her to create stress, other than maybe the physician who is pressuring her to lose weight. At first glance, you may tend to agree with Kathy's analysis. The problem is an internal one, a problem she has within herself and about herself. But is it really? Was Kathy born blaming herself for her ineffective weight control? Where did she get such high standards and learn to be so hard on herself? Why did she not get angry with the doctor for refusing to operate until she lost weight or even give herself the right to argue the case to operate despite her weight? Why did blame fall so easily on her, and acceptance of others' opinions fit so easily?

As we all know, self-blame is not genetic. It emerges from the way we are raised by our families. It is something taught and learned from the interactions with our own parents. In order to survive our childhood experiences in the family, we are often asked inadvertently to surrender our emotions. We spend a lifetime learning to get them back. We bury our reactions to the injustices that befall us, and accept that we as children must be wrong for challenging mom and dad. So as adults, when we need to get angry at some injustice or inequity, we can't feel it or even find it because our anger is so often directed at ourselves. We accept that we must be wrong, and learn to blame ourselves when problems arise.

Kathy is struggling with that emotional dynamic. While the struggle is within her, it is really a struggle to honor her own reaction rather than to adopt the perspective of her parents. She needs to overcome her anxiety about directing her reaction outward and stop turning her anger inward toward herself.

INTERNAL STRESSES: WEIGHT CONTROL

In addition to our internal struggle to separate from our upbringing and the stresses it brings, weight control alone can be a large source of internal stress. By this stage of the book, you realize that Body Burn Rate changes during your life are the major cause of body weight fluctuations. In order to live thinner, most of you will have to battle the reduction in burn rate that will accompany your weight loss. The Burn Rate Diet provides you with the tools to permanently live thinner at a lower burn rate, but it requires time and effort to use these tools. You will need to pay more attention to planning your food intake. You will need to pay some attention to the scale to check your status on a weekly basis.

Some days, you will be ready for that. Other days, you won't want to incur the stress or the burden. The ratio of days "off" to days "on" will depend on how you emotionally react to the workload. You may even experience a type of grief reaction in facing the fact that burn rate cannot be fixed by the next magic diet, exercise, or pill. Only you can fix your weight control by following the Burn Rate Diet.

This recognition alone can bring a strong stress reaction. It is natural and normal to want somebody else to fix our problems. You may cycle through a series of reactions in coming to accept the work that you face. You may try to run away from it, thinking, "There has to be an easier way." You will probably get annoyed at the effort. In the end, you can come to accept it if you are realistic about your expectations so there are no new surprises. Bargaining helps resolve the anger if you say "Well, I'll do the work as long as I get . . . ." If what you get is realistic and achievable, then you will accept the need to do the work. If you bargain for unrealistic outcomes, saying "I'll do the work as long as I never regain a pound," you will be caught off-guard the first time you regain that pound. Unhealthy approaches create unhealthy outcomes.

INTERNAL STRESS: COMPLIANCE

Work is stressful, as is living on your Burn Rate Diet. It is hard to continuously stick to a plan. Compliance is one of the biggest sources of internal stress for many of my patients. There is a delicate balance required to be compliant with the plan. On the one hand, following the plan to the letter is easier in one way. It is already planned for you. You go to the Web site, plan your meal, and you have not only the plan for the next meal, but a meal that can be used over and over again. The structure is comfortable and gives you a feeling of control. On the other hand, variety is the spice of life. You will not be able to plan each situation, and you need to have the flexibility to accommodate many real-life situations, such as parties, going out to eat, eating junk food or fast food, or merely being hungrier one night than another.

BILL'S STORY: PLANNED CHEATING

Because of the depth of guilt and shame about their self-control, many of my patients do not realistically plan around their taste and pleasure needs. Their tendency is to overcontrol, to plan their eating without regard for the strength of appetite and social pressures. Bill is a typical example. Bill was a forty-two-year-old executive who had battled with his weight since he was a teenager. He had not dieted for several years but felt ready to lose weight after his latest physical showed a rise in his cholesterol. Plus, he wanted to feel better about himself. He had hit a dead end at his current job and wanted to find a new job. His excess weight eroded his self-confidence, and he wanted to make a good impression with a new employer. He firmly believed that dieting was an issue of willpower. If he really wanted a new job, he could start by losing some weight.

Bill decided to follow a structured diet plan. He initially did extremely well by limiting his food choices. He avoided even tasting anything not on his diet and cut out all alcohol. He drank soda water with a twist of lime for business functions and parties that included alcohol. After losing 15 pounds, Bill felt his resolve weakening. He felt more tempted with each passing day. Finally, he broke down one night and ate a hamburger at a fast food restaurant with his children. When he got home, he found himself nibbling at some cookies. When he got up in the morning, he rushed to the scale to see what damage he had done. To his disgust, the scale was up by two pounds. Unaware that it was probably a gain in water weight and not fat, Bill became upset. He yelled at his wife for letting him go out with the kids. When he got to the office, he ate the donuts that someone had brought in that day. Feeling that he had already "blown the diet," Bill ordered a hoagie with his colleagues for lunch. The diet was finished.

Bill's case is not uncommon. While the circumstances may vary, the result is often the same. Diets are abandoned for days or weeks at a time, often in response to one small transgression. Because this reaction can have such disastrous effects and is such a source of stress for most of my patients, let's examine what happened to Bill and find a less stressful way to manage his problem. In the first place, Bill should never have lost weight to feel better about himself and to impress an employer. If you lose weight to feel better about yourself, you will feel equally bad about yourself if you regain any weight. It is a setup for failure. Good health is the only valid reason to lose weight and should have been Bill's source of motivation. Secondly, Bill should have followed the Burn Rate Diet, which would have afforded him the flexibility to eat whatever he wanted on a given day. Bill's relapse was a reaction to excessive restrictions. He was literally trying too hard to prove that he still was strong and had willpower. He never planned how to include his most desirable food into his plan. He was dieting for the wrong reasons with the wrong diet plan.

Bill's problems sticking to a diet are not unusual. Actually, reducing the stress for Bill begins with planned cheating. This approach uses the paradoxical power of negative thinking. Rather than believe you will never cheat, cheating is considered normal and expected. Some of you may consider this defeatist thinking because you are being given permission to cheat, rather than being taught ways to be compliant. However, it is realistic and positive, as it recognizes that cheating is a normal response to excessive restriction. If meal planning is done correctly, there should never be a reaction like "I blew the diet." It is more like the diet failed you than the other way around. The Burn Rate Diet can be adapted to suit your situations and stress levels. It also can include all the foods that you need to eat so that you never have to experience excessive restrictions.

To plan effectively, know what stresses require you to flex your diet. Your history is the best clue to these situations. Remaining flexible is important. The more options you give yourself, the more solutions you have. Bill, for example, needed to include fast food in his routine. In addition, he needed to know how to adapt fast food into his diet plan. If he were following the Burn Rate Diet, he would have had the flexibility to accommodate any food that he chose.

INTERNAL AND EXTERNAL STRESS

I believe that "no man (or woman) is an island." The important people in your life affect you. The comments made by your spouse, children, parents, and friends impact you. This is especially true about your ability to control your weight. People mean well, but at times their influence or statements can be very negative. These comments can be a source of high stress for any person who has to watch his or her weight.

One of the most negative comments that my patients mention to me is the question "Do you need that?" To a person, they tell me that this remark makes the hair stand up on their neck. It is an indirect insult. The mere fact that any statement is made reflects the belief that others need to "play policeman" for the overweight person. Even if well intentioned, the comment is destructive because it reinforces the stereotype about mixing weight control with self-control.

Friends, parents, and family all present you with difficult situations. Suppose you go to a party with friends you haven't seen in a long time. While they all comment on how much weight you have lost, someone is bound to say, "Be careful, or you will put it all back on. I know a friend who . . . ." Or how about this? You haven't been over to see your mother for several weeks. She calls you and invites you for dinner. When you arrive, she has made all your favorite food. You're caught in a bind. She is expecting you not only to eat everything she has made but to ask for second helpings. What do you do?

To manage this stress, it is important to realize that your lower burn rate gives you certain rights and privileges. Taking care of yourself first is not being selfish. Go ahead and pick the restaurant that has the food you want. Buy special groceries if they are better for you, even if they cost more. Give yourself extra time to plan your meals, to eat family meals on a schedule, and to ask your spouse and children to do the dishes so that you can go for a walk. You are entitled to these rights because of your biology. Your spouse and others may not realize that fact. Educate them so they don't believe as others and blame you for the problem. If they aren't willing to listen, you may be looking at some unresolved issues in your relationships that surface when you are vulnerable and need support. If this is the case, your weight control is the least of your problems and you need to define the relationship problems that the withdrawal of support has created.

Up to this point, I have been focusing strictly on issues related to diet and weight control, which I have termed internal stresses. External stresses exist as well. These include relationships and other sources of pressure.

TONY'S STORY: FAT AND FORTY

To understand how these can have an impact on eating, consider the case of Tony, a thirty-eight-year-old man who is 45 pounds heavier than his normal weight as a teenager. He became overweight in his late twenties after he got married. He jokingly claims that his wife's cooking is the cause of his excess weight. In reality, Tony's low burn rate was disguised by all the exercise that he did. He used to ride his bicycle 30 miles per week and would enter competitive races. He stopped all the training when he took a job as a salesman for high-tech machinery. A year later, he was married. Two years later, he had his first child. His business was booming, and he worked many long hours to keep up with the demands of a highly competitive market. Marriage and children robbed him of his time to train, so he gave up cycling and hasn't replaced it with any other form of exercise.

Tony first came to see me reluctantly. He had tried to put himself on diet after diet, each of which worked for several weeks before falling apart. He would lose enough weight to make him think he could do it by himself, but he regained more weight than he lost with each diet attempt. The weight regain was so slow that he never noticed the final outcome. Tony's wife accompanied him on the first visit. It became clear very quickly that Tony was under pressure from his wife to lose weight. She was scared about his health, she knew that he pushed himself too hard with his business, and with the new child, she was worried that he would have a heart attack by age forty.

Tony wasn't nearly as worried as she was. He was more worried about meeting his deadlines and getting home at a reasonable hour. He did not have much time to worry about what he ate. As he told me, "I'm lucky if I get to eat a sandwich from 7-11. I sometimes only get to eat a soft pretzel from a street vendor because I don't have the time to stop during the day. Eating is a luxury that I don't have time for." Tony does eat, but haphazardly, and compensates when he gets home at night. He will eat the meal that his wife has prepared and then "graze," as he calls it, all evening long. He might start with some chips an hour or so after dinner, followed by a bowl of popcorn and possibly a bowl of ice cream by ten o'clock. In between, he might eat three or four cookies. Before going to bed, he may take a chunk of cheese or a few pieces of salami to go with his juice.

Tony described his eating as being out of control. I described Tony's life as being out of control. It was clear to me that Tony's eating reflected his chaotic and pressured lifestyle. He didn't have a second to process the emotions that hit him all day long. He rushed from one high-pressure deal to the other, trying to give his customers what they wanted in order to sell his equipment. By the time he got home at night, he was an emotional volcano. Since he had become numb to the feelings, he didn't feel the stress and tension that his eating helped keep at bay. Eating was a distraction used to avoid feeling the delayed stress of the day. It replaced work as the distraction used to avoid feeling the fear and depression that haunted him all day long.

Tony was a workaholic. The first-born son of an immigrant

family, Tony was the one with the brains in the family. He was the one who was going to make something of himself, just like his father had said. He was the athlete in high school, the good student in college.

Tony had been raised with this burden, so he took it on as if it were his. He could not tell the difference between what he wanted and what his parents wanted for him. They were always one and the same. That changed when his wife came along. She did not want a husband who was married to work first and her second. They had plenty of money and didn't need him to work so hard. Tony, on the other hand, never felt that he had enough money. He felt it was all going to disappear as quickly as it came. What if he got sick? Who would make sure his family was okay? Who was going to help his mom and dad when they had to live on Social Security in two years?

In the beginning, Tony's wife accepted his excuses. They were starting out, and all the young couples worked that hard. But it never changed for them the way it did for her friends. Their husbands found a way to get home at a reasonable time. Tony never did. He always had an excuse that made sense, always a reason to keep going at the current killer pace. After a while, his wife began to feel she came third. Work came first, parents second, and her third. She didn't realize it at the time, but she wasn't bringing Tony to me for his weight control. She was bringing him in to restore some emotional balance to his life, and his weight was as good a place as any to get started.

Tony is a good example of how stress outside of dieting—external stress—can interfere with weight control. Tony had a ton of outside stress. His first stress was the inability to separate from his parents. Their values and interests were his values and interests. Their plans for him were his plans for himself. This childlike commitment to please his parents interfered with his marriage. He was not able to compromise or negotiate solutions with his wife. Either he was not available to talk or he became angry at the slightest hint of doing anything differently than the way he had been raised. In his own mind, he was a hard worker and dedicated husband. He was no workaholic. With regard to his eating, he felt that was just the price he had to pay for his hectic schedule. One day when he slows down, he believes the weight will drop off. He doesn't have the time to even think about that now.

STRESS AND HIDDEN EMOTIONS

Tony does not truly understand what is going on emotionally inside of him. He feels pressure from his job requirements but chalks that up to the normal stress of a job. His eating worries him, because his excess weight leaves him huffing and puffing and undermines his confidence. He knows that being overweight can make it difficult to change jobs, so he feels trapped. He is concerned about his level of anger at his wife and child. On numerous occasions, he launched into wild tirades at his wife for the smallest things, to the point of embarrassing himself. That worried him. He didn't know why he had gotten so angry or so out of control. That had never happened before. Each time, he would feel tremendous remorse, apologize, and swear it would never happen again. After the third or fourth time, the apologies lost meaning to his wife. He meant it each and every time but didn't know what to do to stop his rages.

Tony is an excellent example of the hidden emotions that drive us all. You live your life, assuming that you are doing what you want to do. The reactions of your body, your mate, and your children are the test for that assumption. If you are doing what you want, your life will be in balance. You will not overeat, have difficulty sleeping, or show little interest in sex. You will not confuse your spouse or lover. While you may think you are being honest and trustworthy, your spouse or mate feels your anger and sees your sadness. If you are in control of your emotions, your children will know that you care. You won't feel that you have to keep proving it to them. They will not be angry or withdrawn. They will not need explanations about how work requires this or that. They won't be puzzled by angry reactions to childish ways, by hideous faces or loud voices in response to spilled milk or toys on the floor. If you fail the test, then something is wrong. There are emotions that are seen by others but are not felt or recognized by you. They are hidden from your view by the need to keep doing what you think you want, the mission that you have seemingly adopted for yourself. But is it really your mission, or one that you were handed?

This kind of stress is the worst kind of all. It is not stress related to a diet. It is stress that comes from the basic human struggle to be an individual. It requires you to honestly challenge the pressures to live the life your parents want for you, and be true to your own values. This struggle carries an irrational emotional charge. It is the kind of stress that creates overreactions and provides hidden meaning to events in your life. For example, I can have one patient gain weight one week and not be worried. Another, who gains the same weight, is so humiliated or disgusted that I fear I will never see him or her again. The difference is the meaning that each one assigns to the experience. This meaning is based on the hidden emotions that serve as the fuel for those extreme reactions. In order to understand this type of stress, let's look at how family roles impact on the development of your self, and what to do to be in control of your own emotional reactions.

FAMILY ROLES

To understand hidden emotion, the first step is to understand that some of your emotions are the footprints of your parents' impact on you. They are the "inner family," the felt voice of your parents acting upon you. This psychological force is a constellation of powerful emotions and thoughts—anxiety, guilt, and shame—about the "right way" to act, as defined by your parents. This script is outlined by negative emotions that keep you in the right role. Try to behave outside your prescribed role, or even dare to think about it, and you are hit with emotion—you feel weak in the knees, your chest tightens, you feel nauseous, or just plain scared, guilty, or ashamed.

This is not to say that parents are bad people that make you feel terrible. The job of parenting is the most humbling job on the face of the planet. It is the one job that you care most about, and can never get right. You can only get it less wrong. There is no handbook, and there is a bewildering array of your own personal emotional reactions to confuse you even further. Parents are just people, too, a mixture of some good and some bad. The bad is difficult to admit to oneself, let alone admit to your child. When you behave poorly with your own child, you don't want to admit it. You want to see yourself as a good parent, not a bad one. In fact, this desire to see yourself as good becomes the very problem that hurts your children. It makes you deny that you behave or respond in certain destructive ways despite your child's reactions to the contrary. It is a "sore spot" that is insulated from view by your own denial.

This parental denial is at the root of self-doubt and insecurity. Consider for a moment that children are born with the right to react. Toddlers verbalize their anger the minute they feel it. No one has to teach two-year-olds how to have a tantrum, or to whine and cry for what they want. So when and how do they learn to give it up? That depends on parents' reaction. When the toddler's desire threatens the relationship to mom and dad, it is too frightening to hold onto. You give up your honesty when its exposure brings hurt or rejection from others. Playing roles is more comfortable and generates less anxiety than honesty.

A parent's denial can alienate you from your own perceptions and feelings about what is true. It will interfere with your self-confidence and capacity to shape your world in a positive way. Your dependency upon your parents for your survival makes you keenly aware of any inconsistency between your perceptions and theirs. For example, if you feel your father is treating you unfairly, and he says he isn't, you then have a choice to make. Will you stand up for yourself or accept his denial as the truth? The multiple episodes of encounters with your parents' denial collectively form the most important ingredient in your self-esteem. If you are able to hold onto your perceptions in the face of mom and dad, you will survive the ultimate test of yourself and feel strong. If you accept their perception, you will be accepting a role as the basis for your sense of who you are. You will basically be accepting a definition of self based on how well you fit into your parents' beliefs about the world. You will have to surrender your honest reactions and trade them in for the comfort of fitting in.

A family role means that you are not true to your real self but have surrendered it for parental approval. The natural reaction to this capitulation is anger. Your perceptions are being assigned no value. If you show this anger as a child and meet with strong or continuous disapproval, you will learn to hide it, get in line with the denial, and adopt your parents' view of the world for your own. Notice that this is not a healthy process. It is a giving in under the pressure of denial and the need to accept a false truth. I call people who accept their assigned family role the "family hero." Family heroes do not challenge the family system. They are protected by the family system, especially mom and dad, feel comfortable staying within it, and receive much support for their acts of loyalty.

If you continue to protect your right to be angry in the face of parental disapproval, you run the risk of becoming a scapegoat in the family. This family role is a difficult one, as you will experience much isolation and loneliness. The family will gang up on you, so you typically retreat in one form or another, such as moving away from home, never calling on the phone, spending more time with friends than family, and so on. That distance feels safer than being constantly told you are wrong for the way you feel. The fear of being rejected keeps scapegoats from telling others how they feel, or even standing up for themselves after a while. Retreat seems the only way out, surely better than being told you are supersensitive and are always making a big deal out of everything.

Managing Anger: Undoing the Family Role

Anger is a difficult emotion for both heroes and scapegoats. The hero is not allowed to be angry, so he rarely feels it. It is so hidden that it doesn't even surface. Heroes will feel anxiety rather than anger. They dare not risk the exposure to their family because they will be disloyal to the family view. Scapegoats don't have it much better. They will feel the anger and have only one of two options: retreat or explode. In either case, they are blamed for something. If they retreat, they are asked why they didn't speak up. If they explode, they confirm everyone's belief that they are the problem.

Whether you are a hero or a scapegoat, or change from one to the other over time as an adult, being healthy requires walking down the same path. In either case, the recognition or the exposure of the anger is necessary to protect your own reactions and sense of self. Until you can learn to make your anger work for you,

you will never live life on your own terms. Anger is the one emotion that can energize you enough to overcome the fear or guilt that prevents you from asserting your needs. Anger can give you the strength you need to stand your ground. And until you know that you can do this for yourself, you will not protect yourself in your relationships and won't really be able to expose what you feel to the people you love. Fear will always make you hold back and avoid discussions that can lead to solutions.

Most of my patients are confused when I talk about anger. They often equate it with rage. By the time many of them feel anger, they've passed through the whole continuum of feeling and have reached the point where they are capable of scorching the other person with their words. They rarely, if ever, feel anger at its initial level. They may describe it as disappointment, frustration, hurt, upset, and many other terms, but not anger. They hide it because of its anticipated threat to relationships. It becomes the most difficult of human emotions to process. As the famous Greek philosopher Aristotle stated thousands of years ago: "Anyone can become angry—that is easy. But to be angry with the right person, to the right degree, at the right time, for the right purpose, and in the right way—this is not easy." (*The Nicomachean Ethics*)

Anger is one of the most vital emotions to harness in order to be healthy and take care of yourself. It serves multiple purposes. It arises when you feel loss. It is a natural part of the grieving process. It is also a messenger. It reminds you when you forget to take care of yourself and take care of others to excess. It makes you define your needs and present them to others to consider. Its proper use makes you keep your relationships in balance.

Used constructively, anger can help overcome the barriers to a truly shared relationship. If it is suppressed and internalized, however, it can undermine your very sense of self and your physical health. The very energy of it, and ongoing stress from the conflicts and problems that are left unsolved, can drag you into depression; disrupt your natural patterns of eating, elimination, and sleep; and intensify your need for stress relief through excessive drinking and eating. These physical changes are all directly caused by the energy of the suppressed anger. Harnessing this anger is necessary to honor your own reactions and free yourself of the symptoms of your emotional suppression. To accomplish this, you must learn to shed the family role that creates distance between the way you would like to live your life and the way that you do. Your anger is the key to taking control of your life and relearning how to stand up for yourself in a self-respecting way. You change by being honest about your reactions, rather than waiting for others to change.

JERRY'S STORY: IS EVERYBODY HAPPY?

The connection between eating under stress and managing your anger to break your family role is clearly illustrated by the case of Jerry. Jerry is twenty-eight years old and a large man both in stature and body weight. He is 6 feet 6 inches tall and weighs over 400 pounds. Despite his weight, Jerry physically strikes others as a big-and-tall man rather than a fat man. His weight is evenly distributed and well proportioned. He is a physically imposing individual. Whether he is 300 or 400 pounds won't change how people perceive Jerry. He will always turn heads and be noticed for his size.

Jerry believes that he is noticed solely for being overweight and hates himself for it. His social awkwardness has led him to try diet after diet without much success. In fact, the biggest problem he has had has been getting started with each diet. He is highly motivated to be thinner and can't understand why he is unable to stick with any of the diets that he has tried.

I saw Jerry's noncompliance with his dieting as an indication of emotional distress. Here was a person who was motivated yet unable to make his behavior consistent with his words. When that happens, it typically means that some emotion is getting in the way. Knowing the power of the family to evoke strong emotion in people, I asked Jerry about his family life and how his parents felt about his weight. Tears came to Jerry's eyes as he told me how his mother and father have always gotten on him about his weight and continue to do so. He can count on being asked what he is doing about his weight with each and every phone call or visit from his parents.

When I asked Jerry how that affected him, he told me that he knew that his parents loved him, wanted the best for him, and that was their way of showing him that they cared. When I asked him if it made him mad, he said no, that they were just being parents and doing the best they could. He told me that he was mad at himself for failing to take care of the problem. It was his fault, he said, and not their fault because if he fixed the problem, then they would have nothing to criticize.

In discussing Jerry's history further, it became apparent that the requirement for Jerry to please his parents and be a hero was to accept his parents' excessive criticism and lack of support by blaming himself. If he were ever to get angry with them, both mom and dad would tell Jerry that he was being disrespectful and threaten him with some consequence if he persisted. Over time, it became normal for Jerry to deny his anger and to accept what was unreasonable. It was what his family role dictated.

Jerry's suppressed anger interfered with his ability to manage his weight. The anger that Jerry didn't feel was felt as anxiety and tension each time he faced a situation that might require him to use his anger to solve a problem. He lived in fear of situations that might end in conflict and became the consummate people-pleaser. The resulting imbalance between the lack of care for his own needs and the excessive attention to the needs of others left him chronically tense. There was no space to handle the frustration of a diet. There was no room for taking care of himself, taking the time to pay attention to what he ate, or making the time to exercise. Maintaining his family role didn't leave any emotional energy to care for himself.

With treatment, Jerry was able to free himself of his family role. He became less afraid of his anger and learned to take better care of himself. Better self-care translated into an improved ability to take time for himself and control his food intake. As a result, he was finally able to succeed in reaching a healthier weight where other diets had failed.

WORKING WITH YOUR ANGER

Jerry's story illustrates how our anger and our family role can affect weight control. Eating is a biological function that is sensitive to emotion, especially a strong emotion like anger. As children, we learn to fear our anger because of its anticipated threat to our relationship to mom and dad. Many people are likely to feel anxiety before they feel anger. This anxiety is the warning sign that they are deviating from the family role. Staying within the role relieves anxiety, but the anger stays hidden. Whether from the felt anxiety of its presence, or the tensions created by suppression, you will feel anxiety associated with anger. While not true for all people, many do eat when they feel tense. Suppressed anger is not the only reason you may overeat, but it occurs more often than not.

Why is it so hard to realize the energy of anger and its impact on our lives? Most people have not learned to recognize the presence of emotion. It has been hidden from you by following your family roles. As you encounter situations that force reactions to the surface, you are surprised. You are amazed at the fear you may feel when asking the boss for a raise. You may be shocked by how easy it is for you to feel like a little child in the presence of your parents. And you may be overwhelmed by the power that drives you to overeat. Many of my patients describe it as some force that comes over them that they cannot control no matter how hard they try.

The first step in breaking free of your family role is to recognize the presence of your emotions. Fortunately, emotions are an active force that cannot be denied. If you can't recognize them in their raw state, you can recognize what occurs when you try to hide them. If you notice yourself working too hard, obsessing about something, smoking more than usual, or eating or drinking more, they are present in your behavior. If you can't sleep, chances are that you are angry about something. If you have dreams of anger, something or someone probably bothered you more than you realized.

The second step in learning to be honest and free of your family role is to define the problem—that is, to know at whom you are angry. If you get irritable, you may be reacting to more than what is in front of you. Your wife or children may be annoying, but if the size of your reaction is way out of proportion to what just happened, chances are they only caused some of your anger. If you realize later that you overreacted, consider at whom else you may be angry. One thing to decipher is where the emotion is coming from. If you were unable to finish a project on time, are you angry at your boss for unrealistic deadlines, your secretary for typing too slowly, or your parents for requiring you to always get it right? Maybe you were angry with all three and need to discuss each piece separately with each one of them.

The third step in breaking the mold of your role is to know what you need. When you are locked in your role, the exchanges between you and others are not healthy. The needs of others assume more importance than yours. In breaking free, you need to determine what you want before you listen to what others want. It is necessary and healthy to begin a dialogue to resolve any differences you may have with another person by first stating what you want or need. This may feel like you give with strings attached and may feel wrong or selfish. But you can't solve a problem if you don't know what is in it for you. It is a place from which to start to negotiate or compromise.

The final step is to know what to do with your anger. I don't believe that anger should be released in pounding pillows or primal screams to release your rage. Anger is only resolved by fixing the problem that is making you angry. Sometimes you need to hold on to your anger to ensure that all resistances to solving the problem have been overcome. Calmly holding onto your anger can help you surmount the guilt and/or shame you may feel when you first assert yourself. Guilt and shame are the backwash you experience when you break the family role. You break the rules, so you feel guilty. In this case, the guilt is giving you false information. It is the *rules* that are wrong, and the guilt is irrational.

It can require a lot of reflection to define why you are angry, who made you angry, and what you need from the situation. You also have to learn to communicate it in a way that's likely to produce the result you want. One important ingredient is to stay focused on the real problem and avoid getting sidetracked. The other is to avoid attacking, blaming, or ridiculing the other. If done correctly, anger is not a destructive emotion. It is a healing emotion that helps resolve differences between people and remove the obstacles to sharing and closeness.

POINTS TO REMEMBER

- Difficulties getting started with a diet, taking the time to exercise, sticking to the diet, and staying with your exercise program and eating when you are bored are all stress symptoms.

- Food restriction increases stress. If you are highly stressed, you will avoid adding more stress.

- Many of us don't recognize when we are under high stress. Changes in our personal habits—eating, drinking, sleeping, and exercise—are the barometers of our stress.

- Weight control alone is a stress. If you overcontrol, it will increase your stress.

- Suppressed anger is the product of your family role and a source of high tension.

- Freeing yourself from your family role may be necessary in order to take the time and have the patience to be effective at weight control.

- Managing your anger more effectively is a process learned through trial and error. It is not easy, but it is a major contributor to improved self-worth.

11

Four Problems, Four Stories

Nothing describes what I want to say about dieting and weight control better than the real life reactions of my patients to my methods of treatment. The struggle with weight control and the relief provided by applying the Burn Rate Principles can best be understood through the stories of my patients. In this next section, I will share with you several stories to give you a feel for my clinical experience and the value of the Burn Rate approach to weight control in these people's lives. Details have been changed to protect the privacy of my patients.

THE OVERWHELMED DIETER: THE CASE OF BETH

The Story

Beth is a forty-three-year-old mother of three children—two girls and a boy. The girls are thirteen and ten years old, and the boy is seven. She has been married for fifteen years. Beth relocated to this area of the country several years after the birth of her first child to take advantage of a job opportunity for her husband, James. She has lived here for nine years. Her extended family all live back where she grew up, a large metropolitan city two hours away. She is the only family member who has ever "chosen" to leave, according to Beth's mother. James has a sister who lives an hour away, but the rest of his family is scattered all over the country, and his parents live in Arizona.

Beth was employed full-time as manager of a convenience store before she had children. With her husband's new job, the increased money enabled Beth to stay at home to raise the children. The couple found that the costs of childcare took so much of Beth's salary that James's increase in pay more than covered the small gain that her working provided. She had been a homemaker since the birth of their second daughter.

James's job requires him to travel occasionally, but it has flexible hours that enable him to be home to help Beth when she needs it. He will often come home early to drive one girl to Girl Scouts while Beth takes the other to dance lessons and the boy to soccer practice. They are active in their local church and have met several couples with children with whom they socialize on weekends whenever they want.

A friend referred Beth to me shortly after she had regained 50 pounds that she had lost on a diet plan given to her by her physician. She would go for weekly visits to her doctor to check her progress on this diet plan. The plan consisted of two nutritional drinks per day and a regular meal at dinner. She had agreed to follow this diet because she had high blood pressure and her doctor felt that weight loss could potentially relieve her symptoms and enable her to go off her medication. Beth hated taking the medication, which was expensive, and she was worried about suffering a stroke or some heart problem as she got older. The diet plan worked well, and in eight months, she had lost 43 pounds. Her blood pressure had returned to normal and she no longer needed her medication. She felt great, had bought several new outfits that made her feel like a new woman, and felt better about herself because she had been able to lose the weight.

The Problem

I saw her about two years after her weight loss. Beth had not only regained the 43 pounds that she had lost, but 7 pounds more on top of that. She was now at the highest weight she had ever been, and terribly upset. Since I wanted to know what she thought was the problem, I asked her what upset her most. She said, "My lack of willpower is embarrassing. How could I regain all that weight plus more when I know that it is bad for my health? I felt so great when I was lighter. I could do more, didn't have to take that medication, and didn't have to spend the money on it anymore. My life was so much better. And look at me now! I just don't understand myself."

I asked Beth to tell me about her weight history. Beth's mother first took her to a diet doctor when she was eleven years old. She was 5 feet 6 inches tall and weighed 185 pounds. The doctor said she was entirely too heavy and put her on diet pills. She remembers having no appetite and losing 25 pounds in a very short time. Once she went off the pills, she regained that weight plus more. By the time she was a senior in high school, her weight had increased to over 200 pounds. Over the next ten years, she went on and off diets several times. The lowest she got was 165 pounds, and she managed to stay there for several years. She described that time in her life as highly social, going out frequently on dates and worrying constantly about her weight. She would exercise daily for at least one hour and ate only two meals per day. If she went out and partied, she would barely eat the next day and increased her exercise to two hours per day. Since she was living at home and working, she had the time to do what she wanted. She remembered still weighing 165 pounds at her wedding and looked great in her wedding dress.

After the birth of her first child, her weight control problems got worse. She was 175 pounds when she conceived, and weighed 190 pounds six months postpartum. The same thing happened with her two subsequent pregnancies. She retained about 15 pounds each time, leaving her at 220 pounds after the birth of her last child seven years ago. Between then and when I saw her, she had tried to diet several times before doing the liquid nutrition plan with her doctor. She was able to lose only 15 pounds each time, and regained it rather quickly. With the last weight loss effort two years ago, her weight had gone from 225 to 182, but she had not reached her goal weight of 165 pounds. She saw that as a failure, too, but not nearly as bad as having regained all her weight plus more.

When I asked her to explain why she thought it had happened, Beth could only blame herself and her lack of self-control. She said, "I think it is because I eat the wrong things, eat at the wrong time, and I don't exercise like I used to back in my twenties. I pick at my children's food when I make lunches, I snack when I make dinner, and nibble on a cookie or two at night. I just feel so out-of-control."

I asked Beth whether she thought her emotions had anything to do with her eating. She did recognize the connection, but not fully. She said that she was a stress eater but couldn't understand what caused her so much stress. Her life didn't seem that complicated, and she certainly had less stress than some of her friends who were working full-time and hassling with day-care on top of everything else. At least she didn't have to worry about that anymore, so her life was actually less stressful than her friends' lives were. In her mind, then, she had to be the problem. She just couldn't handle the same stresses that everybody else could handle.

I tried to get more specific with her about her emotions but didn't get very far. I described several of the situations in her life and asked her if they bothered her a great deal. For example, her mother's reference to Beth "choosing" to move away didn't seem very supportive, and suggested to me that Beth's mother wanted her children around for her own emotional purposes. Beth didn't bite and said that she hadn't thought of it that way. I asked her if she felt isolated from her family and if it was hard to be the only one apart. Again, there was no reaction. She did hint that her husband didn't seem very emotional and was too easy going but that it was no big deal. Her life seemed fine, and she was totally confused and upset about her inability to handle normal life.

Consistent with the Burn Rate approach, I told Beth that the first step in the treatment process was to do an evaluation. Since no two weight problems are ever the same, I told her that she would be asked to undergo metabolic testing to measure her Burn Rate. She agreed and was tested, using the Burn Rate Test Diet. She lost 3.4 pounds in the two weeks and discovered that her Body Burn Rate was in the normal range. This finding didn't surprise her because she felt that metabolism was just an excuse used by overweight people to avoid responsibility for their problem. She thought that a normal reading meant that her metabolism was not a problem. I explained that, according to the Burn Rate principles, her metabolism should be normal at her current weight. The problem was that when she reduced her weight from 225 to 165 pounds, her Body Burn Rate would drop by 600 calories, from 2,000 calories per day to 1,400 calories per day. Because an intake of 1,400 calories per day is too stressful to maintain long term, I recommended that she experiment with a calorie intake of 1,700 calories that would stabilize her weight at between 190 and 195 pounds, her most reasonable weight.

The Solution

Beth was not very pleased with my recommendation. In fact, she was very annoyed. She said, "It's not even worth the effort. How do you expect me to accept 195 when I even felt heavy at 165? There is no way I will accept that. I maybe can accept 175, but that is it." Beth was not satisfied with my explanation that 175 pounds would require her to eat only 1,500 calories per day and that she would be more susceptible to weight regain. She left the office disappointed, frustrated, and angry. "It's just not fair," she mumbled.

Beth was right. It was not fair. But what Beth didn't understand was that she had fallen into a trap. By refusing to acknowledge her low burn rate at the weight range she wanted, she left herself in a pitched battle with her biology. Any failure would also be on her. If you recall, Beth already had assumed full responsibility for all her past diet failures. In fact, she probably had a low burn rate all along but was able to compensate in her twenties with her exercise and severe food restrictions. After the pregnancies, her burn rate was probably lowered even further. Even the routine that she had used before would still have regulated her weight much higher than 165 pounds.

Treatment did not follow a straight and easy path for Beth. She tried to follow the 1,700 calorie intake that I recommended and still had problems. She would tend to snack and found herself very agitated any time she had to restrict below the 2,200 calories per day that she had been eating before. To her credit, she continued the treatment process without initially losing any weight. Treatment focused on the resolution of the Shame/Guilt Cycle issues, and the acceptance of the Burn Rate Principles. In addition, there was a great deal of hidden emotion in Beth that created low frustration tolerance and an inability to restrict her calories at the recommended level. The sources of hidden emotion included her extended family and her husband. Instead of being supportive of Beth and her husband with his new job, the entire family was angry with Beth for leaving. Initially, Beth felt guilty for leaving her mother, but she came to realize the emotional role reversal that prevented her from engaging her mother about the failure to support Beth. Similarly, Beth's husband had withheld his emotions, and was not giving Beth the support that she needed from him. As the months wore on, Beth was able to identify and better direct her anger from herself to the problems in her close relationships. Her frustration tolerance improved, as did her ability to live on a more restricted range of calories. At her last visit, she had been staying at 1,700 calories for months, and her weight was stable at 193 pounds.

There was one problem that we never fixed. Beth still to this day wants to be 150 pounds and would still settle for 165. She still feels too heavy at 193 pounds, and hates it. The difference now is that she realizes that is the best that she can do. While she doesn't like it, she isn't running from diet to diet that make her fatter and fatter. The Burn Rate Diet has made a real difference in her life.

THE PERFECTIONIST: THE CASE OF JOAN

The Story

Joan seems to have everything a woman would want, but doesn't realize what she has. She is 5 feet 4 inches tall, 125 pounds, and perfectly proportioned. She is the one that most of her women friends mention when they talk about a woman who has a great body. Joan works hard at it. She goes to her local gym at least three times per week, and sometimes more. She will typically attend an hour-long aerobics class, and follow that with a weight training program. In between, she is always active, playing tennis or bicycle riding with her daughter.

Forty-six years old, Joan is in a second marriage to Paul, a fifty-three-year-old corporate executive in a large pharmaceutical company. Her husband travels frequently, and has many foreign guests that visit on business when he is home. He likes to entertain his business clients and his own staff in his home. Since Joan is a great hostess and cook, she enjoys having visitors to her home, and especially likes the stimulation provided by people from foreign countries. Occasionally, she gets to travel with Paul to Europe, where they sightsee together. Her life is full and active.

Joan's first marriage was not as neat and clean. After a series of jobs in public relations after college, she married in her early thirties and regretted it almost immediately. Looking back, she realized that she had married for the wrong reasons. She had felt life was passing her by and wanted to have a child, so she thought she had fallen in love and got married. Her daughter was born two years later, about the same time she discovered that her husband was regularly engaged in extramarital affairs. The divorce was messy, there was little money, and she was left with very little child support and a two-year-old daughter to raise on her own. She went to work for the same pharmaceutical company as Paul, and met him after one year on the job. They were married six months later, and have been happy ever since.

Relative to her weight history, Joan was always extremely conscientious about her weight. She remembers back in high school that she and her friends were constantly dieting to maintain their shape. She recalled one episode of purging for several weeks at one point, but when the vomiting hurt her throat she became scared and didn't continue with that behavior any longer. Exercise was always her key to weight control. If she gained a few pounds, she would run several miles a day for weeks to lose the extra weight. She believed that weighing herself daily was absolutely essential to her weight control. If she gains any weight at all, she cuts way back on her eating for several days until the scale returns to the weight she wants to be.

The Problem

Joan came to see me because she did not weigh the weight she wanted to be, and hoped that I could help her lose the extra 15 pounds she had gained over the years. She explained that no matter how hard she dieted and trained, the scale just didn't want to move. She hated the extra roll in her stomach and the extra weight on her thighs. She absolutely hated saddlebags and the mere thought she was gaining weight on her thighs drove her crazy. From those infomercials on television, she was forever buying thigh cremes and exercise devices aimed at spot reducing the upper thighs. Nothing seemed to work. She was hoping that I could help her lose the 15 pounds and reduce the size of her saddlebags.

As with all patients, the first step in deciding what to do with Joan was to evaluate her metabolic rate. I measured Joan's burn rate through indirect calorimetry using a metabolic cart to measure gas exchange. I discovered that Joan's Body Burn Rate was 1,513 calories, just slightly higher than the lowest intake of 1,500 calories per day that I recommend for women. That meant that Joan's quest to remove her saddlebags would require a reduction of intake to 1,363 calories per day. While a change of only 150 calories per day, it amounted to nearly a 10 percent reduction of intake from a level of intake that was already highly restrictive. She was already highly active and certainly could not stand to increase her exercise level. Plus, Joan was counting on losing some of the weight from her upper thighs, something I could hope would happen but would not be able to guarantee. It was possible that Joan could lose 15 pounds and still have her hated saddlebag thighs.

It was clear that Joan not only was not going to achieve the goal she wanted, but also she placed herself at high risk to regain the weight, potentially in her thighs. I didn't look forward to the next consultation to describe all this to her. I tried to present the data carefully, and hoped that she would come to the same conclusion as I about the feasibility of her weight loss. That was not to be the case. Joan understood my recommendation to maintain her current weight, but could not accept that she could not lose the 15 pounds. Even worse, she told me that I did not know what I was talking about concerning spot reducing, and that her exercise trainer had given her specific exercises designed to eliminate saddlebags. Her position was that if it required her to live at 1,363 calories, then that was exactly what she was going to do. She knew friends that had existed for years on 1200-calorie diets, and that many of the commercial diets were at that level. If it was healthy for them to do, then why was I telling her that she couldn't do it?

The Solution

The situation I faced with Joan was very difficult. If I pushed her to accept the recommendation, I stood to damage my relationship with her and not have the opportunity to help her find a more reasonable and balanced approach to her weight management. On the other hand, I had an obligation to her as a patient to take a stand on what I felt was healthy and not support something that was not in her best interest. I decided to appeal to her perfectionistic tendencies and avoid a confrontation about body weight. I suggested that we first focus on the peak performance and ideal appetite control that the Burn Rate Diet can provide, and then review her body weight once appetite control had been established. She liked that idea, and she began to follow her own Burn Rate Diet. She was extremely conscientious, and had excellent results. She especially liked the fact that she did not get hungry even with the small breakfasts that were recommended. Plus, she could not get over the fact that I recommended that she eat bacon and eggs for breakfast!

When I saw that Joan was being too rigid with the diet, I became concerned. Knowing that flexibility is needed for long-term weight control, I suggested that she have several days where she ate different foods and was more casual about her food. She was extremely resistant to this idea. Everything was going so well. She had lost 3 pounds and was feeling great. Why would I want to wreck it for her?

Joan wasn't buying the flexibility concept. She dug in her heels and refused to be anything but perfect with the Burn Rate Diet. She loved planning the menus from the Internet because it gave her a feeling of total control over her food. I got my opportunity to break her tight hold after one night that Joan lost control and over-ate Chinese food. She had several glasses of wine with Paul and they had ordered in the food. It was a fun night and she was having a good time. She ate far more food than she even realized until the next morning. As she was throwing out the empty cartons, she realized what she had done. She experienced pains in her chest that she had never ever had before, and they scared her. She thought she was having a heart attack, and was very scared. She contacted me over the phone, and I discussed the situation with her. Given that she had just had a full stress test and physical one month earlier, chances were that the pains in her chest were due to anxiety and not a heart attack. I advised her to contact her physician for his opinion, but told her that anxiety can cause chest wall pain, and that anxiety was the most probable cause, given the circumstances.

Joan did contact her physician and he confirmed my opinion. Joan was very frightened by the experience. She had never had to face a situation that created such loss of control. It gave me the opportunity to review her history of obsessiveness about her weight, including the mild dalliance with bulimia. I made it clear to her that an eating disorder is a mask for depression and low self-worth. Extreme eating and weight control are merely symptoms of the larger problems with the emergence of the self, and coping with the adolescent rebellion that is natural and normal. As Joan discovered, she was a tried-and-true family hero. She was the one her parents counted on to represent what they believed. She was their trophy to hold up to the world. As Joan became more aware of her family dynamics, she also became more aware of her hidden anger and how it fueled her perfectionism. She eventually learned to surrender her excessive focus on her weight, and live a more balanced life. She was actually able to lose 5 of the 15 pounds that she wanted to and decided that she could live with her body weight at that point.

THE CHALLENGED PERSON: THE CASE OF JENNIFER

The Story

Jennifer is a thirty-two-year-old single woman who has been overweight as long as she can remember. At 5 feet 6 inches and 245 pounds, her weight places her in the range of medically significant obesity. To Jennifer, being that big has been something she has had to deal with since early childhood. Born to a mother and father who were both overweight, it did not seem that abnormal to Jennifer to be that large. She saw her parents constantly going on and off of diets every couple of years. There were times when one of her parents would have some period of temporary success, only to see it disappear in a very short time.

Eating was important in Jennifer's home. As Jennifer's mother was Italian, food had special significance. Jennifer identified with her mother's Italian heritage and interest in food. She remembers her mother cooking in the kitchen for hours and preparing lavish meals, especially around the holidays. It was also true for her uncles and aunts. Food was always a large part of any visit to a relative's house. As a result, food was important to Jennifer, and she learned to cook like her mother.

As Jennifer grew older, her weight problem continued to get worse. Each time she went to the doctor, she seemed to be heavier. The doctor was always emphasizing the need to go on a diet and to exercise, but Jennifer resisted. She had watched her parents try this method many times, only to have it fail. She didn't want to put herself through that work for no good reason. It didn't make sense to her.

Her doctor's advice did make her reexamine her relationship to food. She tried to adapt her mother's recipes to low-fat variations. She started paying more attention to her own fat intake, especially the saturated fat of the Italian sausages and meatballs. She bought only the lean ground beef and added less sausage than a recipe would call for. She used only the low-fat cheeses for her antipasto.

Despite her size, Jennifer has always loved sports and was an excellent dancer. She was forever taking walks with her dog, and became an avid racquetball player. People were always amazed at her quickness and agility. As she got older, she gave up the racquetball because her knees began to hurt, but she continued to walk as much as she could.

Dating was the one area of her life with which Jennifer was most uncomfortable. Having been teased by boys as a teenager about her weight, she did not trust men very much. Her uncles and aunts used to tease her about hiding from men and would constantly try to set her up on blind dates with men her age. Jennifer would always resist. She secretly wondered if she was hiding behind her weight and was too scared to have a normal relationship with a man.

When Jennifer reached the age of twenty-five, her doctor discovered that her blood sugar was starting to climb and that she had high blood pressure. Her doctor reinforced the idea that she needed to lose weight for health reasons, and Jennifer finally tried her first diet. She lost 40 pounds—down to 215 pounds—and her medical conditions were eliminated. She no longer had to take blood pressure medication or worry that she was developing diabetes. Within two years, she regained some of the weight, but not all. She exercised now faithfully each day and walked twice around the block. Her weight stabilized at 245 pounds, meaning she had kept off 10 of the original 40 that she had lost. Her blood sugar was stable at that weight, but her high blood pressure returned, forcing her to be on medication to keep it under control.

The Problem

When I first met Jennifer at the initial consultation, she was worried about the state of her health. She did not have much faith in diets, but wondered about how she ate and whether she could make any more changes in her diet that could help her live thinner. While she knew that she ate in a healthy way, in the back of her mind she wondered whether food was too important because she had grown up that way. Maybe if she could learn to eat to live, rather than live to eat, as her family did, she could learn to be healthier as a result.

It would be so easy to agree with Jennifer's assessment of the situation. Yes, food was probably too important in her life and was most likely related to the cultural emphasis on food. But she did exercise regularly and did mention the low-fat alternatives that she had incorporated in her life, so something in the story didn't make sense. Again, the first step in determining Jennifer's problem began with the diagnostic evaluation. I evaluated Jennifer's Body Burn Rate with the Burn Rate Test Diet and found that her weight barely changed at the calorie level of the Test Diet. She lost .2 pounds in two weeks, yielding a Body Burn Rate of 1,520 calories.

This low Body Burn Rate at Jennifer's current weight of 245 pounds meant that Jennifer had been doing everything possible to manage her weight. In fact, her natural weight, the weight that her body would weigh if she ate like the average person, was predicted to be 295 pounds. In order to live at less than 295 pounds, Jennifer had to do a whole lot of work, and she was doing it. She had made many significant lifestyle changes in her food intake and had increased her daily exercise. Her Italian heritage had nothing to do with her weight control, nor did her enjoyment of food. Despite what one might think, she had learned to be very careful and cautious in her eating and had learned to eat only those foods that she truly loved. Spaghetti and meatballs were her favorite, but she would eat a small bowl of pasta and only one meatball. She was doing everything that she could to be as healthy as she could be.

So what about her high blood pressure and the threat of diabetes if she gained weight? It was obvious that weight loss was not a treatment of choice for Jennifer. She could not live on fewer calories than she was already eating and could not realistically add any additional exercise to her life. Could Jennifer improve her health or live thinner in any way? Was Jennifer a hopeless case, or was there something that I could do for her?

The Solution

There were two aspects of Jennifer's life that could be improved by the application of the Burn Rate Principles. The first was her physical health. Recent research has shown that "fitness" is more highly correlated to increasing life expectancy than "fatness." Research from the Cooper Institute for Aerobics Research in Dallas, Texas, on over 20,000 men indicated that fit and overweight men had the same health risks as fit and thin men. (Lee, C.D., et al., *International Journal of Obesity*, 1998, 22, 2). This research provided part of the answer to what Jennifer could do to improve her health. The first step for her was to increase the strength of her heart to carry her body weight. Since exercise has been shown to reduce blood pressure and blood sugar in some individuals, there may be a larger health benefit to Jennifer than she realized by increasing the intensity of her walking program. I showed Jennifer the walking program in the Burn Rate Diet, and had her begin to advance through the levels. I had her consult with a podiatrist to make sure that she had the right sneakers and correct alignment to ensure that her knees did not become affected. Jennifer enjoyed the physical challenge of the program, and it did have the intended effect. While her weight has not changed, Jennifer's blood pressure medication has been cut in half, and her blood sugar has remained stable despite her weight.

The second area of treatment called for in the Burn Rate Diet is the reinforcement to Jennifer that she has done nothing wrong and everything right in the management of her health. The little voice in the back of her mind, the doubt and wonder, are the outgrowths of the effects of stereotypes about fat people in American society. Jennifer is as susceptible as anyone to this effect. She too looks at her body size and wonders if she is not to blame. She doubts her love of food, and wonders if her ethnic emphasis on food hasn't been part of the problem. The answer is a resounding "No way" and needs to be stated loud and clear to Jennifer. It also needs to be stated loudly by her parents, relatives, and siblings to help Jennifer remain well adjusted and healthy.

The single biggest psychological scar for Jennifer is her doubt about her interest in dating and attractiveness to men. This is the area where the shame of obesity has done its greatest damage. There is no doubt that Jennifer's weight would be an obstacle for many men. There are other men who would not care about Jennifer's weight, and would see her as a whole person with many great qualities. Finding that man will be difficult and a huge risk for Jennifer. She would have to endure the many trials and tribulations of the dating scene and cope with the rejection that all people face in those settings.

This became the focus of my sessions with Jennifer. As she learned to honor her own reactions, Jennifer became more able to protect herself from people's reactions to her, making their reactions something about them rather than something about her. While she continues to explore relationships with men, she is happier about herself and feels stronger about her strengths, and we have together been successful at quieting that little voice in the back of her mind.

THE OVERWEIGHT CHILD: THE CASE OF KATE

The Story

Katherine, who likes to be called Kate, is an eleven-year-old girl in elementary school. Kate never had a weight problem until fifth grade. In a span of eighteen months, Kate gained 55 pounds for a 4-inch growth spurt. Kate's mother was alarmed, a reaction intensified by both the school nurse and her pediatrician, who both warned her of the dangers of letting Kate continue to gain weight. Kate was shocked by all the changes in her body, and embarrassed. She had gone from being a normal-size girl to being the tallest girl in her class, and one of the largest. The school nurse particularly embarrassed her. At the beginning of school, the entire class is brought down to the nurse's office for their annual health check. The nurse goes over the immunization records and records each child's height and weight. This school nurse used to call out children's weight as she weighed them. Kate was mortified when the nurse called out her weight and heard the mumbling of her classmates in the line behind her.

Kate's frustration grew as she became the target of angry kids looking to pick on somebody. With girls, whenever she got in a verbal fight with one of them, they would always end the fight with the statement, "Well, at least I'm not fat like you." Kate reacted to these comments by becoming really self-conscious. Picking out a bathing suit became a battle with her mother. She would try one on, only to feel ugly and fat in the suit. Her mother would get frustrated after a while and tell her to just go ahead and pick one or she was going to leave the store. It all seemed like such a burden.

Kate's mother, Fran, felt pressure as well. She wondered if she had done something wrong to let Kate gain all that weight. She felt like a good mother who was attentive to her children's needs, but how could she not notice Kate's weight gain? Should she have been restricting her intake more, like not giving her chips in her lunch every day? She had noticed a tone in the voice of the pediatrician that she interpreted as a comment on her negligence as a parent.

In response to the pressure, Fran began to watch Kate's intake more closely and make comments. Any time Kate would ask to go out for ice cream, Fran would say, "I don't think you need that." So Kate would wait until she went out with her friends and would eat the largest sundae should could find. Fran also began to serve smaller portions to Kate at mealtime. If Kate asked for seconds, Fran would once again respond with, "That's not good for you." Kate would often be hungry after dinner and would sneak into the kitchen for leftovers or whatever she could find. One time, Fran caught her getting a large bowl of ice cream from the refrigerator. Fran got very upset and said, "No wonder you are overweight. Do you want to be fat your whole life?"

Kate's father was no help, either. His position on the whole matter was that Fran was making a big deal out of nothing and he couldn't understand why she was so upset. He felt that Kate would outgrow it and that it was Fran who was creating the problem. When Fran would mention what the pediatrician or nurse had said, the father would say that they didn't know what they were talking about, and dismiss their remarks. That was not so easy for Fran to do. She knew her husband had a habit of not emotionally responding to her or to Kate, and she didn't trust his perspective. She felt he was being negligent and ignoring a problem that needed some help.

Fran began to wonder if Kate's weight problem wasn't due to her overeating, as she seemed abnormally interested in food lately. Fran was upset about Kate and her food, but even more worried that Kate's food intake was now becoming a problem in their relationship. Every time Fran commented about Kate's food intake, Kate got angry and withdrew. Fran noticed that they no longer had the mother-daughter chats that they used to have. Kate kept her life much more to herself, and would respond with "I don't have to tell you that" any time Fran would ask Kate about her friends or what was going on in school. Fran felt that Kate was developing a bad attitude. She became more and more worried about her daughter.

The Problem

I saw Fran and Kate together for the first consult. It was obvious that there was a problem there, and Kate's weight was only a small part of it. Fran did all the talking, and Kate barely got a word in edgewise. Each time she tried to correct what her mother had said, Fran would make a sarcastic remark, and Kate would retreat further into the couch. After ten minutes of this exchange, Kate simply got up and walked out of the office, much to the shock and dismay of her mother.

Fran was stunned and didn't know how to react. I reassured her that Kate was not the first child to get up and leave the first session, and wanted her to tell me more about Kate's weight history. She told me the story about how Kate had been normal weight her whole life until recently. Fran said she could not figure out what was going on and felt like an irresponsible parent but also found that the attempt to help was destroying the relationship with her daughter.

Consistent with my treatment approach, I explained to Kate that I needed to get a fix on her metabolic rate to help her with her weight control. I told her that I believed that most weight control problems had less to do with food intake than with metabolism, and that I needed to measure her burn rate to know how to help her. Kate responded to my approach and underwent the metabolic testing to determine her Body Burn Rate through indirect calorimetry using a metabolic cart to measure gas exchange. The results indicated that Kate had a Body Burn Rate of 2,065 calories, well below the 2,200 calories per day for the average female child her age. I explained to Fran and Kate in the next session that burn rate was also a measure of food intake. If a person's weight was stable, then the food intake matched the burn rate that I measured. If her weight had gone up in the past month, I could calculate how much over her burn rate she was eating to cause that amount of weight gain. If her weight had dropped in the past month, then I could calculate how much less than her burn rate she had been eating to cause the weight loss. Since Kate's weight was stable, her food intake had matched her burn rate, meaning that Kate was eating even less than the average child was. Her weight gain, then, was not due in any way to overeating, and Kate was doing nothing wrong to cause this weight gain. In fact, eating like the average child had caused her body weight to react in the way that it had.

The Solution

Fran raised the issue of Kate's "sneak" eating and wondered if that had anything to do with the problem. While Fran could plainly see that Kate did eat more from time to time, she had learned to compensate for it by cutting back at other times. Fran acknowledged that she had noticed this with Kate. She would drink water when her friends had juice or would skip meals from time to time or just eat a piece of fruit for breakfast or lunch.

Reassuring both Fran and Kate that there was nothing wrong with Kate's eating was a critical element in the solution provided by the Burn Rate Diet. Kate could continue doing what she had been doing without Fran's critical review. Fran was reassured that she was being a good mother, and could trust Kate's choices of food intake. While Fran's father was guilty of being negligent and uninvolved, he had been right about leaving Kate alone, but for the wrong reasons. He had been guilty of reacting without knowing, and, in fact, Kate could have been a child who was overeating due to stress and who really had a psychological problem that needed to be addressed. The diagnosis of the problem through identifying her Body Burn Rate had provided the answer. Fran could now legitimately confront her spouse's emotional distance and lack of involvement with the family's needs because she had the facts to support her. They could now reorganize the family in a healthier way on healthier terms.

As for Kate's weight, the most likely explanation is that Kate's body was preparing itself for its final growth stage. By increasing her fat mass, the body was storing the energy that would be later used to add muscle and bone to reach her final height and weight. The answer may one day be provided by medical research, but there is no answer with the current state of our knowledge.

The Burn Rate Diet gave Kate a plan to guide her food intake and define a level of exercise that was comfortable for her. She appreciated the flexibility in the plan and knew that she could eat anything she wanted at a given time and how to compensate to keep her calories in the range that she had selected. She was now doing the best that she could to be healthy, and the rest was up to nature and her genetics. Hopefully, her growth spurt to her final height would alter her body size to make it more normal. If not, at least Kate was armed with the realization that it was not her fault, and that she was doing nothing wrong. She did not need ever to be subjected to going on and off of diets, and would never be made fatter by each apparent attempt to solve the problem. She had been saved from the diet wars and could manage her life with her sense of body and self organized in a healthy way.

EPILOGUE

Beth, Joan, Jennifer, and Kate are just several of the many examples of patients who have misunderstood their weight problem and made matters only worse in the process. In each case, the misdiagnosis of the problem as a psychological problem of willpower or self-control led them down a path that hurt each of them. The Burn Rate Diet offered a different solution, one that provided a new understanding of body weight changes, and a new understanding of themselves.

This can be true for you, too. I look forward to hearing about your experience applying the Burn Rate Principles to your weight management. I can be reached on the Web site in the support network from time to time and am available to answer questions that you may have. Even though we may never get the chance to meet face to face, I still consider myself your doctor and look forward to learning more about you through the Web site. I sincerely hope that by reading this book and taking advantage of the Web site, you too can gain a new understanding of yourself and your weight.

APPENDIX I: Burn Rate Test Diets

BURN RATE
TEST DIET
FOR WOMEN

Daily Calorie Intake: 1,500 calories per day

Breakfast Options

food	amount	total calories	substrate calories carbohydrate	protein	fat
GOAL		**244**	**77**	**42**	**125**
1. Eggs and Bacon					
boiled egg	1 med	75	0	27	48
bacon	3 slices	90	0	24	60
bread	1 slice	75	75	0	0
TOTAL		**240**	**75**	**41**	**108**
2. Cottage Cheese and Fruit with Sausage					
cottage cheese 4%	¼ cup	60	0	44	16
sausage link	1 link	130	0	12	118
cantaloupe	¼ melon	47	47	0	0
TOTAL		**237**	**47**	**56**	**134**

food	amount	total calories	substrate calories carbohydrate	protein	fat
GOAL		**244**	**77**	**42**	**125**

3. Ham and Cheese Open-Faced Sandwich

food	amount	total calories	carbohydrate	protein	fat
ham	1 oz	50	0	25	25
cheese	½ oz	55	0	19	36
margarine	2 tsp	66	0	0	66
bread	1 slice	75	75	0	0
TOTAL		**246**	**75**	**44**	**127**

4. Turkey and Cheese Roll-Up with Fruit

food	amount	total calories	carbohydrate	protein	fat
turkey	1 oz	48	0	32	16
cheese	1 oz	111	0	37	74
banana	½ med	53	53	0	0
TOTAL		**212**	**53**	**62**	**90**

5. Peanut Butter on Rice Cake

food	amount	total calories	carbohydrate	protein	fat
peanut butter	2 tbsp	196	0	64	136
rice cake	1	52	52	0	0
TOTAL		**248**	**52**	**64**	**136**

6. Bagel with Cream Cheese and Lox

food	amount	total calories	carbohydrate	protein	fat
bagel, small	½	80	80	0	0
cream cheese	1 tbsp	100	0	0	100
lox	2 oz	66	0	44	22
TOTAL		**246**	**80**	**44**	**122**

7. Bread and Cheese

food	amount	total calories	carbohydrate	protein	fat
cheese	1 oz	111	0	37	74
bread	1 slice	75	75	0	0
margarine	2 tsp	46	0	0	46
TOTAL		**232**	**75**	**37**	**120**

Lunch Options

food	amount	total calories	substrate calories carbohydrate	protein	fat
GOAL		**418**	**250**	**42**	**125**

1. Tuna Fish Sandwich with Pretzels

food	amount	total calories	carbohydrate	protein	fat
bread	2 slices	150	150	0	0
tuna in water	2 oz	60	0	60	0
mayonnaise	1 tbsp	100	0	0	100
pretzels	1 oz	110	110	0	0
TOTAL		**420**	**260**	**60**	**100**

2. Sausage Pizza and Fruit

food	amount	total calories	carbohydrate	protein	fat
pizza	1 slice	250	108	62	80
sausage	½ oz	65	0	7	58
apple	1 med	81	81	0	0
TOTAL		**396**	**189**	**69**	**138**

3. Soup and Salad with Cottage Cheese and Fruit

salad:

food	amount	total calories	carbohydrate	protein	fat
lettuce	3 cups	39	39	0	0
tomatoes	1 med	26	26	0	0
dressing	2 tsp	80	0	0	80
soup (broth)	2 cups	126	88	18	20
cottage cheese 4%	¼ cup	60	0	44	16
apple	1 med	81	81	0	0
TOTAL		**412**	**234**	**52**	**116**

4. Turkey and Cheese Half-Sandwich with Potato Chips and Fruit

food	amount	total calories	carbohydrate	protein	fat
bread	1 slice	81	81	0	0
cheese	½ oz	55	0	19	36
turkey	1 oz	48	0	32	16
potato chips	1 oz	150	75	0	75
banana	1 med	105	105	0	0
TOTAL		**439**	**261**	**51**	**127**

food	amount	total calories	substrate calories carbohydrate	protein	fat
GOAL		**418**	**250**	**42**	**125**

5. Cottage Cheese and Fruit with Potato Chips

food	amount	total calories	carbohydrate	protein	fat
cottage cheese 4%	¼ cup	60	0	44	16
apple	1 med	81	81	0	0
pear	1 med	98	98	0	0
potato chips	1 oz	150	75	0	75
TOTAL		**389**	**254**	**44**	**91**

6. Grilled Cheese Sandwich with Fruit

food	amount	total calories	carbohydrate	protein	fat
bread	2 slices	162	162	0	0
cheese	1 oz	111	0	37	74
margarine	1 tsp	33	0	0	33
apple	1 med	81	81	0	0
TOTAL		**387**	**243**	**37**	**107**

7. Frankfurter with Sauerkraut, Fruit, and Pretzels

food	amount	total calories	carbohydrate	protein	fat
frankfurter	1 link	150	0	32	118
hot dog roll	1	110	110	0	0
sauerkraut	½ cup	15	15	0	0
mustard	1 tsp	12	4	0	8
orange	1 med	62	62	0	0
pretzels	½ oz	55	55	0	0
TOTAL		**404**	**246**	**32**	**126**

8. Vegetarian Lunch

food	amount	total calories	carbohydrate	protein	fat
rice	½ cup	90	90	0	0
beans, lentils	1 cup	208	160	48	0
margarine	1 tsp	33	0	0	33
olives, black	10	90	0	0	90
TOTAL		**421**	**250**	**48**	**123**

Snack Options

food	amount	total calories	substrate calories carbohydrate	protein	fat
GOAL		**175**	**175**	**0**	**0**
1. pretzels	1½ oz	165	165	0	0
2. two pieces of fruit:					
apple	1 med	81	81	0	0
banana	1 med	105	105	0	0
3. bread, French	2 slices	164	164	0	0

Dinner Options

food	amount	total calories	substrate calories carbohydrate	protein	fat
GOAL		**663**	**323**	**141**	**199**
1. Chicken Parmigiana with Rice and Broccoli					
chicken	4 oz	168	0	88	80
cheese	1 oz	111	0	37	74
tomato sauce	1 cup	74	74	0	0
rice	1 cup	180	180	0	0
margarine	2 tsp	67	0	0	67
broccoli	1½ cups	57	57	0	0
TOTAL		**645**	**311**	**125**	**221**
2. Turkey-Broccoli Casserole with Cantaloupe					
turkey	4 oz	192	0	128	64
broccoli	½ cup	19	19	0	0
noodles	1 cup	196	196	0	0
mayonnaise	3 tsp	100	0	0	100
bread, French	1 slice	82	82	0	0
margarine	1 tsp	33	0	0	33
cantaloupe	¼ melon	47	47	0	0
TOTAL		**669**	**344**	**128**	**197**

food	amount	total calories	substrate calories carbohydrate	protein	fat
GOAL		663	323	141	199

3. Spaghetti and Meatballs with Green Beans
meatballs (1 oz each)	3 oz	246	0	123	123
spaghetti	1 cup	196	196	0	0
tomato sauce	1 cup	74	74	0	0
green beans	1 cup	44	44	0	0
margarine	1 tsp	33	0	0	33
bread	1 slice	82	82	0	0
TOTAL		**675**	**396**	**123**	**156**

4. Fish with Rice, Broccoli, and Fruit
fish, cod	5 oz	150	0	150	0
tartar sauce	6 tsp	200	0	0	200
rice	1 cup	180	180	0	0
broccoli	1½ cups	57	57	0	0
apple	1 med	81	81	0	0
TOTAL		**668**	**318**	**150**	**200**

5. Pasta with Shrimp
pasta	1½ cups	294	294	0	0
olive oil	4 tsp	160	0	0	160
shrimp	5 oz	140	0	140	0
garlic	1 clove	4	4	0	0
onions	1 cup	40	40	0	0
TOTAL		**638**	**338**	**140**	**160**

6. Steak and Potatoes with Green Beans and Cottage Cheese
steak	3 oz	228	0	99	129
potato	1 med	220	220	0	0
sour cream	3 tsp	26	0	0	26
green beans	2 cups	88	88	0	0
cottage cheese 2%	½ cup	109	0	89	20
TOTAL		**671**	**308**	**188**	**175**

food	amount	total calories	substrate calories carbohydrate	protein	fat
GOAL		663	323	141	199

7. Pork Fried Rice with Peas and Carrots

food	amount	total calories	carbohydrate	protein	fat
pork	4 oz	272	0	136	136
rice	1½ cups	250	250	0	0
oil	1 tsp	40	0	0	40
carrots	½ cup	35	35	0	0
peas	½ cup	58	58	0	0
TOTAL		**655**	**343**	**136**	**172**

8. Vegetarian Dinner

food	amount	total calories	carbohydrate	protein	fat
rice	1 cup	180	180	0	0
tofu, raw	6 oz	132	0	54	78
beans, black	1 cup	208	160	48	0
nuts	1 oz	164	0	26	138
TOTAL		**684**	**340**	**128**	**216**

BURN RATE
TEST DIET
FOR MEN

Daily Calorie Intake: 1,800 calories per day

Breakfast Options

food	amount	total calories	substrate calories carbohydrate	protein	fat
GOAL		**293**	**92**	**50**	**151**
1. Eggs and Bacon					
boiled eggs	2 med	144	0	54	96
bacon	2 slices	60	0	16	44
bread	1 slice	75	75	0	0
TOTAL		**279**	**75**	**70**	**140**
2. Cottage Cheese and Sausage with Orange Juice					
cottage cheese 2%	¼ cup	55	0	44	11
sausage link	1 link	130	0	13	117
orange juice	7 oz	98	98	0	0
TOTAL		**283**	**98**	**57**	**128**

food	amount	total calories	substrate calories carbohydrate	protein	fat
GOAL		293	92	50	151

3. Ham and Cheese Open-Faced Sandwich

food	amount	total calories	carbohydrate	protein	fat
ham	1 oz	50	0	25	25
cheese	1 oz	111	0	38	74
margarine	1 tsp	33	0	0	33
bread	1 slice	75	75	0	0
TOTAL		**269**	**75**	**63**	**132**

4. Turkey and Cheese Roll-Up with Fruit

food	amount	total calories	carbohydrate	protein	fat
turkey	2 oz	96	0	48	32
cheese	1 oz	111	0	37	74
apple	1 med	81	81	0	0
TOTAL		**288**	**81**	**85**	**106**

5. Peanut Butter on Rice Cake

food	amount	total calories	carbohydrate	protein	fat
peanut butter	2 tbsp	196	0	64	136
rice cake	2	104	104	0	0
TOTAL		**300**	**104**	**64**	**136**

6. Bagel with Cream Cheese and Lox

food	amount	total calories	carbohydrate	protein	fat
bagel, large	½	105	105	0	0
cream cheese	1 tbsp	100	0	0	100
lox	3 oz	99	0	66	33
TOTAL		**304**	**105**	**66**	**133**

7. Bread and Cheese with Bacon

food	amount	total calories	carbohydrate	protein	fat
cheese	1 oz	111	0	37	74
bread	1 slice	75	75	0	0
margarine	1 tsp	33	0	0	33
bacon	2 slices	60	0	16	44
juice, tomato	4 oz	24	24	0	0
TOTAL		**303**	**99**	**53**	**151**

Lunch Options

food	amount	total calories	substrate calories carbohydrate	protein	fat
GOAL		502	301	50	151

1. Tuna Fish Sandwich with Pretzels and Fruit

food	amount	total calories	carbohydrate	protein	fat
bread	2 slices	150	150	0	0
tuna in water	2 oz	60	0	60	0
mayonnaise	1½ tbsp	150	0	0	150
plum	1 med	27	27	0	0
pretzels	1 oz	110	110	0	0
TOTAL		**497**	**287**	**60**	**150**

2. Pizza with Fruit and Potato Chips

food	amount	total calories	carbohydrate	protein	fat
pizza	1 slice	250	108	62	80
potato chips	1 oz	150	75	0	75
banana	1 med	105	105	0	0
strawberries	2 cups	106	106	0	0
TOTAL		**502**	**394**	**62**	**150**

3. Soup and Salad with Fruit
salad:

food	amount	total calories	carbohydrate	protein	fat
lettuce	1 cup	13	13	0	0
tomatoes	1 med	26	26	0	0
dressing	2 tsp	60	0	0	60
eggs, hard boiled	2	144	0	54	96
soup (broth)	1 cup	63	44	9	10
banana	1 med	105	105	0	0
apple	1 med	81	81	0	0
TOTAL		**492**	**269**	**63**	**166**

4. Turkey Sandwich with Potato Chips and Fruit

food	amount	total calories	carbohydrate	protein	fat
bread	2 slices	162	162	0	0
turkey	2 oz	96	0	64	16
mayonnaise	1 tsp	33	0	0	33
potato chips	1 oz	150	75	0	75
orange	1 med	62	62	0	0
TOTAL		**503**	**299**	**64**	**124**

food	amount	total calories	substrate calories carbohydrate	protein	fat
GOAL		502	301	50	151

5. Cottage Cheese and Fruit with Potato Chips

food	amount	total calories	carbohydrate	protein	fat
cottage cheese 4%	½ cup	120	0	89	31
apple	1 med	81	81	0	0
pear	1 med	98	98	0	0
nectarine	1 med	45	45	0	0
potato chips	1 oz	150	75	0	75
TOTAL		**494**	**299**	**89**	**106**

6. Grilled Cheese Sandwich with Fruit

food	amount	total calories	carbohydrate	protein	fat
bread	2 slices	162	162	0	0
cheese	1 oz	111	0	37	74
margarine	2 tsp	66	0	0	66
banana	1 med	105	105	0	0
orange	1 med	62	62	0	0
TOTAL		**506**	**329**	**37**	**140**

7. Frankfurter with Fruit and Pretzels

food	amount	total calories	carbohydrate	protein	fat
frankfurter	1 link	150	0	32	118
hot dog roll	1	110	110	0	0
sauerkraut	½ cup	15	15	0	0
mustard	1 tsp	12	4	0	8
orange	1 med	62	62	0	0
pretzels	1 oz	110	110	0	0
TOTAL		**459**	**301**	**32**	**126**

8. Vegetarian Lunch

food	amount	total calories	carbohydrate	protein	fat
rice	1 cup	90	90	0	0
beans, lentils	1 cup	208	160	48	0
margarine	2 tsp	66	0	6	66
olives, black	10	90	0	0	90
tomato	1 med	26	26	0	0
celery	1 cup	20	20	0	0
TOTAL		**500**	**296**	**48**	**156**

Snack Options

food	amount	total calories	substrate calories carbohydrate	protein	fat
GOAL		209	209	0	0
1. pretzels	2 oz	220	220	0	0
2. two pieces of fruit:					
pear	1 med	98	98	0	0
banana	1 med	105	105	0	0
3. bread and fruit					
bread, French	2 slices	164	164	0	0
nectarine	1 med	45	45	0	0

Dinner Options

food	amount	total calories	substrate calories carbohydrate	protein	fat
GOAL		796	388	170	239
1. Chicken Parmigiana with Rice and Peas					
chicken	5 oz	210	0	110	100
cheese	1 oz	111	0	37	74
tomato sauce	1 cup	74	74	0	0
rice	1 cup	180	180	0	0
margarine	2 tsp	67	0	0	67
bread	1 slice	75	75	0	0
peas	1 cup	58	58	0	0
TOTAL		**775**	**387**	**147**	**241**
2. Turkey-Broccoli Casserole with Canteloupe					
turkey	5 oz	240	0	160	80
broccoli	½ cup	19	19	0	0
noodles	1 cup	196	196	0	0
mayonnaise	4 tsp	133	0	0	133
bread, French	1 slice	82	82	0	0
margarine	1 tsp	33	0	0	33
canteloupe	½ melon	94	94	0	0
TOTAL		**795**	**391**	**160**	**246**

food	amount	total calories	substrate calories carbohydrate	protein	fat
GOAL		**796**	**388**	**170**	**239**

3. Spaghetti and Meatballs with Green Beans

food	amount	total calories	carbohydrate	protein	fat
meatballs (1 oz each)	4 oz	328	0	164	164
spaghetti	1 cup	196	196	0	0
tomato sauce	1 cup	74	74	0	0
green beans	1 cup	44	44	0	0
margarine	2 tsp	67	0	0	67
bread, French	1 slice	82	82	0	0
TOTAL		**791**	**396**	**164**	**231**

4. Fish with Rice, Broccoli, and Fruit

food	amount	total calories	carbohydrate	protein	fat
fish, cod	6 oz	180	0	180	0
tartar sauce	6 tsp	200	0	0	200
rice	1 cup	180	180	0	0
broccoli	1½ cups	57	57	0	0
bread, French	1 slice	82	82	0	0
margarine	1 tsp	33	0	0	33
orange	1 med	62	62	0	0
TOTAL		**794**	**381**	**180**	**233**

5. Pasta with Shrimp

food	amount	total calories	carbohydrate	protein	fat
pasta	2 cups	392	392	0	0
olive oil	6 tsp	240	0	0	240
shrimp	6 oz	168	0	168	0
garlic	1 clove	4	4	0	0
TOTAL		**804**	**396**	**168**	**240**

6. Steak and Potatoes with Green Beans

food	amount	total calories	carbohydrate	protein	fat
steak	5 oz	380	0	165	215
potato	1 med	220	220	0	0
sour cream	3 tsp	26	0	0	26
bread, French	1 slice	82	82	0	0
green beans	2 cups	88	88	0	0
TOTAL		**796**	**390**	**165**	**241**

food	amount	total calories	substrate calories carbohydrate	protein	fat
GOAL		**796**	**388**	**170**	**239**
7. Pork Fried Rice with Fruit					
pork	5 oz	340	0	170	170
rice	2 cups	360	360	0	0
oil	2 tsp	80	0	0	80
plum	1 med	27	27	0	0
TOTAL		**807**	**387**	**170**	**250**
8. Vegetarian Dinner					
rice	1 cup	180	180	0	0
tofu, raw	6 oz	132	0	54	78
beans, black	1½ cups	312	240	72	0
nuts	1 oz	164	0	26	138
TOTAL		**788**	**420**	**152**	**216**

ADJUSTMENTS TO BURN RATE TEST DIET

Extra Calories

Day 1: _____   Day 2: _____

_____subtotal: _____   _____subtotal: _____

Day 3: _____   Day 4: _____

_____subtotal: _____   _____subtotal: _____

Day 5: _____   Day 6: _____

_____subtotal: _____   _____subtotal: _____

Day 7: _____   Day 8: _____

_____subtotal: _____   _____subtotal: _____

Day 9: _____   Day 10: _____

_____subtotal: _____   _____subtotal: _____

Day 11: _____   Day 12: _____

_____subtotal: _____   _____subtotal: _____

Day 13: _____   Day 14: _____

_____subtotal: _____   _____subtotal: _____

TOTAL EXTRA CALORIES: _____cals

Exercise Calories

Activity	Time	Calories Expended
1._____	_____	_____
2._____	_____	_____
3._____	_____	_____
4._____	_____	_____

TOTAL EXERCISE CALORIES _____

APPENDIX II

Body Burn Rate and Burn Rate Diet Guidelines Manual Calculations

The formulas to perform the manual calculations are listed below for your information. While it is possible to manually calculate your results, it is far easier and simpler to go to the Web site for this purpose at **www.burnratediet.com**. If you do not have access to the Internet, follow the instructions to perform the calculations for yourself.

BURN RATE TEST DIET: MANUAL CALCULATIONS

1. Enter results of Burn Rate Test Diet below:

    Start Weight: _____ lbs

    - End Weight _____ lbs

    = Weight Change _____ lbs Lost / Gained

2. Calculate Current Body Burn Rate

Multiply Weight Change by 200: Add that amount to the respective calorie level of the Burn Rate Test Diet if weight was lost;

Subtract that amount from the calorie level of the Test Diet if weight was gained: Calculate adjustments due to extra eating and exercise:

Burn Rate Test Diet   1,500 or 1,800 cals

Add if loss, subtract if gain:

Weight Change x 200   _____ cals

Adjustments:

Subtract:

Extra Calories ÷ 14   -_____cals

Add:

Exercise Calories ÷ 14   +_____cals

CURRENT BODY BURN RATE   =_____ cals/day

3.   Calculate Predicted Body Burn Rate

You must first determine your Goal Weight to find your Predicted Body Burn Rate. Predicted Body Burn Rate will be the calorie level of the Burn Rate Diet that you will construct. With Burn Rate Principles, Goal Weight must pass a reasonableness test. The Predicted Body Burn Rate must exceed reasonable levels of restriction to be considered acceptable. If the level of calorie restriction is too extreme, you will be asked to revise your Goal Weight until your Predicted Burn Rate falls is greater than the severe range of restriction.

RECOMMENDED RANGES FOR PREDICTED BODY BURN RATE: MODERATE TO MILD

Level of Restriction	Female (cals/day)	Male (cals/day)
Mild	>1,900	>2,200
Moderate	>1,700	>2,000
Severe	>1,500	>1,800

a. Determine Your Goal Weight

Current Weight: _____lbs

Subtract:

Desired Weight - _____lbs

= Amount of Weight You Want to Lose: _____lb

b. Calculate Predicted Body Burn Rate at Desired Weight

Current Body Burn Rate: _____cals/day

Subtract:

Amount of Weight You Want to
Lose x 10: - _____lbs

= Predicted Body Burn Rate: _____cals/day

c. Test Reasonableness of Predicted Body Burn Rate

Test of Reasonableness: Predicted Body Burn Rate must exceed
1500 calories/day for women and 1800 calories/day for men.

Predicted Body Burn Rate _____cals/day

Subtract: - - 1,500 or 1,800

Test Value: _____cals

If Test Value >0, Test of Reasonableness is passed.
Skip Adjustment section

If Test Value <0, eliminate negative sign, and continue
to Adjustment Section

Adjustment Section

d.   Calculate Adjustments to Predicted Body Burn Rate

Predicted Body Burn Rate   _____cals/day

Add:

Test Value   +_____cals

Final Predicted Body Burn Rate   _____ **cals/day**

e.   Calculate Adjustments to Goal Weight

Initial Goal Weight   _____lbs

Subtract:

Test Value ÷ 10   -_____lbs

Final Goal Weight   _____**lbs**

4.   Calculate Burn Rate Diet Guidelines

Your Burn Rate Diet Guidelines are the set of instructions to
match the burn rate of food to your Predicted Body Burn Rate. In
the steps below, you will select a diet composition, and apply the
selected percentages to the calories/hour of your Body Burn Rate.
These values will then be matched to the burn rate of food across
a six-hour time interval. The result will be the calorie values of carbohydrate, protein, and fat for breakfast, lunch, snack, and dinner.

a. Select your Diet Composition:

Standard:	55% Carbohydrate	15% Protein	30% Fat
Medical:	60% Carbohydrate	15% Protein	25% Fat
Athletic:	50% Carbohydrate	20% Protein	30% Fat

b. Calculate Body Burn Rate as Calories/hour

Predicted Body Burn Rate ÷ 24 = _____calories/hour

c. Calculate Burn Rate Diet Nutritional Information:

Enter the values of your selected diet composition in the table below. Determine the calories/hour for any substrate by multiplying the calories/hour of the Predicted Body Burn Rate by the percentage of the Diet Composition. Multiply the cals/hr by 24 to obtain the cals/day values. Grams/day is determined by dividing the cals/day by 4 for carbohydrate and protein and by 9 for fat.

Substrate	Diet Composition	Cals/hr	Cals/day	Grams/day
Carbohydrate	_____%	_____	_____	_____
Protein	_____%	_____	_____	_____
Fat	_____%	_____	_____	_____

d. Calculating Individual Meals in the Burn Rate Diet:

Breakfast: Complete the following table by multiplying the Food Burn Rate times the cals/hour from the chart above

Substrate	Cals/hr	x	Food Burn Rate	=	Calories
Carbohydrate	_____	x	2 hrs	=	_____kcals
Protein	_____	x	4 hrs	=	_____kcals
Fat	_____	x	6 hrs	=	_____kcals
			Breakfast Total	=	_____kcals

Lunch: Lunch is the same as breakfast with the addition of a carbohydrate amount (Ketone Replacement Factor) to replace the calories burned from ketones between breakfast and lunch.

Calculate Ketone Replacement Factor as follows:

Substrate	Cals/hr	Breakfast Calories	Calories from Ketones
Carbohydrate	_____ x6	- _____ =	_____ kcals
Protein	_____ x6	- _____ =	+ _____ kcals
Fat	0	0 =	0
Ketone Replacement Factor (KRF)		=	_____ kcals

Lunch Calories

Substrate	Kcals/hr x	Food Burn Rate	+ KRF =	Calories
Carbohydrate	_____ x	2 hrs	+ _____ =	_____ kcals
Protein	_____ x	4 hrs	+ 00 =	_____ kcals
Fat	_____ x	6 hrs	+ 00 =	_____ kcals
		Total Lunch Calories =		_____ kcals

Snack: Snack calories are the equivalent to the calories of the Ketone Replacement Factor calculated for Lunch.

Carbohydrate Calories = KRF calories = _____ kcals

Dinner: The balance of calories remaining form the basis for the
calories of dinner. Subtract the calories eaten in the other
meals/snack from the total calories per day (cals/day) to
determine the dinner calories.

Dinner Calories

Substrate	Total Cals/day	Breakfast	Lunch	Snack	Dinner
Carbohydrate	_____	- _____	- _____	- _____	= _____
Protein	_____	- _____	- _____	- _____	= _____
Fat	_____	- _____	- _____	- _____	= _____
TOTALS	_____	_____		_____	_____	_____

Burn Rate Diet Guidelines: Fill in the table below from the values
calculated in the table above for the dinner meal.

BURN RATE DIET GUIDELINES

Substrate	Total Cals/day	Breakfast	Lunch	Snack	Dinner
Carbohydrate	_____	_____	_____	_____	_____
Protein	_____	_____	_____	_____	_____
Fat	_____	_____	_____	_____	_____
TOTALS	_____	_____	_____	_____	_____

APPENDIX III

Food and
Calorie Lists

PURE CARBOHYDRATE FOODS

Food	Amount	CALORIES Carbohydrate	Protein	Fat	Total
Category: Fruits					
Apple	½ med	41	0	0	41
	1 med	81	0	0	81
Applesauce	½ cup	60	0	0	60
	1 cup	120	0	0	120
Apricots, fresh	1 med	18	0	0	18
	2 med	36	0	0	36
	3 med	54	0	0	54
	4 med	72	0	0	72
	5 med	90	0	0	90
Apricots, dried	1 oz	70	0	0	70
	1½ oz	105	0	0	105
	2 oz	140	0	0	140
Banana	½ med	52	0	0	52
	1 med	105	0	0	105

CALORIES

Food	Amount	Carbohydrate	Protein	Fat	Total
Blueberries	½ cup	44	0	0	44
	1 cup	88	0	0	88
	1½ cups	132	0	0	132
Canteloupe	¼ melon	47	0	0	47
	½ melon	94	0	0	94
Cherries	½ cup	41	0	0	41
	1 cup	82	0	0	82
	1½ cups	123	0	0	123
Figs	1 med	58	0	0	58
	2 med	116	0	0	116
Grapefruit	½ med	46	0	0	46
	1 med	92	0	0	92
Grapes	½ cup	30	0	0	30
	1 cup	60	0	0	60
	1½ cups	90	0	0	90
Honeydew	¼ melon	46	0	0	46
	½ melon	92	0	0	92
Kiwi	1 med	46	0	0	46
	2 med	92	0	0	92
Mango	½ med	42	0	0	42
	1 med	84	0	0	84
Nectarine	½ med	23	0	0	23
	1 med	45	0	0	45
	2 med	90	0	0	90
Orange	½ med	31	0	0	31
	1 med	62	0	0	62
Papaya	½ med	59	0	0	59
	1 med	117	0	0	117
Peach	1 med	18	0	0	18
	1 med	35	0	0	35
Pear	½ med	18	0	0	18
	1 med	36	0	0	36
Pineapple, fresh	½ cup	39	0	0	39
	1 cup	78	0	0	78

CALORIES

Food	Amount	Carbohydrate	Protein	Fat	Total
Pinapple, canned	1 oz	17	0	0	17
	2 oz	34	0	0	34
	3 oz	51	0	0	51
	4 oz	68	0	0	68
	5 oz	85	0	0	85
	6 oz	102	0	0	102
Plum	1 med	27	0	0	27
	2 med	54	0	0	54
Prunes, dried	½ cup	35	0	0	35
	1 cup	70	0	0	70
Raspberries	½ cup	41	0	0	41
	1 cup	82	0	0	82
Strawberries	½ cup	27	0	0	27
	1 cup	53	0	0	53
	1½ cups	80	0	0	80
	2 cups	106	0	0	106
Tangerine	1 med	38	0	0	38
	2 med	76	0	0	76
Watermelon	½ cup	21	0	0	21
	1 cup	42	0	0	42
	1½ cups	63	0	0	63
	2 cups	84	0	0	84

Category: Fruit Juices

Apple Juice and Cranberry Juice

	Amount	Carbohydrate	Protein	Fat	Total
	1 oz	15	0	0	15
	2 oz	30	0	0	30
	3 oz	45	0	0	45
	4 oz	60	0	0	60
	5 oz	75	0	0	75
	6 oz	90	0	0	90
	7 oz	105	0	0	105
	8 oz	120	0	0	120
	9 oz	135	0	0	135
	10 oz	150	0	0	150

CALORIES

Food	Amount	Carbohydrate	Protein	Fat	Total
Lemonade, Pineapple Juice, and Grape Juice					
	1 oz	18	0	0	18
	2 oz	36	0	0	36
	3 oz	54	0	0	54
	4 oz	72	0	0	72
	5 oz	90	0	0	90
	6 oz	108	0	0	108
	7 oz	126	0	0	126
	8 oz	144	0	0	144
	9 oz	162	0	0	162
	10 oz	180	0	0	180
Orange Juice	1 oz	14	0	0	14
	2 oz	28	0	0	28
	3 oz	42	0	0	42
	4 oz	56	0	0	56
	5 oz	70	0	0	70
	6 oz	84	0	0	84
	7 oz	98	0	0	98
	8 oz	112	0	0	112
	9 oz	126	0	0	126
	10 oz	140	0	0	140
Prune Juice	1 oz	23	0	0	23
	2 oz	46	0	0	46
	3 oz	69	0	0	69
	4 oz	92	0	0	92
	5 oz	115	0	0	115
	6 oz	138	0	0	138
	7 oz	161	0	0	161
	8 oz	184	0	0	184
	9 oz	207	0	0	207
	10 oz	230	0	0	230
Tomato Juice	1 oz	6	0	0	6
	2 oz	12	0	0	12
	3 oz	18	0	0	18
	4 oz	24	0	0	24
	5 oz	30	0	0	30

CALORIES

Food	Amount	Carbohydrate	Protein	Fat	Total
Tomato Juice *(cont.)*	6 oz	36	0	0	36
	7 oz	42	0	0	42
	8 oz	48	0	0	48
	9 oz	54	0	0	54
	10 oz	60	0	0	60

Category: Vegetables

Food	Amount	Carbohydrate	Protein	Fat	Total
Asparagus	3 spears	10	0	0	10
	6 spears	20	0	0	20
	9 spears	30	0	0	30
Beans, green	½ cup	22	0	0	22
	1 cup	44	0	0	44
	1½ cups	66	0	0	66
	2 cups	88	0	0	88
Beets, cooked	½ cup	26	0	0	26
	1 cup	52	0	0	52
	1½ cups	78	0	0	78
	2 cups	104	0	0	104
Broccoli, cooked	½ cup	19	0	0	19
	1 cup	38	0	0	38
	1½ cups	57	0	0	57
	2 cups	76	0	0	76
Brussels sprouts	½ cup	27	0	0	27
	1 cup	54	0	0	54
	1½ cups	81	0	0	81
	2 cups	108	0	0	108
Cabbage, cooked	½ cup	24	0	0	24
	1 cup	48	0	0	48
	1½ cups	72	0	0	72
	2 cups	96	0	0	96
Carrots	½ cup	24	0	0	24
	1 cup	48	0	0	48
	1½ cups	72	0	0	72
	2 cups	96	0	0	96

CALORIES

Food	Amount	Carbohydrate	Protein	Fat	Total
Cauliflower	½ cup	13	0	0	13
	1 cup	26	0	0	26
	1½ cups	39	0	0	39
	2 cups	52	0	0	52
Celery	½ cup	10	0	0	10
	1 cup	20	0	0	20
	1½ cups	30	0	0	30
	2 cups	40	0	0	40
Corn	½ cup	69	0	0	69
	1 cup	138	0	0	138
	1½ cups	207	0	0	207
	2 cups	276	0	0	276
Cucumbers	½ cup	14	0	0	14
	1 cup	28	0	0	28
	1½ cups	42	0	0	42
	2 cups	56	0	0	56
Eggplant	½ cup	13	0	0	13
	1 cup	26	0	0	26
	1½ cups	39	0	0	39
	2 cups	52	0	0	52
Garlic	1 clove	4	0	0	4
	2 cloves	8	0	0	8
	3 cloves	12	0	0	12
	4 cloves	16	0	0	16
Lettuce	1 cup	7	0	0	7
	2 cups	14	0	0	14
	3 cups	21	0	0	21
	4 cups	28	0	0	28
Mushrooms	½ cup	20	0	0	20
	1 cup	40	0	0	40
	1½ cups	60	0	0	60
	2 cups	80	0	0	80
Okra	½ cup	12	0	0	12
	1 cup	24	0	0	24
	1½ cups	36	0	0	36
	2 cups	48	0	0	48

CALORIES

Food	Amount	Carbohydrate	Protein	Fat	Total
Onions, cooked	½ cup	47	0	0	47
	1 cup	94	0	0	94
	1½ cups	141	0	0	141
	2 cups	188	0	0	188
Peas	½ cup	58	0	0	58
	1 cup	116	0	0	116
	1½ cups	174	0	0	174
	2 cups	232	0	0	232
Peppers	1 med	20	0	0	20
	2 med	40	0	0	40
Potato, baked with skin	½ med	110	0	0	110
	1 med	220	0	0	220
boiled, skinless	½ cup	67	0	0	67
	1 cup	134	0	0	134
mashed, milk, butter	½ cup	111	0	0	111
	1 cup	222	0	0	222
	1½ cups	333	0	0	333
	2 cups	444	0	0	444
Sauerkraut	½ cup	15	0	0	15
	1 cup	30	0	0	30
	1½ cups	45	0	0	45
	2 cups	60	0	0	60
Spinach	½ cup	18	0	0	18
	1 cup	36	0	0	36
	1½ cups	54	0	0	54
	2 cups	72	0	0	72
Squash	½ cup	23	0	0	23
	1 cup	46	0	0	46
	1½ cups	69	0	0	69
	2 cups	92	0	0	92
Tomato	½ med	13	0	0	13
	1 med	26	0	0	26
	1½ med	39	0	0	39
	2 med	52	0	0	52

CALORIES

Food	Amount	Carbohydrate	Protein	Fat	Total
Tomato sauce	½ cup	37	0	0	37
	1 cup	74	0	0	74

Category: Breads, Grains, and Cereals

Food	Amount	Carbohydrate	Protein	Fat	Total
Bagel, small	½ bagel	80	0	0	80
	1 bagel	160	0	0	160
Bagel, large	½ bagel	105	0	0	105
	1 bagel	210	0	0	210
Bread	1 slice	75	0	0	75
	2 slices	150	0	0	150
Bread, French	1 slice	82	0	0	82
	2 slices	164	0	0	164
Bread, lo-cal	1 slice	45	0	0	45
	2 slices	90	0	0	90
Cereal, bran	1 oz	70	0	0	70
	2 oz	140	0	0	140
	3 oz	210	0	0	210
	4 oz	280	0	0	280
Cereal, corn flakes	1 oz	100	0	0	100
	2 oz	200	0	0	200
	3 oz	300	0	0	300
	4 oz	400	0	0	400
Cereal, granola	1 oz	130	0	0	130
	2 oz	260	0	0	260
	3 oz	360	0	0	360
	4 oz	480	0	0	480
Muffin, English	½ muffin	65	0	0	65
	1 muffin	130	0	0	130
Muffin, blueberry (1½ oz)	1 muffin	140	0	0	140
Oatmeal	½ cup	66	0	0	66
	1 cup	132	0	0	132
	1½ cups	198	0	0	198
	2 cups	262	0	0	262
Pancakes	1 med	60	0	0	60
	2 med	120	0	0	120

CALORIES

Food	Amount	Carbohydrate	Protein	Fat	Total
Pancakes *(cont.)*	3 med	180	0	0	180
	4 med	240	0	0	240
	5 med	300	0	0	300
Pasta, cooked	½ cup	99	0	0	99
	1 cup	198	0	0	198
	1½ cups	297	0	0	297
	2 cups	396	0	0	396
	2½ cups	495	0	0	495
	3 cups	594	0	0	594
Popcorn, air-popped	½ cup	60	0	0	60
	1 cup	120	0	0	120
	1½ cups	180	0	0	180
	2 cups	240	0	0	240
	2½ cups	300	0	0	300
	3 cups	360	0	0	360
	3½ cups	420	0	0	420
	4 cups	480	0	0	480
Pretzels	½ oz	55	0	0	55
	1 oz	110	0	0	110
	1½ oz	165	0	0	165
	2 oz	220	0	0	220
	2½ oz	275	0	0	275
	3 oz	360	0	0	360
Rice	½ cup	90	0	0	90
	1 cup	180	0	0	180
	1½ cups	270	0	0	270
	2 cups	360	0	0	360
	2½ cups	450	0	0	450
	3 cups	540	0	0	540
Rice cake	1 med	52	0	0	52
	2 med	104	0	0	104
	3 med	156	0	0	156
	4 med	208	0	0	208
Roll, dinner	½ med	45	0	0	45
	1 med	90	0	0	90
Roll, kaiser	½ med	85	0	0	85
	1 med	170	0	0	170

CALORIES

Food	Amount	Carbohydrate	Protein	Fat	Total
Roll, hamburger	1 med	120	0	0	120
Roll, hot dog	1 med	110	0	0	110
Waffle	1 med	80	0	0	80
	2 med	160	0	0	160
	3 med	240	0	0	240
	4 med	320	0	0	320

Category: Sugars

Chewing gum	1 stick	10	0	0	10
Italian ice	2 oz	48	0	0	48
	4 oz	96	0	0	96
	6 oz	144	0	0	144
	8 oz	192	0	0	192
Tootsie Roll Pop	1 pop	111	0	0	111

Category: Beverages

Soda and beer	1 oz	12	0	0	12
	2 oz	24	0	0	24
	3 oz	36	0	0	36
	4 oz	48	0	0	48
	5 oz	60	0	0	60
	6 oz	72	0	0	72
	7 oz	84	0	0	84
	8 oz	96	0	0	96
	9 oz	108	0	0	108
	10 oz	120	0	0	120
	11 oz	132	0	0	132
	12 oz	144	0	0	144
Wine	1 oz	25	0	0	25
	2 oz	50	0	0	50
	3 oz	75	0	0	75
	4 oz	100	0	0	100
	5 oz	125	0	0	125
	6 oz	150	0	0	150

PURE PROTEIN FOODS

Food	Amount	CALORIES Carbohydrate	Protein	Fat	Total

Category: Dairy

Food	Amount	Carbohydrate	Protein	Fat	Total
Egg white	1 white	0	15	0	15
	2 whites	0	30	0	30
	3 whites	0	45	0	45
	4 whites	0	60	0	60
Cottage cheese, light, 1%					
	¼ cup	0	44	0	44
	½ cup	0	89	0	89
	1 cup	0	178	0	178
	1½ cups	0	267	0	267
	2 cups	0	356	0	356

Category: Seafood

Food	Amount	Carbohydrate	Protein	Fat	Total
Crab	1 oz	0	25	0	25
	2 oz	0	50	0	50
	3 oz	0	75	0	75
	4 oz	0	100	0	100
	5 oz	0	125	0	125
	6 oz	0	150	0	150
	7 oz	0	175	0	175
	8 oz	0	200	0	200
Lobster, Shrimp	1 oz	0	28	0	28
	2 oz	0	56	0	56
	3 oz	0	84	0	84
	4 oz	0	112	0	112
	5 oz	0	140	0	140
	6 oz	0	168	0	168
	7 oz	0	196	0	196
	8 oz	0	224	0	224

CALORIES

Food	Amount	Carbohydrate	Protein	Fat	Total
Tuna canned in water, Cod					
	1 oz	0	30	0	30
	2 oz	0	60	0	60
	3 oz	0	90	0	90
	4 oz	0	120	0	120
	5 oz	0	150	0	150
	6 oz	0	180	0	180
	7 oz	0	210	0	210
	8 oz	0	240	0	240
Flounder, Scallops, Haddock					
	1 oz	0	33	0	33
	2 oz	0	66	0	66
	3 oz	0	99	0	99
	4 oz	0	132	0	132
	5 oz	0	165	0	165
	6 oz	0	198	0	198
	7 oz	0	231	0	231
	8 oz	0	264	0	264

PURE FAT FOOD

Category: Dairy

Food	Amount	Carbohydrate	Protein	Fat	Total
Sour cream	1 tsp	0	0	9	9
	2 tsp	0	0	18	18
	3 tsp (1 tbsp)	0	0	27	27
	4 tsp	0	0	36	36
	5 tsp	0	0	45	45
	6 tsp (2 tbsp)	0	0	54	54
Butter, Margarine, Cream cheese (regular), Mayonnaise, Tartar sauce					
	1 tsp	0	0	33	33
	2 tsp	0	0	67	67
	3 tsp (1 tbsp)	0	0	100	100

CALORIES

Food	Amount	Carbohydrate	Protein	Fat	Total

Butter, Margarine, Cream cheese (regular),
Mayonnaise, Tartar sauce *(cont.)*

Food	Amount	Carbohydrate	Protein	Fat	Total
	4 tsp	0	0	133	133
	5 tsp	0	0	167	167
	6 tsp (2 tbsp)	0	0	200	200

Butter or margarine, whipped

	Amount	Carbohydrate	Protein	Fat	Total
	1 tsp	0	0	23	23
	2 tsp	0	0	46	46
	3 tsp (1 tbsp)	0	0	69	69
	4 tsp	0	0	92	92
	5 tsp	0	0	115	115
	6 tsp (2 tbsp)	0	0	138	138

Category: Oils

Oils (all kinds), Salad dressings (French, Ranch, Russian, Italian)

	Amount	Carbohydrate	Protein	Fat	Total
	1 tsp	0	0	40	40
	2 tsp	0	0	80	80
	3 tsp (1 tbsp)	0	0	120	120
	4 tsp	0	0	160	160
	5 tsp	0	0	200	200
	6 tsp (2 tbsp)	0	0	240	240

Salad Dressing, light

	Amount	Carbohydrate	Protein	Fat	Total
	1 tsp	0	0	25	25
	2 tsp	0	0	50	50
	3 tsp (1 tbsp)	0	0	75	75
	4 tsp	0	0	100	100
	5 tsp	0	0	125	125
	6 tsp (2 tbsp)	0	0	150	150

Mayonnaise, light

	Amount	Carbohydrate	Protein	Fat	Total
	1 tsp	0	0	17	17
	2 tsp	0	0	34	34
	3 tsp (1 tbsp)	0	0	51	51
	4 tsp	0	0	68	68
	5 tsp	0	0	85	85
	6 tsp (2 tbsp)	0	0	102	102

CALORIES

Food	Amount	Carbohydrate	Protein	Fat	Total

Category: Vegetables

Food	Amount	Carbohydrate	Protein	Fat	Total
Olives, black	10 large	0	0	90	90
	20 large	0	0	180	180
Olives, green	10 large	0	0	45	45
	20 large	0	0	90	90

MIXED FOODS

Dual Mix: Protein/Fat

Category: Meat, Fish, and Fowl

Food	Amount	Carbohydrate	Protein	Fat	Total
Bacon	1 slice	0	8	22	30
	2 slices	0	16	44	60
	3 slices	0	24	66	90
	4 slices	0	32	88	120
	5 slices	0	40	110	150
Salmon	1 oz	0	20	20	40
	2 oz	0	40	40	80
	3 oz	0	60	60	120
	4 oz	0	80	80	160
	5 oz	0	100	100	200
	6 oz	0	120	120	240
	7 oz	0	140	140	280
	8 oz	0	160	160	320
Chicken, boneless and skinless					
	1 oz	0	22	20	42
	2 oz	0	44	40	84
	3 oz	0	66	60	126
	4 oz	0	88	80	168
	5 oz	0	110	100	210
	6 oz	0	132	120	252
	7 oz	0	154	140	294
	8 oz	0	176	160	336

CALORIES

Food	Amount	Carbohydrate	Protein	Fat	Total
Swordfish	1 oz	0	29	15	44
	2 oz	0	58	30	88
	3 oz	0	87	45	132
	4 oz	0	116	60	176
	5 oz	0	145	75	220
	6 oz	0	174	90	264
	7 oz	0	203	105	308
	8 oz	0	232	120	352
Turkey and Trout	1 oz	0	32	16	48
	2 oz	0	64	32	96
	3 oz	0	96	48	144
	4 oz	0	128	64	192
	5 oz	0	160	80	240
	6 oz	0	192	96	288
	7 oz	0	224	112	336
	8 oz	0	256	128	384
Ham, lean	1 oz	0	25	25	50
	2 oz	0	50	50	100
	3 oz	0	75	75	150
	4 oz	0	100	100	200
	5 oz	0	125	125	250
	6 oz	0	150	150	300
	7 oz	0	175	175	350
	8 oz	0	200	200	400
Veal	1 oz	0	36	17	53
	2 oz	0	72	34	106
	3 oz	0	108	51	159
	4 oz	0	144	68	212
	5 oz	0	180	85	265
	6 oz	0	216	102	318
	7 oz	0	252	119	371
	8 oz	0	288	136	424
Lamb, lean	1 oz	0	29	29	58
	2 oz	0	58	58	116
	3 oz	0	87	87	174

CALORIES

Food	Amount	Carbohydrate	Protein	Fat	Total
Lamb, lean *(cont.)*	4 oz	0	116	116	232
	5 oz	0	145	145	290
	6 oz	0	174	174	348
	7 oz	0	203	203	406
	8 oz	0	232	232	464
Pork	1 oz	0	34	34	68
	2 oz	0	68	68	136
	3 oz	0	102	102	204
	4 oz	0	136	136	272
	5 oz	0	170	170	340
	6 oz	0	204	204	408
	7 oz	0	238	238	476
	8 oz	0	272	272	544
Steak, sirloin	1 oz	0	33	43	76
	2 oz	0	66	86	152
	3 oz	0	99	129	228
	4 oz	0	132	172	304
	5 oz	0	165	215	380
	6 oz	0	198	258	456
	7 oz	0	231	301	532
	8 oz	0	264	344	608
Beef, regular ground	1 oz	0	41	41	82
	2 oz	0	84	84	168
	3 oz	0	123	123	246
	4 oz	0	164	164	328
	5 oz	0	205	205	410
	6 oz	0	246	249	495
	7 oz	0	287	287	574
	8 oz	0	328	328	656
Pork/beef sausage	1 link (1 oz)	0	13	117	130
	2 links	0	26	234	260
	3 links	0	39	351	390
Frankfurter	1 link	0	32	118	150
	2 links	0	64	236	300
	3 links	0	96	354	450

CALORIES

Food	Amount	Carbohydrate	Protein	Fat	Total
Category: Dairy					
Egg	1 med	0	27	48	75
	2 med	0	54	96	150
	3 med	0	71	144	215
Cheese, light	1 oz	0	40	40	80
	2 oz	0	80	80	160
	3 oz	0	120	120	240
	4 oz	0	160	160	320
Cheese, all kinds	1 oz	0	37	74	111
	2 oz	0	74	148	222
	3 oz	0	111	222	333
	4 oz	0	148	296	444
Cottage cheese, 2%	¼ cup	0	44	11	55
	½ cup	0	89	20	109
	1 cup	0	178	40	218
	1½ cups	0	267	60	327
	2 cups	0	356	80	436
Cottage cheese, 4%	¼ cup	0	44	16	60
	½ cup	0	89	31	120
	1 cup	0	178	62	240
	1½ cups	0	267	93	360
	2 cups	0	356	124	480
Category: Nuts					
Nuts, all kinds	½ oz	0	13	69	82
	1 oz	0	26	138	164
	1½	0	39	207	246
	2 oz	0	52	276	328
	4 oz	0	104	552	656
Peanut butter	1 tsp	0	11	23	34
	2 tsp	0	22	46	64
	3 tsp (1 tbsp)	0	33	69	102

CALORIES

Food	Amount	Carbohydrate	Protein	Fat	Total
Peanut butter *(cont.)*	4 tsp	0	44	92	136
	5 tsp	0	55	115	170
	6 tsp (2 tbsp)	0	66	138	204

Dual Mix: Protein/Carbohydrate

Category: Beans

Beans, all kinds

	½ cup	80	24	0	104
	1 cup	160	48	0	208
	1½ cups	240	72	0	312
	2 cups	320	96	0	416

Category: Dairy

Yogurt, low fat , vanilla

	½ cup	83	22	0	105
	1 cup	166	44	0	210
	1½ cups	249	66	0	315
	2 cups	332	88	0	420

Yogurt, low fat, fruited

	½ cup	98	22	0	120
	1 cup	196	44	0	240
	1½ cups	294	66	0	360
	2 cups	392	88	0	480

Milk, skim

	2 oz	10	10	0	20
	4 oz	20	20	0	40
	6 oz	30	30	0	60
	8 oz	40	40	0	80

CALORIES

Food	Amount	Carbohydrate	Protein	Fat	Total

Dual Mix: Carbohydrate/Fat

Category: Condiments

Food	Amount	Carbohydrate	Protein	Fat	Total
Mustard	1 tsp	4	0	8	12
	2 tsp	8	0	16	24
	3 tsp	12	0	24	36
	4 tsp	16	0	32	48

Category: Vegetables

Food	Amount	Carbohydrate	Protein	Fat	Total
Avocado	1 oz	12	0	38	50
	2 oz	24	0	76	100
	3 oz	36	0	114	150
	4 oz	48	0	152	200
Potatoes, french-fried	3 oz	125	0	95	220
	6 oz	250	0	190	480

Category: Crackers and Snacks

Food	Amount	Carbohydrate	Protein	Fat	Total
Potato chips	1 oz	75	0	75	150
	2 oz	150	0	150	300
	3 oz	225	0	225	450
	4 oz	300	0	300	600
Chips, tortilla	1 oz	90	0	50	140
	2 oz	180	0	100	280
	3 oz	270	0	150	420
	4 oz	360	0	200	560
Popcorn, microwave	1 cup	19	0	14	33
	2 cups	38	0	28	66
	3 cups	57	0	42	99
	4 cups	76	0	56	132

CALORIES

Food	Amount	Carbohydrate	Protein	Fat	Total
Crackers	½ oz (2 crackers)	45	0	15	60
	1 oz (4 crackers)	90	0	30	120
	1½ oz (6 crackers)	135	0	45	180
	2 oz (8 crackers)	180	0	60	240

Category: Cakes, Pies, Cookies, Candy, and Chocolate

Food	Amount	Carbohydrate	Protein	Fat	Total
Chocolate	½ oz	40	0	40	80
	1 oz	80	0	80	160
	1½ oz	120	0	120	240
	2 oz	160	0	160	320
Chocolate cake	1 slice	150	0	100	250
	2 slices	300	0	200	500
Cupcake, chocolate	1 cupcake	126	0	54	180
Pie, apple	1 slice	172	0	108	280
Cookies, chocolate chip					
	1 cookie	30	0	20	50
	2 cookies	60	0	40	100
	3 cookies	90	0	60	150
	4 cookies	120	0	80	200
	5 cookies	150	0	100	250
Candy bar, Milky Way	1 bar	168	0	100	268

Triple Mix: Carbohydrate/Protein/Fat

Category: Seafood

Food	Amount	Carbohydrate	Protein	Fat	Total
Oysters	1 oz	7	7	7	21
	2 oz	14	14	14	42
	3 oz	21	21	21	63
	4 oz	28	28	28	84
	5 oz	35	35	35	105
	6 oz	42	42	42	126
	7 oz	49	49	49	147
	8 oz	56	56	56	168

CALORIES

Food	Amount	Carbohydrate	Protein	Fat	Total
Mussels	1 oz	11	11	11	33
	2 oz	22	22	22	66
	3 oz	33	33	33	99
	4 oz	44	44	44	132
	5 oz	55	55	55	165
	6 oz	66	66	66	198
	7 oz	77	77	77	231
	8 oz	88	88	88	264
Clams	1 oz	14	14	14	42
	2 oz	28	28	28	84
	3 oz	42	42	42	126
	4 oz	56	56	56	168
	5 oz	70	70	70	210
	6 oz	84	84	84	252
	7 oz	98	98	98	294
	8 oz	112	112	112	336

Category: Dairy

Food	Amount	Carbohydrate	Protein	Fat	Total
Milk, whole	2 oz	10	10	17	37
	4 oz	20	20	35	75
	6 oz	30	30	53	113
	8 oz	40	40	70	150
Milk, 2%	2 oz	10	10	10	30
	4 oz	20	20	20	60
	6 oz	30	30	30	90
	8 oz	40	40	40	120
Milk, 1%	8 oz	40	40	40	120
	2 oz	10	10	6	26
	4 oz	20	20	12	52
	6 oz	30	30	18	78
	8 oz	40	40	24	104

CALORIES

Food	Amount	Carbohydrate	Protein	Fat	Total

Category: Combination Foods

Food	Amount	Carbohydrate	Protein	Fat	Total
Pizza	1 slice	108	62	80	250
	2 slices	216	124	160	500
Soup, broth	1 cup	44	9	10	63
	2 cups	88	18	20	126
	3 cups	132	27	30	189
Soup, cream	1 cup	46	12	72	130
	2 cups	92	24	144	260
	3 cups	138	36	216	390

INDEX